D0788119

Identity Politics in the United States

For Haley Ann-Helen
May you always know impossible things are happening every day.

Identity Politics in the United States

KHALILAH L. BROWN-DEAN

polity

Copyright © Khalilah Brown-Dean 2019

The right of Khalilah Brown-Dean to be identified as Author of this Work has been asserted in accordance with the UK Copyright, Designs and Patents Act 1988.

First published in 2019 by Polity Press

Polity Press
65 Bridge Street
Cambridge CB2 1UR, UK

Polity Press
101 Station Landing
Suite 300
Medford, MA 02155, USA

All rights reserved. Except for the quotation of short passages for the purpose of criticism and review, no part of this publication may be reproduced, stored in a retrieval system or transmitted, in any form or by any means, electronic, mechanical, photocopying, recording or otherwise, without the prior permission of the publisher.

ISBN-13: 978-0-7456-5411-9
ISBN-13: 978-0-7456-5412-6 (pb)

A catalogue record for this book is available from the British Library.

Library of Congress Cataloging-in-Publication Data
Names: Brown-Dean, Khalilah L., author.
Title: Identity politics in the United States / Khalilah Brown-Dean.
Description: Cambridge, UK ; Medford, MA : Polity Press, 2019. | Includes
  bibliographical references and index.
Identifiers: LCCN 2019008489 (print) | LCCN 2019019979 (ebook) | ISBN
  9781509538829 (Epub) | ISBN 9780745654119 (hardback) | ISBN 9780745654126
  (pbk.)
Subjects: LCSH: Identity politics–United States. | Political
  participation–Social aspects–United States. | Race–Political
  aspects–United States. | Ethnicity–Political aspects–United States. |
  Gender identity–Political aspects–United States. | Identification
  (Religion)–Political aspects–United States.
Classification: LCC JK1764 (ebook) | LCC JK1764 .B77 2019 (print) | DDC
  320.97308–dc23
LC record available at https://lccn.loc.gov/2019008489

Typeset in 10/13pt Swift Light by
Servis Filmsetting Ltd, Stockport, Cheshire
Printed and bound in Great Britain by TJ International Limited

The publisher has used its best endeavours to ensure that the URLs for external websites referred to in this book are correct and active at the time of going to press. However, the publisher has no responsibility for the websites and can make no guarantee that a site will remain live or that the content is or will remain appropriate.

Every effort has been made to trace all copyright holders, but if any have been overlooked the publisher will be pleased to include any necessary credits in any subsequent reprint or edition.

For further information on Polity, visit our website: politybooks.com

Contents

Tables

Figures

Boxes

Illustrations

Acknowledgements

Fifty years after 600 peaceful protesters were brutally beaten during what would become known as Bloody Sunday, my family and I gathered at the base of the Edmund Pettus Bridge in Selma, Alabama. We were there to honor brave visionaries who created political opportunities that many people take for granted. As we approached the bridge, my husband and I noticed our daughter's hesitance. She was afraid of what was waiting for us on the other side. We reassured her, then paused to reflect on what those footsoldiers must have felt when they encountered a phalanx of people armed with billy clubs, dogs, tear gas, and a vicious disdain for their very existence. As we stood on the bridge, we heard a group of marchers singing "We Shall Overcome": in that moment we questioned just how much had changed since 1965, when Jimmie Lee Jackson and Viola Liuzzo were shot to death simply for demanding access to democracy and equality.

We looked into the crowd and spotted the first two women to legally marry in the state of Alabama. We mouthed a silent "thank you" as Reverend William Barber II, architect of the Moral Monday movement, marched by. We watched as elders in wheelchairs were escorted by young people whose first introduction to Bloody Sunday happened via a movie screen. We listened as an interfaith group voiced their demands for immigration reform. We stood in solidarity with the formerly incarcerated whose banner advocated not for a second chance but for a viable *first* chance at achieving the American Dream. We looked back over the bridge and remembered that, less than twenty-four hours earlier, we had stood shoulder to shoulder with people from all over the world as the United States' first Black president acknowledged John Lewis, a man who was savagely beaten by state troopers during that fateful march yet overcame permanent injuries to become a member of the United States Congress. We critiqued our own hubris as we listened to the stories of local veterans who had fought for democracy abroad, only to return home and be denied the vote. These men and women removed their hats, held their hands to their hearts, and closed their eyes in reverence as a choir sang the words to "Lift Ev'ry Voice." There on that bridge we better understood that American democracy is cloaked in the blood, prayers, and sacrifices of elders who were willing to fight for a future more powerful than the present. That bridge is sacred ground.

The trip to Selma provided the fuel to write this book. Completing it would not have been possible without a legion of supporters. I am grateful to the many students I have taught at the Ohio State University, Yale University, and Quinnipiac University. Portions of this research have been presented at Texas A&M University, Claflin University, Northeastern University, Harvard University, DePauw University, the University of Connecticut Graduate School of Social Work, the College of William and Mary, and the University of North Carolina-Greensboro.

Many thanks to Brandee Blocker Anderson, Nisha Gandhi, Christopher Pagliarella, Corey Scott, and Danielle Tomlinson for research assistance. My colleagues at Quinnipiac have provided support and an overall sense of collegiality that gave me the confidence to embark on this ambitious project. This research has been supported by various grants from the Quinnipiac College of Arts and Sciences and the Provost's Innovation Grants. A special thanks to the Eli's Crew for end of semester debriefs and affirmations.

Being an academic is often a lonely enterprise, but my journey has been enriched by a number of colleagues and friends who challenge me, pray for me, inspire me, and, when necessary, laugh with me. Chief among them was the late Professor Mark Sawyer, who was at once my sharpest critic and fiercest advocate. Thanks for teaching me to listen for the sound of el coqui, my friend.

Saladin Ambar, Domonic Bearfield, Niambi Carter, Wartyna Davis, Michael Fauntroy, Jelani Favors, Christina Greer, L'Heureux Lewis-McCoy, Shayla Nunnally, D'Andra Orey, Ravi Perry, Clarissa Peterson, Kathy Powers, Melanye Price, Melynda Price, Gabe Sanchez, Valeria Sinclair Chapman, Wendy Smooth, James Taylor, Alvin Tillery, Derrick White, and David C. Wilson provided me with valuable feedback and critique on various parts of the project via drafts, affiliated articles, and conference presentations. They are exceptional scholars and even better friends. Thank you to the many people who provided a forum for me to debate and defend the core arguments of this text – especially the NCOBPS family. I owe a special debt of gratitude to the hardest working person I know, Jessica Lavariega Monforti, for her copious comments on the early chapters.

I am eternally grateful to Professors Matthew Holden, Paula McClain, and the late William E. Nelson, Jr, for setting the standard and convincing me to pursue a PhD instead of a JD.

Thank you to the anonymous reviewers for insightful critiques that challenged my thinking and helped make the final product much stronger. This book would not be possible without Polity Press, my gracious editor Louise Knight, and Sophie Wright. Thank you for your patience, your guidance, and your unwavering commitment to this project.

Jamal Watson, executive editor of *Diverse: Issues in Higher Education*, provided me with a weekly blog column to flesh out the ideas that form the intellectual heart of this book. Charles Ellison and WURD Radio gave me a weekly segment to address the historical context and contemporary controversies of identity politics. Jamal, Charles, and my friends at Connecticut Public and WTNH helped me develop a platform to make public scholarship relevant and accessible. Conversations with Tarana Burke, Danny Glover, Gary Winfield and Reginald Dwayne Betts made real the possibilities of bridging the gap between theory and practice. I remain inspired by the T.R.U.E. Unit at Cheshire CI. Thank you to the Mitchell Public Library (especially Mr Bostic) and Manjares Café for providing physical space for me to write and try out new ideas.

   This is a book about identity politics, so I have to acknowledge those who have shaped my identity as a scholar and a citizen. Lynchburg, Virginia, will always be the place where I learned about democracy's promise and the perils of ignoring rather than addressing difference. Chestnut Grove is where I return for spiritual refueling. The women of Alpha Kappa Alpha Sorority, Incorporated – especially Theta Kappa and Theta Epsilon Omega chapters – continue to be the women I seek to emulate. Thank you to my prayer team for their covering. Tuere McElroy and Stacyanne Headley astound me with their uncanny ability to send a much-needed text message or pop up to visit when things seem overwhelming. The Patton, Williams, Spearman, and Pegues families are a tremendous gift.

   My amazing family – the Browns, Deans, Martins, and Pendletons – remind me who I am and *whose* I am. My mother JoAnn Brown Martin is my greatest cheerleader and the one who first showed me the value of civic education. She is a consummate public servant. My sisters, Megan and Courtney, provide life's soundtrack, while conversations with my Aunts Veda, Wanda, and Vay have addressed nearly every controversy contained in this book. My nieces and nephews (JaBrille, John, Mikayla, Jacob, Jessica, Lennon, Dean, and Myles) are a constant reminder of life's true purpose. I wish my grandparents, Ted Louis Brown and Helen Pendleton Brown, were here to read this book. So much of my interest in politics and identity is the result of their commitment to community.

   My husband, William R. Dean, Jr, calmed my fears and refused to allow me to give up on this project. I thank him for believing in me even in the moments I couldn't believe in myself. I am eternally grateful for every additional load of laundry, meal prep, schedule change, and school drop-off he took on so I could carve out more space to write.

   Finally, I dedicate this book to our daughter, Haley Ann-Helen, who is named after her two grandmothers and a great-grandmother. She is the reason I refuse to give up on the hope that, someday, we will get this thing called American democracy right so that she can inherit a more just world. Thank you for every encouraging note you secretly tucked into my notebook, for every "Good job, Mommy," and for never complaining about the extra trips to the library. May you always know that impossible things are happening every day.

For Fannie Lou, Sojourner, Carrie, MumBett, Ida B., Ethel, Nellie, Barbara, Coretta, Helen, Elizabeth, Maxine, Septima, Ella, Eunice, Marion, Shirley, Tiny, Louise, Mary, Amelia, Maya, and every elder who paved the way, I thank you.

1

The Personal is Political

I first discovered the work of poet and essayist Maya Angelou in middle school. Even though the themes in *I Know Why the Caged Bird Sings* were mature, I felt a deep connection to the story she told of growing up in Stamps, Arkansas. I flinched when she recounted being raped by her mother's boy-friend. I cried when Uncle Willie hid in the potato bin to avoid the Ku Klux Klan. Klan leaders throughout the United States included sheriffs, judges, prosecutors, and ministers. It seemed ominous that the very people responsi-ble for protecting vulnerable communities routinely engaged in terrorizing them.

Maya Angelou's voice let me know that it was OK to be a little brown girl with a big Arabic name in a place called Lynchburg, Virginia, with the audacity to imagine possibilities unbound by geography. I vowed to someday thank Dr Angelou in person for inspiring me. At seventeen I finally had the chance – or so I thought. That year Angelou arrived at my high school as part of a citywide Black History Month observance. I was selected as one of the students who would get to speak with her. Being a nerd has its perks. I rehearsed what I would say to her a thousand times. I was determined not to come across as some naïve kid in search of an autograph. With dog-eared copy of my notebook in hand I patiently waited for my turn. But I was awe-struck. The words simply wouldn't come. Angelou looked at me and said with that beautiful, commanding lilt, "Would you like to say hello?" I eagerly shook my head and squeaked out, "Hello?!" She smiled and took the time to nod her reassurance. I knew in that moment she realized the impact she had on me. Angelou was my intellectual rock star.

Quite literally, Angelou made it possible for me to be the first person in my immediate family to earn a four-year degree. I competed in oratorical competitions in high school and earned college scholarships using a number of her poems and essays. I discovered the poem "Our Grandmothers" while trying to understand why the contributions of women were so overlooked in the retelling of American freedom movements. I knew about Harriett Tubman and could recite Sojourner Truth's "Ain't I a Woman" line by line. But "Our Grandmothers" highlighted the ways that everyday acts of resistance chal-lenge exclusion. It is a beautifully complex poem that affirms the power of women who make personal sacrifices to inspire, protect, challenge, and build

Dr Maya Angelou was a poet, performer, and essayist. She delivered a poem at the 1993 inauguration of President Bill Clinton and received the 2011 Presidential Medal of Freedom.

communities. I have always been struck by a line from it that reads "When you get, give. And when you learn, teach."

I grew up in a town where the specter of Jerry Falwell's **Moral Majority movement** loomed large. The Moral Majority was a concentrated effort in the 1980s to raise the political voice of the Christian Right. Despite my Southern Baptist upbringing, it didn't make sense that one minister could convince local government officials to change the day my friends and I would trick or treat when Halloween fell on a Sunday. I looked to Angelou's prose to give me the strength to speak before our city council to protest moving a busy fire station to the heart of our working-class neighborhood. I wondered why the demands of our neighbors weren't enough to convince the board to change its decisions. Where was *our* power?

When Maya Angelou passed in 2014, a reporter asked me to choose my favorite work. At first it seemed like an impossible task, and then I remembered her essay titled "The Graduation." Angelou reflects on her 1940 graduation from high school and paints a clear picture of how separate education is inherently unequal. She talks about the tattered textbooks and outdated science equipment that she and her classmates shared, while students at white schools had more equipment than they could actually use. **Black** graduates were expected to bring honor to their communities by becoming athletes, janitors, and entertainers. White graduates were encouraged to become physicians, lawyers, and teachers. Even then, the lens of **identity** was incredibly narrow. It didn't matter that Angelou and her classmates had memorized Shakespeare's "The Rape of Lucrece" or could recite "Invictus" with great conviction. Their destiny was predetermined. The name of schools for Black children in the South reinforced a sense of inferiority: training schools. I remember seeing my maternal grandmother's class ring inscribed with "Amherst County Training School" and wondering why it wasn't called a "high school." In the 1940s, Black students were trained to serve society. White students were educated to shape it. That one essay helped me understand the necessity of the 1954 *Brown v. Board of Education* decision better than any legal or historical text I have ever read. Sixty years later we are still trying to figure out how to educate students equally.

I lacked the language of intersectionality at the time, but I knew these disparate experiences were bound together by a tradition of treating groups differently based on their perceived worth. In her seminal work "Mapping the Margins: Intersectionality, Identity Politics, and Violence against Women of Color," Kimberlé Crenshaw (1991) cautions that "the problem with **identity politics** is not that it fails to transcend difference, as some critics charge, but rather the opposite – that it frequently conflates or ignores intra group differences." My neighborhood friends and I learned that lesson every morning as we passed three elementary schools en route to the suburban school we were chosen to integrate. We didn't fully understand why we had to take the long bus ride to Paul Munro Elementary School instead of the short walk to Garland Rhodes. We dreaded the mandatory neighborhood walking tours with our teachers and classmates because it reminded us that we were perpetual interlopers. Our classmates would pass through familiar streets, pointing out their expansive homes and eagerly waving to neighbors heading to lunch at the country club, where people who looked like us were not allowed to join. Four years of field trips and the streets never felt familiar or welcoming to us. Those barriers, both real and imagined, made it clear that the meaning of our presence in multiple spaces was structured by interlocking systems related to education, religion, region, class, gender, and **race**. But it wasn't just *our* personal experiences of being bussed to new schools or observing Halloween. It was a collective experience shared by various groups navigating identity politics in the United States.

Why This Book?

This book grows out of that interest fueled decades ago in Virginia. Democracy in the United States is built upon the battle of ideas related to how we see ourselves, how we see others, and the mechanisms available to reinforce these distinctions. To some the term *identity politics* has become a pejorative term used to decry the tendency to promote group solidarity at the expense of mutual progress. I reject this description because it is often lobbed against groups whose relationship to traditional spheres of influence and inclusion remains tenuous. Understanding lived political experiences across multiple identity markers isn't an attempt to create a hierarchy of oppression based on who has suffered the most or who is entitled to the greatest political rewards. That approach is both intellectually lazy and fundamentally uninteresting. The solution, however, isn't to tell people to strip away the layers of their identity or to ignore how those layers structure opportunities. The notion that people should stop talking about or stop affirming the groups to which they belong is inconsistent with the longstanding political practice of creating and reinforcing identity-based cleavages in US politics.

Consider, for example, contemporary efforts to address the growing opioid crisis sweeping the United States. President Donald J. Trump has declared a public health crisis as advocates argue for a kinder, gentler approach to addiction that promotes rehabilitation and support over punishment and incarceration. Some question why this new approach to opioid addiction varies from the 1990s political response to the crack epidemic that mostly ensnared Blacks and Latinos in urban areas, who were demonized as morally reprehensible (Forman 2018; Alexander 2010; Fortner 2015; Muhammad 2011; Hinton 2016). Indeed, the former mayor of Baltimore (Kurt Schmoke) was ridiculed for suggesting that addiction should be treated as a public health crisis rather than simply a criminal justice problem.[1] Since the War on Drugs was formally launched in the 1970s during the Nixon administration, over $50 billion has been spent to significantly increase the arrests, prosecutions, and incarceration of millions of people in the United States. The result hasn't made the country safer, nor has it significantly reduced addiction (Mauer and King 2007; Hart 2013). Instead, this massive collection of public policies has had a disproportionate impact on certain groups, even if members of those groups don't perceive it as "their problem." That type of divide makes it important to address and understand identity politics rather than demonize its existence.

Over the last fifteen years as a university professor, I've taught thousands of students in both public and private university settings, from Ivy League institutions to large public universities. I've taught first-generation students and those whose family names are chiseled into the archways of university buildings. I've taught courses on US politics during contentious elections and debated the merits of the death penalty during high-profile court cases. Against the backdrop of new efforts to limit the movement of Muslims in the United States, my courses on race and **ethnicity** in US politics address the historical fear that Irish immigrants would "pollute" American society by importing their Catholic faith and the importance of military service to helping immigrants "belong." I've taught a course on American **political movements** at the height of mass demonstrations to denounce violence and sexual assault while helping freshmen navigate the heightened tensions sparked by debates over freedom of speech on college campuses in the wake of violent clashes at schools such as the University of Missouri and UC Berkeley.

Without fail, some pressing political event will occur that forces me to help students make sense of our increasingly complex and contentious political world. It's important to note, however, that the challenges of identity politics supersede any one election, political party, or public official. Understanding issues of identity, power, and conflict are central to understanding US politics for students and casual observers alike. Some might wonder why a country founded on the principle of revolutionary freedom periodically devolves into intense and at times violent clashes that deny the sense of personal liberty that rests at the heart of American democracy.

For example, the 2017 gathering of white supremacists on the campus of the University of Virginia forced important conversations about the defense of Southern heritage vis-à-vis the failure to protect Jewish Americans. It also raised the question of how exercising constitutionally protected rights to speech and assembly prompt judicial and extralegal efforts to reinforce the boundaries of belonging. Placing contemporary tensions into traditional frameworks of understanding rests as the central motivation for this book. These tensions aren't bound by classrooms and shouldn't be pondered just by students. The historic context sets the stage for contemporary controversies that affect all of us.

Politics is a battle over resources such as power, leadership, economic development, and legal standing. At times the battle over resources is an attempt to stave off perceived challenges to power. The quest for power has been marked by legal means to substantiate claims to authority. Likewise, extralegal methods to counter challenges inhibit group claims to representation. It follows then that political maneuvering that centers on group identities is an essential feature of US politics. Indeed, the very founding of this nation was forged as an attempt to craft a cohesive national identity distinct from the British Crown.

Identity politics is at its core, a persistent negotiation over the meaning, limits, requirements, and protections of citizenship. Even as individual members gain success, the tendency to effect boundaries to political inclusion based on group attributes has been a ubiquitous feature of American political development since its founding. Identity politics isn't merely an effort to gain access to power. Rather, it shapes and is shaped by the very practice of governance that renders certain groups vulnerable to legal justifications of their subordinate status. Examples of the practical implications of this battle appear as groups fight to add an Equal Rights Amendment to the Constitution that would protect gender equality in courtrooms where undocumented minors appeal for amnesty to stay in the only country they have known. And the practical implications are found in houses of worship where parishioners determine how to balance their faith with concerns about their safety. My hope is that this book will help elevate conversations for those who are at once fascinated or disgusted by the enterprise of US politics.

Intersectionality as an Organizing Framework

In a 2018 address celebrating the twenty-fifth anniversary of Rice University's Baker Institute for Public Policy, former President Barack Obama reflected on the tensions surrounding identity in the United States:

> When I hear people say they don't like identity politics I think it's impor-tant to remember that identity politics doesn't just apply to when it's white people or gay people or women. The folks that really originated identity politics were folks who said the three-fifths clause and all that stuff. That's identity politics . . . Jim Crow was identity politics. Part of what's happened is that when people find their status is being jostled and threatened, they react.

Individuals perceive their identities, and those of others, in complex ways that define their political preferences. The tendency of governments and the political process, however, is to lump people together and treat them as group members regardless of individual differences (Shaw et al. 2015). This institutional treatment triggers the individual-level responses referenced in Obama's remarks based on perceived threats to status and well-being. At times various government actors, institutions, and choices work to construct group identities (Hawkesworth 2003; Simien 2007). At other points, the prac-tice of politics structures which groups have access to political power and representation vis-à-vis policy-making, voting behavior, legislative decision-making, and judicial rulings. The political meaning of identity is shaped by interlocking structures of power that define the meaning of multiple statuses at once.

Consider, for example, the passage of the **Civil Rights Act of 1964**. The Act was intended to strike down laws and practices that justified denying African Americans access to transportation, water fountains, jobs, and schools. Although the bill had the support of President Lyndon B. Johnson, it faced fierce opposition within Congress. Opponents of the bill, such as Representative Howard W. Smith (R-VA), included sex-based **discrimination** in an effort to kill it. Ironically, the bill successfully passed and ended up extending federal protection to women in the workplace. The Civil Rights Act was a monumental piece of legislation because it demonstrated that the federal government could play a role in safeguarding the rights of citizens at the state and local levels. What began as an effort to protect Black citizens against discrimination has over time been used to protect all Americans from race- and gender-based discrimination in employment.

In 2009, the US Supreme Court presided over a groundbreaking case, *Ricci v. DeStefano*, which involved nineteen white firefighters and one Hispanic firefighter who were denied promotions. After a series of oral and written exams, the city of New Haven, Connecticut, scrapped the final promotion list out of fear that people of color would file a racial discrimination lawsuit because the highest scoring applicants were all white. The Court ruled in favor of the twenty firefighters and, in turn, upheld the view that the Civil Rights Act guarded against racial discrimination in all forms.

Patricia Hill Collins (1989) cautions us to consider how systems mutually construct one another: "As opposed to examining gender, race, class, and nation as separate systems of oppression, intersectionality explores how these systems mutually construct one another . . . across multiple systems of oppression and serve as focal points or privileged social locations for those intersecting systems." Given this, it is useful to consider how institutional structures shape exclusion and how political actors react to/reason through this exclusion.

It may seem contradictory to employ the lens of intersectionality in a book whose chapters reference particular categories of difference. However, my approach is to examine the complex ways the political process defines political incorporation within and across categories. For example, a number of pundits, journalists, and activists declared 2018 the Year of the Woman, citing the record number of women running for office. While those numbers are promising, a proper intersectional account of those trends must account for the structural challenges wrought by issues such as fundraising that limit the number of women of color able to pursue elected office. Similarly, policies such as the California Voting Rights Act were originally meant to protect the ability of communities of color to elect candidates of their choice. However, these provisions rarely increase the number of elected officials from underrepresented communities. Dismantling at-large districts must be done in tandem with broader efforts to limit the institutional barriers to office-holding.

Intersectionality as an organizing framework recognizes that no one group possesses absolute privilege or absolute disadvantage. While some individuals from marginalized groups may be able to transcend categories in some instances, they are not completely inoculated from broader social negotiations (Purdie-Vaughns and Eibach 2008; Alexander-Floyd 2012). In short, individual political experiences are inextricably bound by broader notions of belonging that shape differences within and between groups. This book examines the interlocking political experiences derived from categories of race, ethnicity, gender, religion, and sexual orientation to explore the quest for power in the United States. Although there are a number of texts that deal with identity politics by focusing on a singular racial/ethnic group, this book evaluates political power through the lens of *multiple* group identities.

Power and Politics

In a seminal work, Robert Dahl (1957) defines power as follows: "*A* has power over *B* to the extent that he can get *B* to do something that *B* would not otherwise do." Clarissa Hayward (2000), drawing on Michel Foucault, criticizes Dahl and his interlocutors for seeing power as an instrument exercised by individuals rather than as existing in networks that restrain action. In this book I adopt a more nuanced emphasis on what Khalilah L. Brown-Dean and Benjamin Jones (2017) term **authentic power**. Specifically, authentic power refers to the extent to which a group harmed by a policy can get policy-makers and other government officials to acknowledge this harm and, ultimately, to change the policy to the group's benefit.

This definition emphasizes that authentic power, rather than becoming observable only with a policy change, can reveal itself beforehand through shifts in the public debate that force officials to admit previously ignored problems with a policy. This definition also is intentionally broad and encompasses a wide range of political phenomena. Policies can detrimentally impact well-established groups with significant power – for example, new gun-control legislation hurting gun owners – so the exercise of authentic power is by no means limited to underrepresented groups. In many instances of authentic power, it remains largely static: an already powerful group responds to a harmful policy or push for political inclusion by mobilizing existing resources to oppose it. Some of the more interesting instances of authentic power, however, involve a more dynamic process: policies are detrimental to already underrepresented groups, creating further barriers to their ability to influence the political process; yet, over time, the harm caused by these policies becomes a galvanizing force for groups to become politically engaged in ways not seen before. In turn, the value of US citizenship is politicized to shape political power, access, participation, and representation.

A Note about Terms

Names and labels are important for conveying notions of power, worth, and inclusion. I purposely avoid using the terms "minority" or "marginalized" to refer to underrepresented groups in the United States because it implies a sense of inferiority and subordinate status. The term *underrepresented* applies to groups whose political presence within decision-making arenas does not mirror their statistical share of the US population. For example,

Signage at a Black Lives Matter rally in Minnesota: the death of unarmed motorist Philando Castile mobilized communities around the nation to demand change.

women comprise 51 percent of the total population and only 24 percent of the 535 members serving in the US Congress. They are therefore numerically underrepresented in these influential halls of power (Dolan et al. 2016). Women of color make up about 36 percent of women in Congress.[2]

The concept of race that I employ in this text applies to social definitions of race rather than biological differences. For the purpose of this book, race refers to socially constructed groupings of individuals based on common traits such as skin tone, hair texture, and other phenotypical attributes. These designations have changed over time and have been codified by law and practice to bestow differences in social, political, legal, and economic standing. To say that race is a social construct is to acknowledge that the meaning and substance of racial categorizations have changed over time. As a result, defining who is entitled to lay claim to or preside over racial identities varies across space, place, and context. Consider, for example, champion golfer Tiger Woods, who drew tremendous criticism during a 1997 interview on *The Oprah Winfrey Show*. Winfrey asked the mixed-race, multiethnic golfer whether it offended him to be called "**African American**." Woods responded that he preferred to be called "Cablinasian" to capture fully his African American, Thai, Chinese, Dutch, and American Indian ancestry: "I'm just who I am, whoever you see in front of you."[3]

To some, Woods's new term was a fitting homage to his parents, and it wasn't confined by narrow definitions of race that forced him to choose a singular category. Others countered that he had deployed a sense of **social distancing** or the calculated assessment of the relative costs and benefits of affiliating with a particular group. Regardless of how Woods identified himself, to many of his fellow players his racial identity was predetermined.

That same year Tiger Woods became the youngest golfer ever to play in the prestigious US Masters, with analysts deeming him the first Black player to win. His fellow competitor Fuzzy Zoeller urged Tiger not to order collard greens and fried chicken at the Augusta National Club – a nod to racial stereotypes about African American food preferences.

In my courses on race and ethnicity in US politics, I play a game I created with students called "Who Is/Who Isn't?" It involves showing photos of various public figures and allowing students to guess their racial identity. Most of them are shocked to learn, for example, that South African-born actress Charlize Theron could be considered African American or that rapper Drake could be classified as Jewish on account of his mother's heritage. These examples highlight the variable nature of racial categories codified by law, practice, and perception. Politically, the assumptions and judgements that we attach to these perceptions reference what scholars call **racial categorization** as the product of intense battles over which groups we belong to, the meaning of those assignments, and changing contexts for altering outcomes. The challenge of **social categorization** occurs because of a lack of consensus – or unified sense of belonging.

For example, the 1992 Los Angeles riots erupted after the acquittal of four white police officers in the beating of Black motorist Rodney King. The rioting and looting led to the deaths of fifty people and over $1 billion in property damage. The aftermath of the acquittal highlighted tensions between groups under the umbrella of Asian American identity. Some shopkeepers posted signs that read "Not Korean," hoping to distance themselves from decades of conflict between residents and store owners ignited by the shooting death of Black teen Latasha Harlins by Korean store owner Soon Ja Du (Kim 2000).

In many cases the appropriateness of terminology shifts in response to changing political realities and nodes of understanding. I employ the terms **LGBTQI** and **LGBT** based on the time period and context of discussion. LGBTQI references those who identify as lesbian, gay, bisexual, trans, queer, or intersexed.[4] I do not make distinctions in the text between cisgendered (those whose current **gender identity** matches their sex assignment at birth) and those who transition to their current gender identity. Where appropriate, however, I do reference policy debates over inclusion that rest on distinguishing between biological sex and gender identity.

I use the terms Latinx, Latino/a, and Hispanic interchangeably. I concede that the use of these common labels may oversimplify the experiences, histories, and preferences of various subgroups, and I also acknowledge that much of US politics rests on reducing groups to the lowest common denominator with little input from those being defined. It is easier, for example, to pass "English only" legislation that affects "Latinos" without examining the differential impact of these policies based on country of origin and racial identity. Similarly, political candidates find it easier and more cost-effective to deploy Latino outreach efforts without adequately capturing how and why the interests of Puerto Rican voters may differ from those of Cuban Americans. Further complicating this choice is considering how generational status, age, citizenship, and gender identity may shape group labels.

For example, various scholars have criticized the use of the term *Hispanic* because it privileges groups who trace their ancestry to Spain and masks the internal diversity of these communities (Gonzalez 1992; Flores and Yudice 1990; Alcoff 2005). Others see the term as having no internal significance because it was imposed by governmental agencies such as the Census Bureau to classify communities more easily. The term *Latino* is often preferable to those who want to acknowledge the non-European aspects of ancestry and historical experiences. Here, Latinos reference residents of the United States who trace their ancestry to Spanish-speaking regions of Latin America and the Caribbean (Garcia Bedolla 2003). In accordance with the intersectionality lens, at times I use *Latinx* as a gender-neutral term of reference for individuals and groups commonly referred to as Latino/a and Hispanic. All of these appellations come with their own sets of preferences and critiques while highlighting the social and political structuring of identity. I rely on context when choosing which to employ.[5]

I use the term *ethnicity* to refer to distinctions based on culture, language, or common descent that shape political standing. The notion of what Yen Le Espiritu (1992) calls *panethnicity* reflects a sense of group identity based on political opportunities and threats. At times subordinate groups may embrace a broader shared identity in order to reap political advantages or in response to wider threats. In other cases, groups will emphasize their differences to reject negative connotations and behaviors that target "a collectivity within the larger society having a real or putative common ancestry, memories of a shared historical past, or a cultural focus on one or more symbolic elements defined as the epitome of their peoplehood" (Schermerhorn 1970).

In this text, race and ethnicity are relational but not oppositional. Their meaning is shaped by factors external to the group, such as legal decrees (e.g. **Plessy v. Ferguson**), government agencies (e.g. the Bureau of Indian Affairs), and actors (e.g. police officers). Group standing can be shaped by both racial and ethnic notions based on the question of interest. This view was codified into law by the 1987 Supreme Court decision in *St Francis College* v. *Al-Khazraji*. Al-Khazraji was an Iraqi-born US citizen and professor at St Francis College in Pennsylvania who argued that he had been discriminated against based on his "Arabian race." After being denied tenure, he sued the school for violating the Civil Rights Act of 1964. His attorneys argued that the protections should be extended to people who were not considered Black or white. The justices ruled in his favor and decided that the protections should apply to people of Arab descent and whites as well. Justice Brennan wrote in his concurrence with the opinion, "Pernicious distinctions among individuals based solely on their ancestry are antithetical to the doctrine of equality upon which this nation is founded" (481 US 604).

Different and Diverse

It's necessary to acknowledge the unique political standing of American Indians and people of African descent within US politics. Enslaved Africans were used to create wealth that permanently structured US institutions. The experiences of enslaved Africans and their descendants don't neatly fit into the narratives of immigrant groups who had the opportunity to pursue citizenship from their arrival on American shores. Throughout this book I use the terms *African American* and *Black* interchangeably to reference people of African descent now living in the United States.

The use of the seemingly innocuous term "Native American" implies a sense of acceptance and full citizenship standing that many tribal nations have never enjoyed. The rejection of Indian citizenship created nations within a nation who continue to demand recognition and respect of ancestral ties. Indeed, the 2016 protests of the Dakota Pipeline Access project highlight tensions over cultural preservation and its impact on public policy. For example, bills to limit or criminalize protests have been introduced in thirty states since the protests at Standing Rock (Carpenter and Williams 2018). According to political scientist David Wilkins, "the terms Indian and American Indian remain the most common appellations used by indigenous and nonindigenous persons and institutions" (2002: xvii). To be sure, most members refer to themselves based on their tribal affiliation (e.g. Blackfoot or Lakota), just as many immigrants identify based on their country of origin (e.g. Trinidadian or Laotian) rather than a global identifier. However, the political differences for American Indians and African Americans were codified into law and reinforced by political practice.

Acknowledging this reality is not an attempt to situate American Indian and African American experiences as more painful than those of other groups. Nor is it an attempt to elevate their political identities as more important. Rather, it is a recognition of the failure of traditional treatments of identity to adequately capture efforts to permanently define certain groups as beyond the scope of belonging. This oversight is reflected in the longstanding battle to determine the practical meaning of federal recognition for American Indians:

> Federal recognition has historically had two distinctive meanings. Before the 1870s, "recognize" or "recognition" was used in the cognitive sense. In other words, federal officials simply acknowledged that a tribe existed, usually by negotiating treaties with them or enacting specific laws to fulfill specific treaty pledges. During the 1870s however, "recognition" or more accurately, "acknowledgement" began to be used in a formal jurisdictional sense. It is this later usage that the federal government

most often employs to describe its relationship to tribes. In short, federal acknowledgement is a formal act that establishes a political relationship between a tribe and the United States. It affirms a tribe's sovereign status. Simultaneously, it outlines the federal government's responsibilities to the tribe. More specifically, federal acknowledgement meant that a tribe is not only entitled to the immunities and privileges available to other tribes, but is also subject to the same federal powers, limitations, and other obligations of recognized tribes. (Wilkins 2002)

Understanding identity politics requires acknowledging the divergent opportunities for groups to navigate and derive benefits from the political system. These benefits may be material, such as a tax break or a grant to help fund education. Political incorporation may also promote purposive benefits such as the sense of accomplishment you feel after voting. Finally, the political process provides instrumental benefits that help us do things we could not do on our own, such as creating civilian review boards to enhance public safety.

My Vision

Battles over the meaning and scope of group membership play out on NFL football fields as players kneel in protest at the deaths of unarmed civilians. These challenges occur at school board meetings when educators debate whether to provide gender-neutral bathrooms to accommodate students whose gender identity doesn't fit with the designations on their birth certificates. Group identity matters in boardrooms, where the lines between harassment and compliment are drawn, in legislative chambers, where opportunities to express political beliefs are crafted, and in courtrooms, where decisions are made to determine against whom we are allowed to discriminate. The United States, like many other nations, is becoming increasingly polarized. Too often allegations of "alternative facts" in response to things we don't like or with which we disagree limit opportunities to have meaningful conversations about our differences. The proliferation of social media outlets creates echo chambers that allow us to filter out things that make us uncomfortable. It is those moments of discomfort, however, that force us to reflect on what we believe and why we believe it.

The decline of civility and dialogue weakens democracy and our opportunities to engage one another on matters of mutual interest and benefit. My vision is that this book will help spark discussion and debate while prompting each of us to consider the requirements and limits of democracy. I don't expect readers always to agree with me or with each other. What I do hope is that the discussions stimulated by this book will be guided by a commitment to intellectual curiosity that helps each of us better navigate the fault lines embedded in political life. Be willing to be uncomfortable.

The Plan

It is impossible to cover every group-based affiliation in a single text. Instead I focus on the major identity groups that have been most regulated and/ or politicized while framing how notions of inclusion, citizenship, and recognition can be applied to any group of interest. I begin with an introduction to how these identities have been created and politicized in the United States through the lens of citizenship. For example, the 1857 **Dred Scott v. Sandford** decision declared that anyone descended from Africans could not be a citizen of the United States. This denial set in motion African Americans' perpetual struggle to be recognized and afforded the basic rights of American citizenship. The case and its subsequent progeny determined political incorporation for other communities while also shaping strategies for inclusion. These legal definitions provide a framework for understanding the challenges that groups face in both acquiring and protecting their political standing.

Each chapter addresses political forces in identity formation and the means through which historical exclusions shape contemporary battles for power. I weave in a discussion of the impact of law, policy, and socio-economic realities on the strength, salience, and function of identity in US politics. Within each chapter you will find contemporary examples that move beyond theories of difference to examine how battles over political incorporation play out. This emphasis on real-world applications of identity politics challenges us to move beyond the simplistic rejection of group affiliations to better consider whether these categorizations are an immutable feature of US politics. Each chapter also includes key terms, discussion questions, and a "controversy box" that examines how a particular political event or policy question (e.g. the rise of Christian Evangelicals as an organized political force) raises constitutional questions that test the boundaries of identity and inclusion. It is my hope that you will form your own views on whether allegiance to identity undermines the broader goal of American kinship or whether the dynamics of American politics force residents to cling to and organize around identities.

Chapter Overview

Chapter 2 explores the key theoretical traditions that connect group identity and US politics by examining intragroup differences as sites of cooperation and conflict. It introduces readers to the work of scholars such as Robert Dahl, Kimberlé Crenshaw, Cristina Beltrán, and Michael Dawson to specify the political meaning of identity.

Chapter 3 builds on these intragroup differences to situate historical efforts to limit citizenship within broader notions of group identity and competition.

Participants gather for a naturalization ceremony held in 2018 at the Paterson Great Falls National Park in New Jersey. Changes in US immigration laws over time have shaped the number of naturalized citizens as well as their countries of origin.

I place a particular emphasis on key parts of the system such as actors, institutions, and processes that reinforce the boundaries between citizens and non-citizens. These components create differences among citizens in terms of their ability to fully exercise the associated rights and privileges. The salience of a particularly identity, or set of identities, is shaped by elite cues, campaign rhetoric, institutional constraints, and policy framing. This suggests a very complex structure of identity that can vary across individuals, issues, and spaces. Chapter 3 challenges the belief that social groups are monolithic communities with uniform priorities in order to better understand how members of these groups reason through their position in America's political and social hierarchy. The emphasis on intersectionality provides a useful foundation for understanding how growing levels of diversity have changed the complexity of the American polity while simultaneously creating new sites of political pressure.

Chapter 4 focuses on the meaning of racial identity in US politics by tracing the relationship between racial categorizations and efforts to achieve freedom. Its goal is to understand how historical exclusions shape the contemporary contours of race, citizenship, and political standing. I embrace Dr Ronald Walters's view, in *Freedom is Not Enough* (2005), that securing access to the franchise has been a chief focus of African Americans' vision of freedom. Fifty years after the passage of the **Voting Rights Act of 1965** (VRA) that prohibited discriminatory electoral devices, African Americans have raised their profile as both voters and candidates while contending with new threats related to gerrymandering, redistricting, and restrictive photo ID requirements. What are the implications of this emergence? Are policies such as the VRA still relevant, given such gains? The chapter also analyzes the impact of growing internal cleavages (e.g. increased immigration from African, Caribbean, and Latin American countries; a growing Black middle class) on political agendas and priorities to better understand how intergroup political interactions shape intragroup dynamics.

Chapter 5 focuses on ethnic identity in US politics by exploring the challenges groups such as Latinx and Asian Americans have faced in navigating the American political space. It emphasizes the need to place their contemporary political status within the broader context of historical denials of citizenship and membership based on differing experiences with immigration and migration. I discuss the historic candidacies of Ted Cruz and Marco Rubio and their connection to broader questions of authenticity, inclusion, and incorporation. For example, does a Latino leader have to have a Spanish surname? What constraints exist for those who hold individual policy positions that may not be in the best interest of the group as a whole? How does the political process exacerbate internal debates over nationalism and pan-ethnicity?

Chapter 6 examines the role of stereotypes and difference in shaping the meaning of gender and **sexual identity** in the United States. I trace the increased presence of women in elected office while discussing the challenges they face in running. For example, although women make up the largest share of the US population, they comprise only 24 percent of the congressional delegation. Further, various studies document the challenges women face in raising campaign funds. This emphasis on gender identity revisits the concept of intersectionality and the need to understand how notions of difference may persist across other cleavages such as race, religion, and class. **Federalism** rests as the foundation for understanding the emergence of policy concerns and judicial decisions related to sexual identity and gender expression. Recent events such as the Women's March and the Me Too movement highlight the difficult conversations about leadership, message, and strategy.

Chapter 7 examines the impact of religious affiliation on public policy and political behavior. What, for example, was the significance of John F. Kennedy's 1960 bid for the White House in bringing issues of religious diversity and politics to the fore? I highlight attitudes toward religious diversity and how these attitudes shape evaluations of candidates and policies. The contemporary relationship between **religious identity** and US politics has been shaped by the rise of the world's largest evangelical university (Liberty University) and its commitment to inserting the voices of conservative Christians into the public sphere. From efforts to repeal the **Johnson Amendment** limiting churches' partisan activities to state-level efforts to resist the "spread of Islam," religious affiliation has re-emerged as a key fault line. This chapter also introduces readers to less mainstream religious concepts, such as liberation theology, that are deeply embedded within particular communities. Readers should consider the significance of these traditions both for the people who practice them and for those who may be less familiar with them. This emphasis on religious affiliation also highlights the challenges posed when various layers of one's identity may dictate very different political choices.

While chapters 1 to 7 detail how the intersection of law, politics, and policy heightens the salience of identity politics, chapter 8 explores how underrepresented groups challenge their exclusion via political movements to pursue rights and resources. This pursuit of authentic power positions the United States as a movement society where identity becomes a constant source of potential conflict and cooperation. From early organizing efforts such as the Abolitionist movement to the contemporary demands posited by young people in the Never Again movement, the necessity of **collective action** is heightened for groups whose membership in the polity is threatened.

Finally, chapter 9 offers a cautionary note on the growing impact of identity-based conflicts in the United States and around the globe. As demographic shifts continue, economic challenges persist, and fault lines around immigration status, race, ethnicity, gender, and sexual identity widen, it is imperative that both casual observers and astute scholars assess the impact of identity on the process of politics. The results of the 2018 midterm elections point to a potential shift in voters' willingness to embrace difference. I survey the landscape to address my view that identity politics will remain a necessary yet complicated fixture of American politics.

My goal is to help readers make sense of contemporary political realities by evaluating longstanding tensions over the purpose, strength, and function of identity in US politics. In *Notes of a Native Son* (1955), essayist and cultural critic James Baldwin writes: "I love America more than any other country in this world, and, exactly for that reason I insist on the right to criticize her perpetually." This book is inspired by a Twi (Ghanaian) concept, *Sankofa*, which loosely translates to "go back and get it." *Sankofa* is a reminder that understanding the past can help us navigate the present while preparing for the future. Let's get it. Together.

2

Identity Politics and the Boundaries of Belonging

Lessons from the 2016 Presidential Election

I spent election night 2016 at a television station. That evening was the culmination of eighteen months of analyzing what became one of the most divisive, vicious, and dynamic elections I've ever studied. As the election returns began to pour in from various states, it became clear that the person most people expected to be the victor would not be taking the oath of office as president of the United States. Viewers began emailing, tweeting, and calling us to express their reactions. We heard from people who were ecstatic that the White House would be occupied by a Republican after eight years of Democratic control. We saw tweets from local business owners who thought having a fellow entrepreneur in office would foster a pro-business climate that put American manufacturers and laborers first. Other viewers lamented that their daughters would have to wait, again, to see the election of the United States' first woman president. A few criticized the overall structure of US elections, which suppress the voices of independent voters while reinforcing the dominance of two major political parties that may or may not represent the rapidly diversifying electorate.

For millions of people, the 2016 election and its aftermath were bigger than deciding whether Hillary Clinton or Donald Trump would become president. It forced many to consider, often for the first time, the meaning of a collective identity while exposing longstanding fault lines over issues once thought settled for some and ever-present for others. The election unfolded against the backdrop of broader global debates over the best way to address changing demographics wrought by shifts in migration and immigration. For example, Britons voted to withdraw the United Kingdom from the European Union just five months before the American election. The historic Brexit vote rested on brewing tensions over labor, religion, and increased immigration. The battle over who belongs is not unique to the United States, but the factors that shape the importance of group affiliations in politics are indeed a sign of **American exceptionalism**.

President Donald J. Trump at a campaign rally in Iowa, 2018: "Make America Great Again" was the key slogan for Trump and his supporters.

The Context

In the months leading up to the 2016 presidential election analysts and casual observers debated the tremendous amount of **dark money** that would be used to motivate voters and shape campaign strategies. Following the Supreme Court's 2010 ruling in *Citizens United* v. *Federal Election Commission*, a record $1.6 billion was funneled through non-profit organizations to influence the outcome of the election. Campaign ads touted the dangers of contemporary immigration while demanding strict reforms to promote border security. Immigration was portrayed as a drain on American society that excused criminals to the detriment of innocent Americans. Candidate Donald Trump recounted the story of Jose Ines Garcia Zarate, who was deported five times before being accused of murdering Kate Steinle in San Francisco. The Democratic National Committee sought to counter this narrative by introducing Khizr and Ghazala Khan, two Pakistani-born American citizens whose son, Humayun Khan, was killed while fighting in the Iraqi War. The deaths of both Kate Steinle and Humayun Khan resonated with voters. Yet these tropes of the "violent illegal" and the "hardworking patriot" oversimplified the longstanding debates over who deserves the opportunity to pursue the American Dream.

Exit-poll data for the election highlighted the surge in political organizing among Evangelicals, who perceived a war on their values in favor of political correctness. Senator Ted Cruz announced his bid for the Republican nomination for president during convocation at Liberty University. To some it seemed odd that a Congressman from Texas would kick off his pursuit of the presidency in a small Virginia town, at a college he did not attend, in front of students with historically low rates of voting. However, Liberty is now the world's largest evangelical university, with over 110,000 students and a dedicated commitment to training conservative Christians to influence every facet of public life. Democratic hopeful Bernie Sanders stunned some by speaking at the university on Rosh Hashanah, one of the holiest days in Judaism. Ben Carson, an African American neurosurgeon and presidential contender, visited the school to warn students against "secular progressives" who seek to remove God from public life and punish Christians for their beliefs. Months later Donald Trump returned to the school to deliver the annual Dr Martin Luther King Jr Day speech. The persistent tension within the pursuit of the religious vote emanates from an assumption that equates evangelical with white while failing to acknowledge the high number of voters of color who identify with this faith tradition. Tables 2.1 and 2.2 show changes in self-reported religious affiliation and vote choice between 2000 and 2016. Although the share of Americans identifying as Christian has remained fairly constant over time, gaps in presidential vote choice have widened across the intersection of race, ethnicity, and religious affiliation.

Beyond choosing the next president, the 2016 election cycle prompted reflection on the legacy of America's first African American incumbent of the post. Some wondered whether the election and subsequent re-election of Barack Obama signaled a post-racial era that transcended the admonition from scholars such as Gunnar Myrdal, W. E. B. DuBois, and Alexis de Tocqueville that issues of race represented America's great dilemma. The eight years of the Obama presidency were filled with racial contestations over belonging, from the infamous "Beer Summit" following the controversial arrest of Harvard Professor Henry Louis "Skip" Gates, Jr, to repeated uprisings in cities such

Table 2.1 Religious affiliation, 2000–2016 (percentages)

	2000	2004	2008	2012	2016	Net change 2000–2016
Protestant/other Christian	54	54	54	53	52	−2
White evangelical Christian	n/a	23	26	26	26	n/a
Catholic	26	27	27	25	23	−3
Jewish	4	3	2	2	3	−1
Other faiths	6	7	6	7	8	+2
Unaffiliated	9	10	12	12	15	+6

SOURCE: Based on data from Pew Research Center (2015).

Table 2.2 Presidential vote choice by religious affiliation, 2000–2016 (percentages)

	2000		2004		2008		2012		2016		Dem change '12–'16
	Gore %	Bush %	Kerry %	Bush %	Obama %	McCain %	Obama %	Romney %	Clinton %	Trump %	%
Protestant/other Christian	42	56	40	59	45	54	42	57	39	58	−3
Catholic	50	47	47	52	54	45	50	48	45	52	−5
White Catholic	45	52	43	56	47	52	40	59	37	60	−3
Hispanic Catholic	65	33	65	33	72	26	75	21	67	26	−8
Jewish	79	19	74	25	78	21	69	30	71	24	+2
Other faiths	62	28	74	23	73	22	74	23	62	29	−12
Religiously unaffiliated	61	30	67	31	75	23	70	26	68	26	−2
White, born-again/evangelical Christian	n/a	n/a	21	78	24	74	21	78	16	81	−5
Mormon	n/a	n/a	19	80	n/a	n/a	21	78	25	61	+4

Source: Pew Research Center, "How the Faithful Voted: A Preliminary 2016 Analysis," November 9, 2016.

as Ferguson, Missouri; Baltimore, Maryland; and Charlotte, North Carolina, following the shooting deaths of unarmed Black residents at the hands of local police. Immigration activists condemned Obama as the "deporter-in-chief" for deporting more undocumented immigrants than his predecessors, as undocumented students organized as "Dreamers" to demand state-level changes in public education access.

Against the election backdrop rest ongoing questions about the willingness of elected officials to protect the lives of underrepresented communities in Flint, Michigan, and on the Standing Rock reservation. The stakes were high for groups struggling to navigate an increasingly precarious political space that often felt indifferent at best and openly hostile at worst. Some feared that the gains in criminal justice reform, pay equity, and reproductive rights would be erased by a new president with the power to make fresh appointments to the Supreme Court (Rodrik 2016). State-level efforts to adopt bans on Sharia law made clear the mounting fear of and hostility toward the spread of Islam in the United States. This fear was codified by a 2018 Supreme Court decision upholding a ban on travel from six Muslim countries.

Grassroots organizations advocated for the protection of young people via the Delayed Action for Childhood Arrivals (DACA) program that deferred deportation for undocumented youth, while other interest groups such as Focus on the Family saw the election as a conduit for channeling conservative angst over the Supreme Court's affirmation of marriage equality, the dismantling of bans on military service by gay, lesbian, and **transgender** service members, and health-care reform that, to some, felt like a government handout. These battles over immigration, voting rights, economic development, foreign policy, **tribal sovereignty**, and environmental justice are bound together by fundamental tensions over the boundaries of belonging. Though many people believed that the election of Barack Obama signaled a movement toward greater inclusion in the US polity, the 2016 election highlighted unsettled questions over rights, responsibilities, and protections that divide Americans in important ways. The emergence of new groups and the increased political visibility of existing groups challenge the status quo and, by extension, the social order.

This change, or the perception of change, prompted resentment across a range of identities related to race, ethnicity, religion, and sexual orientation. At times this resentment manifested as violence, such as the targeted execution of partygoers at the Pulse nightclub in Orlando and subsequent debates over the meaning of "domestic terrorism." Others channel their resentment by rejecting policies perceived as privileging certain groups over others or demanding judicial interpretations of efforts to protect group beliefs.

The 2016 election and its aftermath captured the attention of people around the globe. However, the chaos that has ensued from threats of tariffs, the retrenchment of civil rights protections, heightened deportations of undocumented immigrants, and decisions to ban transgender troops is grounded in longstanding conflicts over the political meaning of identity. Across various institutions of government, across various political actors, and across various policy spaces, the interaction between political decision-making, public support, and historical circumstance produces public policies that stratify access and representation. Negotiating the complex ways in which identity shapes and is shaped by the American political spaces forms the intellectual heart of this book.

As American as Apple Pie

The story of American political development is one of constant invention and reinvention. What began as an experiment in liberation from the British Crown has evolved into a global blueprint for governance. Wars have been fought, alliances tested, and institutions built to cement the belief that each citizen should have a say in the affairs of government. And yet even at its founding the United States struggled to come to terms with the most basic denial of rights to groups such as American Indians, women, and enslaved Africans. *Discrimination*, or the practice of treating certain groups differently, has been a ubiquitous feature of American political development. Alexis de Tocqueville observes, in his seminal work *Democracy in America* (1835), "Americans are so enamored of equality that they would rather be equal in slavery than unequal in freedom." How, then, does a country tasked with being the architect for modern democracy grapple with the persistent cleavages that both shape and are shaped by the democratic process?

Understanding Identity

At its core, *identity* refers to the attachments we hold to the groups to which we belong, or want to belong. Some aspects of our identity derive from groups into which we are born. Others connect to groups we adopt or are placed into by others. The salience and priority of these attachments vary across a range of factors, such as the available policy options, geographic location, media socialization, and social norms. Quite simply, context matters.

In 2015, paparazzi snapped lucrative photos of former Olympian and reality-show star Bruce Jenner amid speculation that his changing physical appearance signaled an evolving identity. Activists cautioned the public to offer Jenner and his family privacy to manage a deeply personal conversation away from the public gaze.[1] That same year, the former head of the Spokane

National Association for Colored People (NAACP) resigned after claims that she lied about being the victim of hate crimes because of her race. When asked about her identity, Rachel Dolezal, the daughter of two white parents, responded, "Well, I definitely am not white."[2]

Some observers hoped Bruce Jenner's transition to Caitlyn Jenner would help educate the public about the myriad challenges faced by the transgender community. However, activist Janet Mock cautioned against media attempts to exalt Jenner as a representative of the trans community: "To make any trans person a symbol for an entire community is an unfair task. No one can speak about the varying intersecting and layered ways in which trans people experience the world. That is why it's necessary to create a space for nuance and to amplify the voices of those who often are not heard."[3] Mock joined with actress Laverne Cox to highlight how Jenner's wealth provided her with access to medical treatments that are often difficult to obtain by others trying to align their **self-identity** with their physical presentation. The privilege of wealth, they argued, masked the structural barriers for people seeking to transition from the sex assigned at birth to their current gender identity. Jenner's transition also raised the question of whether people can be prejudiced against members of their own community after a *Time Magazine* article quoted her as saying that trans people who "look like a man in a dress" make others uncomfortable.[4]

The notion that attempts at self-definition may make others uncomfortable fueled Dolezal's decision to liken her struggle to that of Jenner by offering that she was born white but felt Black, and thus transracial. The tanning of her skin, adoption of intricately braided hairstyles popular with women of color, and embrace of civil rights struggles reflected Dolezal's controversial belief that she had in fact evolved beyond the racial classification of her birth. Her presentation triggered a mountain of backlash from people who accused her of not understanding trans identity as being deeper than just a "feeling." Others argued that "passing" as Black mocked the contested history of racial tension.

Denying one's racial identity to pass as a member of a different racial group has a long history in the United States. That practice is most commonly associated with fairer skinned people of color passing as white. In Douglas Sirk's 1959 film *Imitation of Life*, the character Sarah Jane tries to convince everyone she encounters that she is white. "Passing" was Sarah Jane's way of rejecting her mother's racial identity and occupation as a domestic worker to overcome the restrictive racial and class castes that ordered American society. However, it's Sarah Jane who is rejected when her classmates discover that her mother is in fact Black.

The varied reactions to Caitlyn Jenner, Rachel Dolezal (now known as Nkechi Diallo), and Sarah Jane highlight two important dimensions of group identity. The first is the extent to which an individual feels they are part of a group (*self-identity*). The second dimension is the extent to which society views them as belonging to a particular group (*social categorization*). At times, social categorization may be a determinant more of group membership than of self-identity (Tajfel 1979). The tension that arises when the way in which an individual sees themselves doesn't align with how others see them mobilizes some groups to push for inclusion. It also highlights the challenge of determining the boundaries of belonging and the penalties for violating them.

BOX 2.1 Key themes of identity politics

Individual identity: how individuals view themselves and their relationship to the political process
Group identity: our proximity to and affinity for those with whom we share certain characteristics and experiences
Group conflict: how the political process both organizes and resolves tension over resources

---

The Boundaries of Belonging

In their classic work *Racial Formations in the United States*, sociologists Michael Omi and Howard Winant (1986) describe the complexity of resolving these tensions through the legal battles of Susie Guillory Phipps, who earnestly believed that she and her six siblings were in fact white. It wasn't until she applied for a passport in 1977 that Phipps learned the state of Louisiana had classified her as "colored"[5] because she was the descendant of an enslaved woman who, some 200 years earlier, had borne the children of a white planter. According to the state of Louisiana, Phipps was 1/32 Black and thus sufficiently colored:

> "I told the clerk that it was wrong and to take it off," remembers Susie. "But she said she couldn't. She said it was the official record. I was mad. My mother and daddy weren't colored. They were white. My daddy even had blue eyes. If it was the other way around, if I was black, I'd be just as shocked and would want it fixed right." (Demaret 1982)

Outraged by the state's refusal to change the law governing her racial classification, Susie Guillory Phipps lost her appeal to change her racial identity on official records.[6] The state eventually repealed the law in 1983 after a public outcry. The Phipps case raises broader questions about how identity is socially constructed and negotiated. In the next section I detail some of the major approaches to understanding identity politics and examine how these negotiations help structure political preferences.

Social Constructions of Identity

The influence and function of group identity are determined by various laws, norms, customs, and policies. Identity, then, is a social construct that both shapes and is shaped by the practice of politics. For some groups, social norms and political practice shape and limit their ability to navigate the political space. At times, exclusion forces groups to collapse inward and organize internally. For others, exclusion encourages them to denounce their unique markers in favor of broader acceptance.

In *The Content of Our Character*, Shelby Steele (1990) argues that having a strong attachment to a particular group creates hostility toward mainstream society while also promoting a mentality of victimization. Steele and others see group-based mobilization strategies as antithetical to the American tradition because they promote separatism and divisiveness. Groups who find themselves shut out of the political process should work hard to adopt and assimilate into American life.

Gordon (1964) offers seven distinct stages of **assimilation** that form a two-stage process. Immigrants and groups seeking recognition must prove themselves worthy by rejecting the markers of their native community and embracing the traditions, preferences, and practices of the host country. Over time, society will include these aspirants if they sufficiently cast off their markers of difference.

BOX 2.2 Gordon's seven stages of assimilation

Cultural assimilation	Rejecting customs of your home country in favor of host-country traditions
Structural assimilation	Embracing the host country's institutions, e.g. civic groups and fraternal organizations
Marital assimilation	Large-scale choosing of marriage partners from groups different from your own
Identificational assimilation	Basing one's sense of self on alignment with the host country
Receptional assimilation	Rejection of bias and prejudice toward new(er) groups
Behavioral reception	Lack of discrimination
Civic assimilation	Lack of conflict over values and power-sharing

---

In the first stage, *cultural assimilation*, groups disregard home customs such as dress, names, religion, holidays, music, and language in favor of the traditions of the host country. The failure to actively embrace the cultural norms of the host community often results in legal efforts to promote conformity. In 1993, the US Supreme Court heard arguments in the case of the *Church of the Lukumi Babalu Aye* v. *City of Hialeah, Florida*. At issue was whether members of the church could practice key tenets of their Santeria faith. The most notable opposition was to ritual animal sacrifice. *Santeria* is a **syncretic** religious faith that combines elements of the Yoruba tradition with Roman Catholicism and is popular in many Afro-Caribbean communities.

Hialeah public officials passed a city ordinance prohibiting the possession of animals for sacrifice or slaughter with limited exceptions. The Court unanimously ruled in favor of the church, arguing that the city had violated the **Free Exercise Clause** of the First Amendment that protects freedom of and freedom from religion. Although the Church of the Lukumi won their legal battle, congregants' failure to distance themselves from their traditional beliefs created longstanding tensions within the Hialeah community. Similar efforts to resolve tensions between religious observance and cultural norms have prompted court cases involving vaccinations and blood transfusions, wearing the hijab in driver's license photos, the banning of ethnic hairstyles in workplaces, and the use of certain hallucinogens during religious sacraments.

The second stage is *structural assimilation* based on an embrace of institutions such as civic groups and fraternal networks. Gordon believed that groups who sought to join longstanding organizations as opposed to identity-based societies would be able to show their appreciation for the host community while personalizing contact to overcome notions of difference. Some of these organizations included the Rotary, business and trade associations, and country clubs. As private organizations, however, these groups often exercised their authority to deny membership to those who didn't "fit" with their desired profile. Many country clubs, for example, explicitly barred women, Jews, and non-citizens from joining. This exclusion from private associations had a direct impact on the ability to form social and business networks.

Stage three requires *marital assimilation* or the large-scale practice of choosing marriage partners from different groups. Recent data from the Pew Center show the rapidly changing rates of intermarriage in the United States across various racial and ethnic groups (Lugo 2013). As figure 2.1 illustrates, rates of intermarriage are highest among Asian American women and Black men, while there are lower rates among Orthodox Jewish men. While intermarriage may be a goal for some, the emphasis on marital assimilation overlooks the history of legal barriers and the glut of *anti-miscegenation laws* that dominated the landscape until 1967. Laws prohibiting "race-mixing" in the United States date back as early as 1661 and were common in many states until the Supreme Court ruling in *Loving* v. *Virginia* that deemed Virginia's miscegenation laws unconstitutional.

In 1967, thirty-four states had provisions that fully banned interracial relationships, with punishments ranging from a $300 penalty to a felony

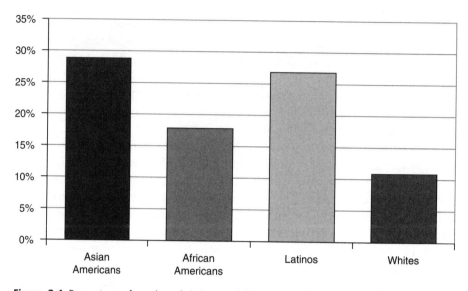

Figure 2.1 Percentage of newlyweds in interracial marriages, 2015
SOURCE: Gretchen Livingston and Anna Brown, *Intermarriage in the US 50 Years after Loving* v. *Virginia*, Pew Research Center, May 18, 2017.

life sentence. To some scholars, the laws were created based on racism and a desire to maintain a strict racial hierarchy. For others, the major motivation was economic. By keeping groups separate and maintaining purer blood lines, the ruling class could ensure that they would have a consistent labor supply. For example, many feared that alliances between enslaved Africans and Indians would lead them to rebel against whites.

The enduring legacy of *Loving* is an increase in the number of individuals who identify as "mixed race" or "multiracial." Until 2000, the US census forced respondents to choose one racial category from among five options. Now, as table 2.3 shows, respondents may choose one or more categories from five options: white, Black/African American, American Indian or Alaska Native, Asian, and Native Hawaiian or other Pacific Islander.

Stage four is *identificational assimilation*, where the sense of self is based on being in alignment with the host country. Identifying ties to the country of origin becomes less important than identifying as "American" first. Once groups can successfully navigate these first four stages, the host country promotes stage five, *receptional assimilation*, characterized by the rejection of bias and prejudice against these groups. Overt acts of prejudice are limited because society eases stereotypes that group members violate cherished American values and traditions. Thus, mistreating groups is viewed as an aberration sharply condemned by the broader society. Closely related is stage six, *behavioral reception*, which is a lack of discrimination. Finally, stage seven is *civic assimilation*, which reflects the absence of conflict over values and power-sharing.

Table 2.3 US census race categories

White	A person having origins in any of the original peoples of Europe, the Middle East, or North Africa
Black/African American	A person having origins in any of the Black racial groups of Africa
American Indian or Alaska Native	A person having origins in any of the original peoples of North and South America (including Central America) and who maintains tribal affiliations or community attachment
Asian	A person having origins in any of the original people of the Far East, Southeast Asia, or the Indian subcontinent, including, for example, Cambodia, China, India, Japan, Korea, Malaysia, Pakistan, the Philippines, Thailand, and Vietnam
Native Hawaiian or other Pacific Islander	A person having origins in any of the original people of Hawaii, Guam, Samoa, or other Pacific islands

SOURCE: US Census Bureau.

This view of assimilation sees discrimination as the consequence of a group's failure to adopt and adapt to American life. To be sure, full assimilation is an aspirational goal that may never be fully realized for groups who begin as an "other" and seek acceptance. Some groups are better able to navigate these stages based on characteristics such as command of the English language, access to social mobility, and skin tone. What's less clear, however, is how we align the experiences of American Indian tribes and native-born Blacks who don't share the experience of immigration. Similarly, Mexican Americans and Puerto Ricans who inherit the legacies of colonization and conquest encounter a more tenuous path toward full assimilation. Emerging immigration patterns within communities of color add a different challenge to assimilation that highlights racial distinctions within ethnic groups (Schmidt et al. 2009).

The Substance of Citizenship

Understanding how assimilation varies across multiple markers helps us better understand the difference between self-identity (how individuals and groups perceive themselves) and social identity (how individuals and groups are perceived by society). This distinction is of particular importance in the context of what it means to "be American" and who is accepted as a citizen. Social psychologists Thierry Devos and Mahzarin Banaji have pioneered research on the degree to which members of certain groups (particularly African, Asian, and white) are associated with American identity. They draw on the work of Swedish sociologist Gunnar Myrdal, who called the gap between American ideals and the American practice of exclusion and discrimination "the great dilemma."

Devos and Banaji (2005) find that, while most people in the United States express a firm commitment to the values of fairness and egalitarianism, they implicitly associate "Americanness" with "whiteness." The authors use thirteen questions that gauge various actions (e.g. voting in elections), beliefs (e.g. faith in God), and conditions (e.g. born in the US) to constitute their definition of Americanness. Respondents were asked to evaluate how closely they associated certain groups with these indicators. The results indicate that the overwhelming majority of participants believe that African Americans, whites, and Asian Americans should be treated equally and with respect. However, Asian Americans were perceived as having weaker ties to US culture and, thus, as "less American":

> To be American is to be white. This finding is itself noteworthy, particularly because it sits in opposition to the explicit assessment that to be American is to endorse civic values such as equality and expressed commitment to egalitarian principles. On the most generic and straightforward explicit measure of ethnic American associations, Asian Americans, and to a lesser extent African Americans, are not viewed as being as American as white Americans. (Devos and Banaji 2005: 453)

This tendency to conflate American identity with whiteness speaks to the ongoing challenge of reconciling formal statements of citizenship with the practice of denying inclusion to groups asserting their membership in the polity. It also helps us address why group attachment may be a necessary coping skill in US politics.

The Psychology of Attachment

For those who feel rejected by society or who reject the notion of assimilation, group identification may serve as a source of empowerment. Various scholars show that group attachment provides such psychological resources as increased efficacy, political trust, and aspirations that, in turn, help connect individual members to a larger community (Nunnally 2012; Wilson and Hunt 2013; Dawson 1993; Anderson 2010; Sanchez and Vargas 2016). Through this connection, individuals are better able to recognize the need for political engagement. For some groups, a shared history and identity leads to the formation of internal networks designed to strengthen community and promote full participation in the polity (McAdam 1982; Morris 1984; Sherrill 1993). Other groups develop out of a shared sense of animosity toward others or a fear over those groups becoming too large or too powerful. Group identity may serve as a coping mechanism for individuals who feel shut out by the broader society or as a conduit for those seeking to block others from participating fully in society.

BOX 2.3 Promoting group solidarity on college campuses

Alpha Phi Alpha Fraternity was founded on the campus of Cornell University on December 4, 1906, as the first intercollegiate fraternity for African American men. At the time of its creation, African American students were largely barred from attending public colleges and universities, and their numbers on private campuses remained small. Those students who did attend found themselves shut out from participating in existing organizations and often created their own networks, affiliations, and institutions to promote civic engagement, cultural awareness, and scholastic excellence. Alpha Kappa Alpha Sorority became the first sorority created by African American women, on January 15, 1908. Since that time, seven other fraternities and sororities have been created for and by Black students: Delta Sigma Theta Sorority, Zeta Phi Beta Sorority, Iota Phi Theta Fraternity, Kappa Alpha Psi Fraternity, Sigma Gamma Rho Sorority, Phi Beta Sigma Fraternity, and Omega Psi Phi Fraternity (Ross 2001).

Over time other groups have created their own fraternal organizations designed to address the unique needs and interests of their constituents while helping members navigate the complexities of being underrepresented on college campuses. Some of those affinity-based organizations include Native American[7] sorority Alpha Pi Omega, Jewish fraternity Alpha Epsilon Pi, the oldest Hispanic fraternity in existence, Phi Iota Alpha fraternity, and Delta Phi Kappa, the oldest Asian American interest sorority. Theta Omega Phi was founded as the first LGBT-centered fraternity in 1956. Other fraternal organizations have also been formed to support the interests of Muslim, Christian, and multicultural students on campuses across the country. These groups are historically but not exclusively populated by students with shared demographic profiles.

The Dimensions of Group Identity

At times, "group membership is a powerful basis for the development of self-identity and perceptions of individual interest" (Bobo 1983). The political meaning of group identity is broader than just placement in a category. Instead, the salience of that membership varies across two key

Indian tribes and their allies across the United States protested the use of derogatory symbols and cultural references. Here a Minnesota resident expresses opposition to the name of the Washington, DC, NFL team.

dimensions. First, the extent to which an individual feels that they are part of a group. Our level of attachment to a particular group (or a particular layer of our identity) varies across a number of factors, such as the primacy of the issue at hand or the options presented by particular allegiances and affiliations.

The second characteristic of group identity is the extent to which society views an individual as belonging to a particular group. Together, these dimensions make certain groups more susceptible to changes in the political environment that can, in turn, shape public opinions, political behavior, and discontent. Below I examine how the external process of exclusion shapes internal cohesion.

Linked Fate

Scholar Michael Dawson (1993) asserts that the political beliefs and actions of individual citizens are related to their perceptions of *group* interests. These individual preferences are shaped by the following components:

1. *Ties to a broader community* These ties are created and reinforced by institutions within the community that help to reinforce elements of your identity and promote a shared affinity – for example, membership in cultural

associations and civic groups, attending a women's college, or participating in worship services conducted in one's native language.

2. *Perception(s) of group interests* This calculation rests on understanding the key policy concerns of the group such as access to affordable health care, the ability to practice one's religious beliefs freely, or limiting immigration. It also shapes support for particular candidates and issues that may affect the group as a whole.

3. *One's place in the class structure* Class functions differently within various racial and ethnic groups. For example, the creation of Japanese Mutual Aid Societies made the purchase of cemetery plots more affordable for indigent families. The development of these support networks grew out of the fact that many underrepresented groups were denied access to traditional modes of support such as bank loans and the right freely to choose their preferred final resting place. For example, Zelinsky (2001) documents that, until the 1950s, 90 percent of American cemeteries were segregated based on race, ethnicity, religious denomination, and fraternal association. He argues that the "spatial segregation of the dead" represents an ongoing effort to define the relative desirability of groups.

4. *One's place in America's broader social hierarchy* The historical experiences of a group coupled with these individual considerations create a sense of cognitive transformation among marginalized groups.

Group Consciousness

Group consciousness is a more politicized view of membership that focuses on using political action to improve the group's position in society. It can invoke an awareness of group interests and a shared collective struggle that encourages members to challenge limits on their inclusion (Dawson 1993; McAdam 1982; Gurin et al. 1980; Harris 2012; Tyson 2017). Drawing upon the indigenous strengths and resources of the communities, what follows is an assessment of the most effective tools for achieving empowerment and promoting development. Examples of indigenous resources are culturally relevant houses of worship, institutions of higher learning with distinct ties to the community (e.g. historically Black colleges and universities and Hispanic serving institutions), and political action committees that raise funds for candidates and issues of mutual concern. At times, these group-based efforts to promote incorporation create tensions that shape and are shaped by the broader process of politics.

Identity, Democratic Theory, and Group Competition

Democratic theory posits that participation in the decision-making process by the mass public is essential to the well-being of a society because "citizen participation is at the heart of democracy ... political participation is an important activity with the intent of influencing government action" (Verba et al. 1995: 38). This helps channel the needs and preferences of communities to political decision-makers and provides the means to pressure a response. Democracy rests on the assumption that the purpose of the political system is to aggregate and collect the preferences of the governed. Essential to that configuration is a system that is both open *and* responsive to all. Gunnar Myrdal documents the persistent gap between the promise of democracy and the realities of its exclusions in his classic study *An American Dilemma*:

> The extreme democracy in the American system of justice ... turns out to be the greatest menace to legal tradition when it is based on restricted political participation ... what America is constantly reaching for is democracy at home and abroad ... In this sense the Negro problem is not only America's greatest failure but also America's incomparably great opportunity for the future ... if America in actual practice could show the world a progressive trend by which the Negro became finally integrated into modern democracy, all mankind would be given faith again. (1944: 1021)

The relative openness of this system can be a key catalyst for political movements designed to pressure inclusion (Hero 1992, 1998; Hochschild 1984; Cohen 1999).

Pluralism

Who Governs? by Robert Dahl (1961) offers the classic statement of pluralist theory. According to pluralists, the political system is open, with no upper limits to participation. Power is diffused across various arenas, and no one group or set of groups has a monopoly on control. Dahl posits the existence of a two-step decision-making process where the masses articulate their needs to sub-leaders, who in turn convey these needs to the leaders. This interactive exchange produces an anticipatory reaction where leaders predict what the masses want and oblige without having to be asked. Pluralists believe this two-step process is democratic because officials are held accountable by elections. Therefore, the right to participate in elections becomes the ultimate guarantee of democracy by insuring that everyone has the opportunity to participate in the process.

Critics of **pluralism** (Bachrach and Baratz 1973; Gamson 1975; Manley 1983; Parenti 1983) point to the interests and individuals that are systematically *excluded* from the decision-making process. Through the **mobilization of bias**, certain interests and groups are organized out of the political process by creating disincentives that discourage participation. For example, seventeen states have adopted laws that make it harder to vote for people without a valid government-issued form of photo identification. A report issued by the Brennan Center for Justice (2006) found that people who make less than $25,000 a year are twice as likely not to have the documentation needed to prove their citizenship and eligibility to vote.

The existence of a system that is open to all is a necessary but certainly not a sufficient condition for a pluralist democracy. An equally important condition is a system that is uniformly responsive to citizens, so that "the claims of a significant number of members as the rules, policies, etc., to be adopted by binding decisions are valid and equally valid, and that no members' claims are, taken all around, superior or overriding in relation to this set of members" (Dahl 1989: 135). The United States is idealized by many as a grand melting pot where anyone can achieve the American Dream if they work hard enough. That aspirational vision has always been hampered at times by competing visions of progress. The unique brand of American democracy – what Tocqueville called "American exceptionalism" – has been contested since the founding of this nation. As Thomas Jefferson penned the words "we hold these truths to be self-evident that all men are created equal," he enslaved nearly 200 Africans, including his wife's sister, Sally Hemings. Hemings gave birth to at least six children who, by Virginia law, remained enslaved and thus ineligible to inherit the land, property, and freedom of their white father (Gordon-Reed 1998).

Recall from chapter 1 that politics is a constant battle for resources, both material and symbolic. The zero-sum approach to political power sparks persistent clashes over access, control, and social standing that moderates conflicts within and between groups.

Group Competition and Conflict

The contemporary group competition and conflict literature grew from the social psychology tradition of emphasizing the existence and importance of intergroup relations (Tajfel and Turner 1979; Levine and Campbell 1972). Social identity refers to "that part of an individual's self-concept which derives from his knowledge of his membership in a group (or groups) together with the value and emotional significance attached to the membership" (Tajfel 1979). Social identity theory rests on the belief that individuals and the groups to which they belong have meaningful interactions with other groups. These interactions are characterized by three primary processes. The first is the ethnocentrism effect, which is characterized by strong in-group attachment and identification (Park et al. 1992). In-group members are rated more favorably than those of the out-group. The second process is the out-group homogeneity effect where out-group members are perceived as being less diverse and more stereotypic than in-group members. This process often leads to greater hostility toward the out-group and heightens competition over resources, cultural values, and political power.

Competition occurs when two or more groups strive for the same finite objectives and have roots in different cultures (McClain 1993). Competition may exist over tangible benefits such as jobs and government services or over more symbolic benefits such as formal recognition and representation of the group's interests. The success of one group may imply a reduced probability that the other will attain its goals and, in turn, influences political attitudes and behaviors, especially as underrepresented groups become more numerous: "an increase in minority percentage should result in an increase in discrimination . . . because of heightened perceived competition and increased power threat" (Blalock 1967: 154). Groups may perceive competitive threat from another group based on self-interest, classical prejudice, stratification beliefs, and an overall sense of group position.

Self-Interest

Self-interest is the "short to medium term impact on the material well-being of an individual's personal life" (Sears and Funk 1991). These explanations suggest an objective basis for conflict of three primary assumptions. The first assumption is that people are rational actors who reach decisions through a cost–benefit analysis that accounts for the uncertainty associated with achieving a desired outcome (Ajzen and Fishbein 1980). The second assumption states that physiological needs take precedence over all other needs, including safety and affection (Maslow 1954). The last assumption is that one's own costs and benefits take precedence over those that may be incurred by society as a whole. Personal vulnerability to political change or loss is the direct basis for hostility as a clash of material interests.

The results of the 2016 presidential election prompted several scholars to examine the relationship between class status and support for Donald Trump (Sides et al. 2018). Some suggested that working-class whites chose Trump out of concern for their economic well-being. Other studies showed that vote choice was shaped not by economic concerns but by a broader sense of resentment related to issues of race, immigration, and religion. Table 2.4 shows how these factors shaped who voted and for whom. For example, 46 percent of those who didn't vote in 2012 cast their ballots for Donald Trump in 2016.

Table 2.4 Trump voters in 2016

Voters in 2016	Among those who voted in both 2012 and 2016, the percentage that voted for Obama in 2012 and Trump in 2016	Among those who did not vote in 2012 but did vote in 2016, the percentage that voted for Trump	Percentage of all WONH voters in 2016
All voters	12.7	46.1	N/A
	(1.4)	(3.0)	
WONH voters only			
Working class	27.2	58.5	25.8
	(4.1)	(5.7)	
Not working class	13.1	62.0	74.2
	(1.7)	(4.3)	
Working class	28.7	59.7	29.4
(broad measure)	(4.6)	(5.5)	
Not working class	11.8	61.4	70.6
(broad measure)	(1.4)	(4.5)	

NOTE: "WONH" refers to voters who are white only and non-Hispanic.

SOURCE: Stephen L. Morgan and Jiwon Lee, "Trump Voters and the White Working Class," *Sociological Science*, April 16, 2018.

Similarly, 59 percent of working-class voters who didn't participate in 2012 preferred Trump over other candidates. Determining which out-groups pose a threat to in-group interests and the best means of countering these threats are shaped by a broader sense of bias.

Classical Prejudice

The classical prejudice model focuses on individual psychological dispositions as opposed to objective reality. This approach differs dramatically from the self-interest approach because it focuses on the shared, collective feelings of society. These feelings do not have to be based on real experiences and processes. Perception, which can be distorted by fear, ethnocentrism, and out-group hostility, is much more important than objective reality (Pettigrew 1982; Kinder and Sears 1981; Eagly and Chaiken 1993; Krauss and Fussell 1996). Since prejudice is learned via socio-cultural sharing and development, perceptions of threat need not be based on actual competitive experiences. Instead, the need for social distance and stereotypes may be crucial for fueling the collective dislike of a particular group.[8] Negative stereotypes of under-represented groups result from perceptual distortion motivated by the threat, both real and imagined, that new groups pose to the majority's interests.[9] Whereas the self-interest model suggests a more cognitive calculation of threat, the classical prejudice model emphasizes an affective perception of threat.

Stratification Beliefs

Individualism suggests that hard-working individuals are rewarded for their efforts. Proponents of this model argue that inequality of outcomes results not from prejudice but from differences in individual effort. Here, group dynamics are rendered unimportant because they do nothing to further an individual's pursuit of the American Dream. In fact, policies aimed at elevating the status of a particular group actually undermine and perhaps discriminate against those pursuing this dream. Lawrence Bobo and Vincent Hutchings (1996) suggest that this emphasis on the individual leads many to criticize social policies such as affirmative action and welfare for rewarding people who may have done nothing to deserve a change in their material condition (Sowell 1984; Cose 1995). Under this conception, individualist citizens do not perceive a group-based threat until some type of policy change occurs that elevates the status of the group over the efforts of the individual. As a result, an emphasis on features of the broader political and social structure has greatly influenced the **symbolic racism** approach to explaining contemporary racism.

The term *symbolic racism* first originated with Sears and Kinder's *Racial Tension and Voting in Los Angeles* (1971). The authors define symbolic racism as being distinct from old-fashioned Jim Crow racism, which is predicted to influence contemporary racial attitudes only weakly. Included in this belief are negative affect and stereotypes of Blacks blended with the perception that Blacks violate cherished American values such as individualism, the Protestant work ethic, meritocracy, self-reliance, freedom, discipline, and impulse control (Esses et al. 1993). It also reflects the attitude that Blacks are no longer significantly hampered by discrimination and should therefore try harder to make it on their own rather than pressing for government assistance. In this respect, symbolic racism suggests that Blacks are making illegitimate demands for, and receiving special treatment from, government and other elites.

Various scholars (Gilens 1996; Schram et al. 2003) find that the public tends to perceive racial and ethnic groups as being the primary recipients of public welfare programs. In addition, data from the National Election Study show that voters who supported the 2016 Republican candidate were twice as likely to attribute racial inequality to irresponsibility and lack of individual effort than voters who supported the Democratic candidate. However, figure 2.2

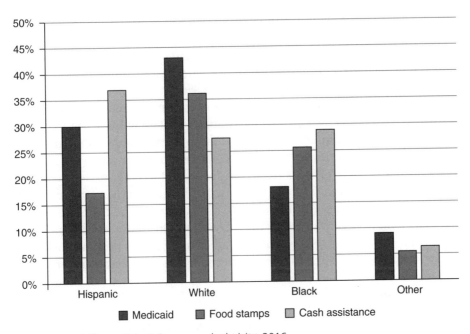

Figure 2.2 Welfare recipients by race and ethnicity, 2016
SOURCE: Caitlin Dewey, "White America's Racial Resentment is the Real Impetus for Welfare Cuts, Study Says," *Washington Post,* May 30, 2018.

illustrates the gap between perceptions and objective data on the major beneficiaries of social welfare. Across three major public welfare programs, whites receive a higher share of benefits than Blacks, Latinos, and other groups. The beneficiary gap is greatest among citizens who receive support from Medicaid, which provides free and reduced-cost health-care coverage for the elderly, the indigent, pregnant women, and people with a range of disabilities.[10]

Whereas the literature on symbolic racism suggests an intentional evaluation of groups, Banaji and Greenwald (2013) offer **implicit bias** as a concept that captures the "thoughts about people you didn't know you had." Bias is a product of the messages, stereotypes, and experiences we encounter that shape implicit associations that may not align with our stated beliefs. Everyone, according to the authors, holds biases that may be difficult to detect. These biases can lead to discrimination in hiring, housing, social interactions, the criminal justice system, and other systemic determinants that shape quality of life (Pager 2007; Carnes and Holbein 2018; Butler and Broockman 2012).

The Sense of Group Position Model

The sense of group position model combines an understanding of the affective and cognitive underpinnings of prejudice with realistic conflict over group interests *and* perceptions of threats from inferior groups. People differentiate themselves from others through the use of group categories accompanied by beliefs that other groups are qualitatively different from the in-group. Members of the dominant group develop feelings of superiority to other groups but readily perceive threats from members of lower-status groups who desire a greater share of those resources. The model has four basic tenets. The first involves a preference for the in-group that leads to stereotyping members of the out-group. The second tenet is that members of the dominant group assume claim over certain rights and privileges. This sense of entitlement is important for shaping the in-group's belief about what its position should be in the overall order. The third tenet of the model suggests that members of the in-group believe that out-group members want a greater share of these rights and privileges:

> Sociologically it is not a mere reflection of the objective relations between racial groups. Rather it stands for "what ought to be" rather than "what is." It is a sense of where the two racial groups belong . . .. In its own way, the sense of group position is a norm and imperative – indeed a very powerful one. It guides, incites, cues, and coerces. It should be borne in mind that this sense of group position stands for and involves a fundamental kind of group affiliation. (Blumer 1958: 5)

The sense of group position posits that perceptions of group competition are connected to broader historical, cultural, and social forces that lead individuals to develop or adopt negative feelings toward out-group members. This hostility is also fueled by views regarding where one's own group should be vis-à-vis the out-group. Further, competition is heightened as control over resources is in question.

Conclusion: Group Identity as Intersectional Construction

Identity in the United States is necessarily fluid, temporal, and contextual. Individuals are members of multiple groups at once. However, the political importance of various group affiliations is often decided by institutions and actors external to those groups. The dynamic nature of US politics creates a constant battle for power that often shapes perceptions of group conflict and opportunities for group coalescence. The factors that limit access to some arenas of political influence may simultaneously promote greater attachment to and identification with group categorizations. The tendency to align one's individual preferences with overall group standing rests on a complex evaluation of group standing that varies across historical era, issue arena, and the structure of opportunities for inclusion. The remaining chapters of this book explore how contestations over the meaning of identity and inclusion have unfolded over time and how these negotiations define the citizenship and standing of various groups based on shared characteristics.

Controversy box: Scouts' honor

Single-sex programs have been a staple of the United States for centuries. Schools such as Spelman College, Hampden-Sydney College, and Wellesley College maintain the view that single-sex education provides meaningful opportunities for growth and self-reflection that promote achievement. Opponents see gender-separate programs as reinforcing gender norms that are incongruent with current realities. Sororities and fraternities maintain gender distinctions while debates rage on college campuses about the availability of gender-neutral housing and restrooms. As schools grapple with evolving understandings of gender identity, youth organizations are facing the same questions.

Each year 2.5 million members of the Boy Scouts of America (BSA) make the same pledge: "On my honor I will do my best to do my duty to God and my country and to obey the Scout Law; to help other people at all times; to keep myself physically strong, mentally awake, and morally straight." BSA's purpose is to instill the values of patriotism, good citizenship, and self-reliance in young men destined to become leaders and contributors in their community. Maintaining that goal some 110 years after its founding has proven to be a major challenge for the scouts.

In 2004 the Boy Scouts adopted a policy preventing "openly gay" adults from serving as scout leaders after a US Supreme Court ruling (*Boy Scouts of America* v. *Dale*) that private organizations had the First Amendment right to set membership standards based on the freedom of association. The move sparked allegations of discrimination and prompted several high-profile sponsors severing ties with the organization. In 2016 a scout in New Jersey was asked to resign from the organization after other members learned that he had been born a girl and so felt his presence undermined the purpose of the organization. In 2017, the Boy Scouts of America announced that it would allow transgender youth who identify as boys to enroll in its programs and would change its name to "Scouts BSA" to allow interested girls to participate. The decision was a significant departure from the organization's past stance and was met with criticism from organizers of the Girl Scouts of America, who defended the need for single-sex scouting.

What do you think? Are single-sex organizations still necessary? And, if so, should trans students be allowed to join the organization that aligns with their identity?

Questions for Debate

- What does it mean to say that identity shapes and is shaped by politics?
- How has group identity been the source of conflict and coalescence?
- How do social categorizations shape group access to authentic power?

Key Terms

- implicit bias
- assimilation
- symbolic racism
- pluralism
- group consciousness
- social categorization
- self-identity
- linked fate

3

The Substance of US Citizenship

José Gutierrez was born near Guatemala City. Over 80 percent of Guatemala's 17 million residents live below the poverty line, and some 40 percent are in extreme poverty. Gutierrez was orphaned at the age of eight and tried to find his way as a "street child" in slums filled with violence and uncertainty. Determined to live a better life, he fled his home country at the age of sixteen and illegally entered the United States. He became one of nearly 5 million undocumented immigrants in the United States who live in constant fear of being detected and deported. After bouncing from various foster homes, Gutierrez eventually settled with an adoptive family in California who encouraged him to earn a green card and pursue his education. He later enlisted in the US Marines, hoping to better his life and build a future in his adopted country.

Citizenship has never been a requirement for US military service. Immigrants and non-citizens have fought in every American military conflict since the Revolutionary War. On any given day, over 35,000 non-citizens serve in the military. Some, like José Gutierrez, entered the country illegally and eventually became green card holders eligible for citizenship after three years' service. Others came to the US as children and have lived here longer than in their country of birth. The US has a long history of immigrants pursuing military service as a way to prove their loyalty and to establish that they are fit to enjoy the benefits, responsibilities, and protections of American citizenship. For example, the massive waves of Irish immigrants who fled the potato famine were greeted with job posters and classified ads that stated "No Irish Need Apply." Fighting in the American Civil War became the chief vehicle for people of Irish descent to prove their loyalty. Over 140,000 Irish immigrants fought on behalf of the Union Army and the Confederacy. Their allegiance to US interests helped them gain acceptance while also heightening tensions with other excluded groups.

In 1863 the federal government announced a new law that included in the draft lottery all male citizens – and those *eligible* for citizenship – between the ages of twenty and thirty-five. The **Enrollment Act of 1863** stated that unmarried men who were between thirty-five and forty-five could also be enlisted. Many Irish immigrants were outraged that the citizenship requirement automatically exempted Black men from being drafted. Without the money

Members of the US Infantry Regiment carry out military funeral honors for US Army Sergeant Chaturbhuj Gidwani. Military service has long been an avenue for underrepresented groups to assert their allegiance and citizenship.

necessary to buy a deferment, Irish residents resented having to risk their lives while other groups watched from the sidelines. In July 1863, the New York City draft riots ignited a powder keg of discontent that had been festering for years. Decades of competition for scarce jobs and deplorable living conditions in New York made Black residents the primary targets of rage. Three days of mayhem resulted in the murder of eighteen Black residents and millions in property damage.

Military service has also been used to compel a sense of patriotism among groups long thought "unsuitable" for US citizenship. For example, members of the Navajo Nation were drafted into the Marine Corps during World War II to protect US troops by secretly transmitting messages via indigenous languages. Over time, members of Navajo, Comanche, Choctaw, and Hopi Nations were drafted into service even as the US government resisted growing demands for the protection of tribal sovereignty. By the war's end, 45,000 members of Native Nations had served in the US military.[1]

Robert Heinlein's science fiction classic *Starship Troopers* rests as an impressive statement of the notion that full citizenship status should be conferred only upon those who have embraced social responsibility over individual concerns. Heinlein highlights the moral dimensions of citizenship and the conditions under which access should be denied. Through the lens of the book's main character, Juan "Johnnie" Risco, Heinlein promotes the view that individuals who have completed military service personify the pursuit of the common good over selfish gain. It is this pursuit of civic virtue that affords military personnel the right to claim full citizenship. Upon leaving the infantry and re-entering civilization, Johnnie finds that he has changed, his views of the world have changed, and society's perceptions of him have changed. Citizenship is viewed as a reward for giving oneself to the community to think above one's own needs. Citizenship confers certain rights and privileges social responsibility over individual standing.

In 2001, US Senators Orrin Hatch and Dick Durbin introduced the Development, Relief, and Education for Alien Minors (DREAM) Act to provide temporary residency to young people who were illegally brought to the country before they were eighteen. If passed, the Act would allow "Dreamers" who have registered for the selective service and contributed to the military to pursue a path to permanent residency and eventual citizenship. Though supporters argue that those willing to risk their lives for the US have proven their allegiance, the *DREAM Act* has failed to garner enough support each session it has been introduced. Some opponents fear that passing the Act will only reward undocumented immigrants for subverting traditional routes to citizenship.

Fighting to Belong

Lance Corporal José Gutierrez enlisted because he wanted to uphold the values and safety of the United States and its residents. He died in combat in Iraq in 2003 not as a citizen but as a patriot. As the United States and countries around the world debate the meaning of citizenship, Gutierrez's death reminds us of the many people who have given their lives fighting for countries that never fully embraced them. Military personnel from diverse backgrounds have risked their lives to protect US interests. However, the fight to determine which values are being protected, and for whom, is a ubiquitous feature of American politics. The US Constitution doesn't prohibit treating groups differently. The parameters for the practice of treating individuals and groups differently – termed discrimination – are enshrined in the very document that structures the key institutions responsible for implementing and enforcing these boundaries. The three branches of government created by the Constitution (legislative, executive, and judicial) preside over the laws, policies, and actions that determine the limits of citizenship.

Persistent tensions over whom we can discriminate against have an impact on both domestic and foreign affairs. In earlier periods of US history, men who didn't own land weren't allowed to vote. Immigrants coming from certain parts of Europe were barred from holding political office, and, until the 1960s, married women weren't allowed to have a credit card in their name. These boundaries are reinforced by law (***de jure***) and by practice (***de facto***). The tension between creating a democracy that is open and inclusive and creating spaces that exclude certain groups has been a constant feature of US political development.

Formal statements of US citizenship are often prompted by efforts of new groups to gain access to the protections that accompany being included in the polity. The country originally had few formal requirements for who could be included. Over time, changing demographic compositions of immigrant populations coupled with increased demands for autonomy from original populations ushered in a host of policies designed to limit the meaning of and opportunities for American citizenship.

In this chapter, I examine the basic conceptions of citizenship that guide American political development. The Constitution offers certain protections to citizens and non-citizens alike. However, defining the boundaries of belonging has shaped a host of laws and policies based on group identity. The 1876 Supreme Court ruling in **United States** v. **Cruikshank** highlights that "citizens are members of the political community to which they belong. They are the people who compose the community, and who, in their associated capacity, have established or committed themselves to the dominion of a government for the promotion of their general welfare and the protection of their individual as well as collective rights" (92 US 542). I analyze how these conceptions define citizenship based on group identity and, in turn, necessitate a constant reimagining of membership in the polity. This overview of identity and citizenship provides a firm foundation for understanding how the very essence of US democracy demands an emphasis on identity politics as a pathway to power.

The Context

American democracy is a dynamic process built on competing norms, conflicting ideals, and persistent tension. Political institutions and the norms that sustain them are structured to uphold the notion that citizens should have a voice in the affairs of government. The persistent challenge, however, is determining which voices should matter and for whom political engagement should be encouraged. Relatedly, the opportunities for engagement vary across issue, policy space, and level of government. From the earliest efforts to declare American independence to contemporary debates over balancing domestic priorities with international concerns, the path toward forming a more perfect union is predicated on defining the limits and boundaries of inclusion. As a result, efforts to incorporate new political voices often develop in tandem with broader efforts to minimize disruptions to the balance of power. This context of American political development reveals a persistent paradox for various identity-based groups between the promise of democratic inclusion and the realities of exclusion.

The Structure of American Government

The political importance of group identity is shaped by the overall structure of US government, which provides myriad opportunities to reward and stigmatize groups based on shared characteristics. Although the word "federal" never appears in the Constitution, the relationship between the national government and the states is clearly outlined. Throughout history this system and the rules that guide it have been continually stretched, reshaped, and reinterpreted by crises, historical evolution, public expectation, and judicial interpretation. All these forces have tremendous influence on who makes policy decisions and how such decisions get made.

Issues involving the distribution of power between the national government and the states affect US residents, regardless of citizenship status, on a daily basis. We do not need, for example, a passport to go from Texas to Oklahoma. There is one national currency and a national minimum wage. But many differences exist among the laws of the various states: the age at which you may marry is a state issue, as are laws governing divorce, child custody, voter eligibility, and the purchase of guns. Both the age at which one is considered old enough to consent to an intimate relationship and the type of photo identification you need to vote vary depending on where you reside.

The concept of *federalism* endows states with a unique set of responsibilities and authority over the well-being of residents. Federalism is defined as the division of power between a central authority and various subordinates. In the United States, power is shared between the federal government, states, and various localities. The distinct nature of this power-sharing shapes how certain issues become viewed as a problem in need of a policy response as well as the resources available for addressing them. The policies set by institutions reflect the presence of a diverse set of actors with differing levels of influence and, often, competing interests. The **Tenth Amendment** provides states with the authority to make laws regarding the health, safety, and well-being of its residents. Ernst Freund affirms the importance of understanding states' power: "the maxim of this power is that every individual must submit to such restraints to remove or reduce the danger of the abuse of these rights on the part of those who are unskillful, careless, or unscrupulous" (1904: 6).

Over the last thirty years, debates over federalism have increased in response to federal mandates and growing internal pressure caused by changing migration patterns and political shifts. For example, a number of localities have adopted **sanctuary city** status to determine how they will cooperate with federal authorities to enforce immigration statutes.[2] Public officials in Newark, New Jersey, for example, argue that cities have to carefully determine how to allocate scarce resources such as law-enforcement staffing and support for English as a second language programs. These cities prefer to cooperate with the federal government only when there is a clear concern for public safety and when it does not create economic hardship for the city to enforce what is essentially a federal function (Mazzola and Yi 2017). Critics argue that these cities are shirking their duties to the detriment of public safety and national security.

Federalism affords states tremendous discretion in implementing public policies that can either affirm or undermine the meaning of citizenship. Federalism divides groups *and* creates divisions within these groups. In her discussion of the New Deal, Suzanne Mettler (1998) finds that those policies institutionalized gendered distinctions by privileging men over women and wealthy men over working-class men. The division of power coupled with multiple access points means that citizenship exists on a fluid dynamic continuum rather than resting as a fixed status. Socially constructed notions of worth determine one's place on the continuum (Schneider and Ingram 1993; Ingram and Schneider 2005) and shape policy-making decisions. This negotiation process moderates the impact of these policies on society as a whole. The consequences are particularly harsh for underrepresented groups, who often lack the political resources necessary to challenge their diminished standing. Some groups are deemed unworthy of full citizenship based on inherent traits, while others are excluded because of perceived challenges to security and public welfare. Some groups are able to overcome this exclusion by proving that they have embraced prevailing norms and beliefs held by the dominant society (assimilation), while others are deemed permanently incapable of inclusion.

BOX 3.1 Three conceptions of US citizenship

Jus soli	Automatically confers citizenship to anyone born on US soil regardless of the parents' nationality
Jus sanguinis	Grants citizenship to anyone who has at least one parent who is a US citizen
Naturalization	The formal process that allows individuals born in other countries to pursue full status as a US citizen

---

Conceptions of Citizenship

Rogers Smith speaks of the challenge of defining citizenship:

> In common parlance, to say that someone is an American citizen often simply means that the person is legally recognized as having American nationality or is eligible to carry a U.S. passport. At times, American courts and executive officials have endorsed that view. But the term "citizenship"

has always carried more demanding connotations that courts and other American political leaders have often endorsed. (Smith 1999: 14)

Citizenship is a political construct that guides negotiations over which groups can lay legitimate claims to the rights, privileges, and protections of membership. This view of citizenship, as more than simply a condition of birth, represents a struggle to define who belongs *and* what benefits should be attached to that belonging. Here, I adopt a more politicized notion of citizenship that distinguishes between those who are able to influence the political process and those who are simply ruled by it. Efforts to define the meaning of citizenship are as much about including individuals as it is about excluding them. Since its inception in 1789, the US Supreme Court has been a chief arbiter – along with Congress – in defining three key conceptions of citizenship.

Birthright Citizenship

The first conception of citizenship, *jus soli*, loosely translates to "right of the soil." This conception automatically confers citizenship to anyone born on US soil regardless of their parents' nationality (Bhaba 2011). For more than a century, "birthright citizenship" was assumed as a condition for anyone born in the US except for indigenous tribes and African Americans. This exclusion was tested in two key court cases. The first was the 1857 case *Dred Scott v. Sandford*. Dred Scott was born enslaved in the commonwealth of Virginia. After his master died he was transferred to the non-slave holding state of Illinois and later appealed to the Court to adjudicate his freedom. Led by Chief Justice Roger Taney, the Supreme Court effectively ruled that Blacks – both enslaved and free – could never become citizens of the United States. In justifying this declaration, Taney wrote that, in spite of the Constitution, Blacks "had no rights which the white man was bound to respect; and that the negro might justly and lawfully be reduced to slavery for his benefit. He was bought and sold, and treated as an ordinary article of merchandise and traffic, whenever profit could be made by it." Taney further argued that "it is too clear for dispute, that the enslaved African race were not intended to be included, and formed no part of the people who framed and adopted this declaration" (60 US 393).

Four years after the Court's ruling, the start of the Civil War forced the United States to rethink notions of citizenship and belonging. Debates over slavery and the supremacy of the national government over individual states filtered into discussions of citizenship and immigration. This shift is reflected in the adoption in 1868 of the Fourteenth Amendment, which was ratified five years after President Abraham Lincoln issued the Emancipation Proclamation that suggested enslaved Africans *should* be freed. With no federal enforcement power, the proclamation was little more than a request. The Fourteenth Amendment was one of three Civil War amendments designed to carve out citizenship status for the formerly enslaved and their descendants. It prohibited states from making or enforcing laws that abridged the privileges and immunities of citizenship and provided that "all persons born or nationalized in the United States and subject to the jurisdiction thereof, are citizens of the United States and of the State wherein they reside." By guaranteeing citizenship to all people born in the United States regardless of race, class, or gender, the Fourteenth effectively overturned the *Dred Scott* decision while simultaneously raising new questions regarding its applicability to other previously excluded groups, such as people of Asian descent.

BOX 3.2 Civil War amendments

Thirteenth Amendment (1865)	"Neither slavery nor involuntary servitude, except as a punishment for crime whereof the party shall have been duly convicted, shall exist within the United States, or any place subject to their jurisdiction."
Fourteenth Amendment (1868)	Grants citizenship to "all persons born or naturalized in the United States" and forbids states from denying any person "life, liberty or property, without due process of law" or "any person within its jurisdiction the equal protection of the laws."
Fifteenth Amendment (1870)	Grants the franchise to African American men so that the "right of citizens of the United States to vote shall not be denied or abridged by the United States or by any state on account of race, color, or previous condition of servitude."

Citizenship Based on Nationality

Wong Kim Ark was born in San Francisco to native-born Chinese parents just five years after Congress passed the monumental Chinese Exclusion Act of 1882. The Act represented the first time in US history that an immigration restriction had been adopted based on race:

> Whereas in the opinion of the Government of the United States the coming of Chinese laborers to this country endangers the good order of certain localities within the territory of ... that hereafter no State court or court of the United States shall admit Chinese to citizenship; and all laws in conflict with this act are hereby repealed.[3]

After visiting his parents in China, Wong was denied re-entry to the United States on the grounds that he was a laborer and not a true citizen. He sued on the basis that the US violated the Fourteenth Amendment by denying his citizenship. The Court ruled in his favor based on the Civil Rights Act of 1866 and the Fourteenth Amendment, which together upheld "the fundamental principle of citizenship by birth." The case helped protect the citizenship status of children born in the United States regardless of their parents' nationality. However, it did not fully prevent future efforts to limit citizenship based on country of origin.[4] Further, the Court did not address the lingering question of Indian citizenship.

Indian Citizenship and Sovereignty

Although American Indians were the original inhabitants of the territory that became the United States, they were viewed as a separate nation and described as uncivilized and as an alien people unworthy of inclusion. These beliefs shaped persistent battles for tribes to maintain their independence and retain their own sense of power. In the simplest terms, *sovereignty* in this context recognizes the rights of over 560 tribal nations to self-governance and

A participant in a Prairie Island Community Wacipi (pow wow). The United States is comprised of over 560 tribal nations, all with a unique set of traditions, principles, and governing bodies. The tension over tribal sovereignty and self-governance directly shapes the citizenship status of American Indians.

control in various areas of decision-making. This includes traditional areas of public affairs (e.g. education, public safety, and environmental oversight) as well as cultural-specific domains (e.g. preservation of spiritual practices and ancestral lands). This notion of self-rule is codified by a complex maze of judicial decrees, constitutional provisions, and legal treaties that have been frequently challenged and redefined. Although sovereignty rests as a recognition that tribes have the right to make decisions over their own affairs and retain their independent systems of governance, tribal autonomy was never meant to replace the benefits and protections of US citizenship.

The Constitution made no provisions for naturalizing American Indians or defining the status of those who chose to live beyond reservations. However, Justice Taney's opinion in the *Dred Scott* decision held that American Indians could become citizens with the proper legal oversight. A major test of this premise was the 1884 case, *Elk v. Wilkins*. The case raised the question of whether American Indians were entitled to the status and accompanying benefits of citizenship. Beginning in the 1880s, some American Indians left their reservations to live and work in cities across the Midwest. The plaintiff, John Elk, left his tribal nation and moved to Nebraska. Having been turned away after attempting to vote in a local city council election, he argued that he met the residency requirements and was entitled to vote based on the Fourteenth and Fifteenth Amendments, which barred discrimination on the basis of race or color. The case raised two major questions:

1 Can American Indians become naturalized citizens?
2 Are American Indians entitled to the full rights and privileges of citizenship?

BOX 3.3 Tribal sovereignty

A recognition of the rights of over 560 federally recognized tribal nations to self-governance and control: members are citizens of their tribal nations *and* of the United States.

The Court never addressed Elk's right to vote. Instead, the primary question rested on his citizenship. Even though he had been born on American soil and had denounced his tribal affiliation, the Court ruled that Elk could not pass the allegiance test mandated by the country's **naturalization** provisions. As a result, Elk and others like him were explicitly barred from citizenship because "they were never deemed citizens of the United States, except under explicit provisions of treaty or statute to that effect, either declaring a certain tribe, or such members of it as chose to remain behind on the removal of the tribe westward, to be citizens, or authorizing individuals of particular tribes to become citizens" (112 US 94).

The question of citizenship was not settled until the passage of the Indian Citizenship Act of 1924, which automatically granted citizenship to all Indians. Individual members now have dual citizenship as citizens both of their tribes and of the United States. Before that, the 1887 Dawes Act had granted citizenship only to American Indians willing to accept land grants from the federal government (Pevar 2012). This battle over land ownership and tribal sovereignty further compromised the protections afforded tribes and their members.[5] Although the Indian Citizenship Act conferred the status of citizenship, it did not guarantee access to things such as voting that were administered by the state. As a result, federalism allowed many states to continue to discriminate against those American Indians attempting to participate fully in political affairs.

Citizenship as Inheritance

The second conception of citizenship, ***jus sanguinis***, translates to "citizenship by blood." This principle confers citizenship to anyone who has at least one parent who is a US citizen (Cohen 2010; Collins 2014). In 2016, Senator Ted Cruz of Texas sought to become the Republican nominee for president of the United States. Since he was born in Canada, his opponents questioned whether he met the requirement of being a "natural born citizen" to be eligible to serve as president: "No person, except a natural born citizen, or a citizen of the United States, at the time of the adoption of this Constitution shall be eligible to that Office who shall not have attained to the age of thirty-five years, and been fourteen years a resident of the United States."[6] Cruz's chief competitor, Donald J. Trump, threatened to file an injunction even as constitutional law scholars affirmed Cruz's eligibility based on his mother's status as a natural-born US citizen. The debate reignited longstanding questions over whether citizenship is derived from the mother or the father and how this evolving standard has been used to stigmatize certain groups and deny their path to citizenship.[7]

Becoming American

The third conception of citizenship, *naturalization*, allows people born elsewhere to formally pursue citizenship in the United States. The Naturalization Act of March 26, 1790, created a path to citizenship for certain foreign-born residents. Section 1 allowed "any alien, being a free white person," to apply for citizenship who had been in the United States for at least two years and a resident of the state in which they sought citizenship for at least two years. The language of the Act explicitly barred indentured servants and enslaved

Africans from being eligible. It also prevented the formerly enslaved from applying for citizenship because they were still viewed by the law as "property" rather than "people."

BOX 3.4 Naturalization Act of 1790

". . . the right of citizenship shall not descend to persons whose *fathers* have never been resident in the United States . . .."

The Act codified the belief that citizenship in the United States centered on men by declaring that "children of citizens of the United States that may be born beyond Sea, or out of the limits of the United States, shall be considered as natural born Citizens." It also demanded that "the right of citizenship shall not descend to persons whose fathers have never been resident in the United States" (preamble). This distinction was not removed until 1934, and then it was by an act of Congress rather than a constitutional amendment. Supporters viewed the Naturalization Act as necessary to protect the US government from foreign influence. It also helped limit those who could legitimately access government and, in turn, make demands for redress.

This Act highlighted an inherent ambiguity in our conception of US citizenship that was noted by early scholars such as de Tocqueville. Congress viewed the residency requirement as an opportunity for foreigners to appreciate American freedom and democracy while determining their contributions to the polity. However, by denying American Indians and Blacks the opportunity to be naturalized, the Act established that American citizenship was based on a racial hierarchy. Over the next decade, politicians sharply debated whether it should be amended to reflect growing tensions and debates concerning the benefits of citizenship. As the number of immigrants to the US grew, many politicians argued that the residency requirement should be lengthened to further prevent foreign influence. The 1798 Naturalization Act permanently extended the residency requirement to fourteen years.

These restrictions reflected what Rogers Smith (1985) and others have called **nativism**. Nativist policies favor native-born citizens over immigrants and reflect a fear of immigrants' growing influence. These policies are an attempt to preserve what is unique about US citizenship even at the expense of group interests. Nativism is not unique to the United States. Such beliefs shape immigration policies and pathways to citizenship in countries across the world, including Canada, Japan, the UK, Sweden, France, and Austria. The challenge rests on who gets to define what makes aspirants desirable and how this negotiation challenges longstanding values associated with US citizenship.

The Values of Citizenship

Three major principles (**liberalism**, **republicanism**, and **ethno-nationalism**), define the values of American citizenship while setting the parameters for how various groups experience it. Liberalism emphasizes the importance of personal freedom. Individuals possess certain rights that are universal and equally distributed. Individuals are rational actors who define and pursue their best interests rather than acting according to a community's interests or demands. The role of the state, then, is to reinforce these individualized pursuits and prevent other actors from interfering with these rights (Hartz 1955). In the liberal tradition, individual rights are acknowledged by all and protected by the state.

BOX 3.5 Three values associated with American citizenship

Liberalism	Emphasizes person liberty/freedom
Republicanism	The people hold popular sovereignty
Ethno-nationalism	Membership in ethnic and national communities

---

In his *Second Treatise on Government* (1689), John Locke invokes the notion of a social contract that defines the relationship between citizens and the state and affirms the importance of citizens' consent. Locke's view of the social contract has a moral foundation but also implies a contractual relationship with government. Government's worth is contingent upon citizens' willingness to engage and participate in it, not on government's desire to limit access. Therefore, individuals can show their gratitude for the state's protection by voting or through military service. The defining characteristic of the liberal tradition is that citizenship does not hold any intrinsic value. Its value is defined by the pursuit of each individual of their own self-interest.

John Rawls (1971) extends the view that citizenship is an appropriate means of recognizing the diversity of thought, behavior, and cultures that is prominent in society. Society, according to Rawls, must provide a space for this diversity to flourish without political infringements. It is this respect for the individual and individual rights that creates consensus and, in turn, a more stable view of citizenship. Critics of the liberal tradition question whether ignoring cultural differences and ascriptive distinctions truly respects the individual. The existence of a neutral state that does not consider individual conceptions of the good seems implausible. The liberal tradition more aptly applies to an abstract notion of the citizen because it cannot properly account for the traits that form identities and, successively, shared communities of interest.

In the republican tradition, citizenship provides its own value because it ties one to a community, or set of communities, and, in turn, shapes political preferences and allegiances. These communities are marked by shared values and common goals. Citizenship and membership help promote a civic virtue that guides the quest for the common good (Hume 1875). Consecutively, attaching duties and responsibilities to citizenship enhances the moral character of communal life while also providing a direct benefit to the individual. Therefore, the republican view of citizenship focuses on individual contributions to a common good that supersedes individual needs and, in turn, fosters a moralistic adherence to the community. Measures of worth and fit often vary based on who is governing debates over citizenship. For some, worth is reflected by wealth and ownership. To others, worth is defined simply by overall fit with the community. The key point here is that, if social responsibility is the governing standard, then groups should have equal opportunities to prove their commitment to civic virtue and have the opportunity to be re-evaluated rather than permanently denied.

The last value associated with citizenship, ethno-nationalism, focuses on membership in ethnic and national communities. Citizenship is a reflection of one's relationship to a common, homogeneous group. This implies a more intimate relationship between the state and the community that may alleviate potential conflict in certain areas. Communities exist within the state and are often defined by and in relationship to the state (Connor 1993). Unlike the liberal tradition, which ignores any differences, the ethno-nationalist approach recognizes cultural differences such as language, dress, religion, and experience. Citizenship, then, reflects these cultural distinctions. Nations are distinct and vary based on cultural markers rather than simply masking cleavages (Greenfeld 1993).

This discussion does not imply that these three values are completely separate or that they can describe the entire course of American development. Rather, such notions often exist in tandem with one another and describe various points in time for various groups (Smith 1993). These traditions grant different explanatory power in describing political life in theory versus in practice.

Fractured Citizenship

American citizenship has always been relational such that citizens with full rights and protections have not been women, slaves, or white men who did not own property. Judith Shklar discusses the tension between America's professed embrace of liberal values and its wholesale exclusion of certain groups by writing that American society was "actively and purposefully false to its own vaunted principles" (1991: 14). She cautions us not to lump these underrepresented groups together completely and to dismiss the view that such groups perceive a common fate or need to work together to challenge their excluded standing. Hierarchies, or what Shklar terms differences in social standing, shape the actions of those in power *and* those who are excluded. The quest for recognition between and the quest for differentiation within groups exist in tandem. Excluded groups perceive their status vis-à-vis those in power and in relation to those who are also excluded. The struggle for citizenship represents a means of achieving particular group interests rather than some broader virtue.

Citizenship and Intersectionality

American political development has been marked by various attempts to carve out a formal, legal citizenship status for some groups while denying access to others. Although issues of identity have been a major force in shaping American political development, notions of citizenship must be properly accounted for within the context of other identities. Patricia Hill Collins offers: "As opposed to examining gender, race, class, and nation as separate systems of oppression, intersectionality explores how these systems mutually construct one another ... across multiple systems of oppression and serve as focal points or privileged social locations for those intersecting systems" (1998: 63). Given this, it is useful to consider what happens when the boundaries meant to exclude certain groups encroach upon the standing of others. How do institutional structures shape this exclusion and how do political actors react to or reason through this exclusion?

Understanding the multiple layers of citizenship is particularly important for groups who contend with many systems of discrimination. Thus, a more appropriate vision of citizenship must recognize distinctions across federal and state domains *and* acknowledge how policies have induced cleavages *within* and not just between groups. These cleavages may include lines of class, gender, region, immigrant status, and urbanicity. Figure 3.1 illustrates how social constructions of groups may enhance or inhibit access to political power. The presence of these manifold fault lines constrains opportunities to critically examine such policies and, in turn, redefine the meaning of citizenship. Just as public policies may make citizens, they can also diminish and deny citizens.[8]

Citizenship is not an absolute, undeniable status. I offer the concept of **fractured citizenship** to imply that citizenship in the United States is hierarchical, relational, and contingent on historical time period and overall context. Citizenship, then, is not simply a condition of birth. It is a construct that results from a collection of political decisions, strategies, and beliefs. Citizenship as an indicator of standing moderates the relationship between public policies and various indicators of political incorporation. Figure 3.2 illustrates this relationship.

Full citizenship status means that groups are completely recognized as members of the polity, are protected from discrimination, and have access

Social Constructions

	Positive	Negative
Stronger political power	**"Advantaged"** Senior citizens Veterans	**"Contender"** Wall Street executives Labor unions
Weaker political power	**"Dependants"** Medicaid recipients Supplemental security income recipients	**"Deviants"** Undocumented immigrants Felons

Figure 3.1 Social constructions of target populations

to the rights to vote, hold office, and participate in the overall decision-making process. Diminished citizenship means that a group may possess legal status but may not be accepted as full members, or that their rights may be abridged in practice by subordinate layers of government. Recall the previous discussion of the Fifteenth Amendment and the Indian Citizenship Act of 1924. Together these two measures extended the vote to men, finally recognized American Indians as citizens and created federal recognition. However, states continued to deny access to voting, office-holding, and representation.

In practice, these two measures provided little more than the *promise* of full citizenship. The Voting Rights Act of 1965 (VRA)[9] and its subsequent extensions directly challenged state-supported measures that denied Indian access to the political process. The Act prohibited states from using any "voting qualifica-

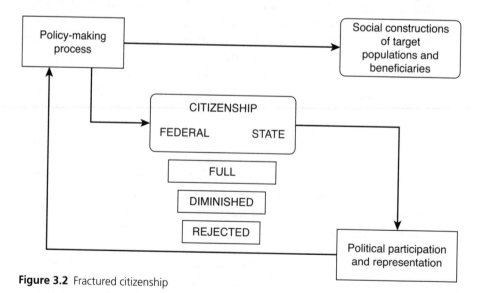

Figure 3.2 Fractured citizenship

tion or prerequisite to voting, or standard practice, or procedure . . . to deny or abridge the request of any citizen of the United States to vote on account of race or color." That the VRA was even needed highlights the challenge of reconciling competing interests across multiple layers of government. Groups such as the Native American Voting Rights Coalition, the Puerto Rican Legal Defense and Education Fund, and the Asian American Legal Defense and Education Fund continue to fight challenges to voting rights for their constituent groups.

This framework of citizenship helps us better understand the development of restrictions on immigration and migration to the United States. While institutions may establish the legal parameters of citizenship, the elites who staff them face the task of translating these mandates into practice. In addition, public sentiment may play a prominent role in both creating policy demands and pressuring a response.

Conclusion: Citizenship as Intersectional Construction

Citizenship in the United States rests at the intersection of policy, legal precedent, and practice shaped by competing visions of inclusion based on the identities of those seeking to belong. For much of US history, citizenship has been assumed as a condition of birth for many groups deemed "white" by socially agreed upon standards. The dominant notion of whiteness as a precondition for citizenship superseded other identity markers such as gender, tribal affiliation, and country of origin. As a result, the notion of birthright citizenship and access to the full rights and protections of that status has been contested for groups such as women, American Indians, African Americans, and various Asian and Latin American subgroups. This practice of differentiating between citizens and "others" has been buttressed by a combination of judicial decisions, constitutional provisions, legislative choices, and informal practices. Debates over the substance, values, and benefits of citizenship often emerge in reaction to new demands for inclusion. This struggle represents a sense of nativism that prioritizes current citizens over immigrants and creates formidable obstacles for groups who want to belong. The quest for full rather than fractured citizenship has shaped enduring debates over access and benefit. The next chapter takes up this premise by examining how racial identity politics challenge the dominant narrative of political inclusion.

Controversy box: Who votes?

People in the United States love to vote. We vote for dancing celebrities and vocalists in search of stardom. We vote for pageant contestants chasing sashes and scholarships, and we vote in community forums to prioritize public investments. We hold more elections than other democratic nations to fill an array of public offices, for justices of the peace, school board members, voter registrars, and prosecutors. We've created a bizarre maze of registration requirements to determine when and how people can participate in political elections. And yet the US still manages to elicit relatively low rates of voter participation.

The framers crafted a Constitution that doesn't include an affirmative right to vote; 230 years after its ratification, the Constitution still grants states the authority to set the time, place, and manner of elections, and, by extension, voter eligibility requirements. America is exceptional in her professed commitment to democracy and the limits she places on voting.

Today millions of Americans are denied access to the franchise because of a criminal conviction. Felon disenfranchisement laws prohibit current and, in many states, formerly incarcerated individuals from voting. According to the nonpartisan think tank Prison Policy Initiative, there are 2.3 million people behind bars in the United States in facilities ranging from local jails to federal immigrant detention facilities. In every state except Maine and Vermont, people behind bars are prohibited from voting. In thirteen states and the District of Columbia, voting rights are automatically restored upon release from prison. However, nine states, including Delaware, Alabama, and Iowa, require the formerly incarcerated to petition for restoration, with acceptance being contingent upon the type of crime committed and the level of government oversight. In 2018 Florida voters supported a ballot measure that restored voting rights to people convicted of crimes other than murder and felony sexual assault. The measure re-enfranchised over 1.5 million people, accounting for 20 percent of voting-age Florida residents of color.

Should people convicted of crimes be allowed to vote after release? What about while they're in prison? Should voting be an inalienable right of citizenship?

Questions for Debate

- What does it mean to be a US citizen?
- How has this definition changed over time and why?
- Who should determine the boundaries and benefits of citizenship?

Key Terms

- liberalism
- intersectionality
- federalism
- nativism
- sanctuary city
- DREAM Act

4

Racial Identity, Citizenship, and Voting

Whom Shall I Fear?

On a balmy Saturday morning in June 2015, Bree Newsome scaled a 30-foot flagpole outside the South Carolina Statehouse to remove the Confederate flag that had towered over the Capitol since 1961. It was a bold move that engendered tremendous risk and criticism. Newsome conspired with fellow *activist*, James Tyson, to dismantle arguably one of the most controversial and recognizable symbols of the United States' complex racial history.[1] To some, the flag reverences Southern heritage and the fiercely independent spirit thought to dwell below the Mason–Dixon line. For others, the flag is a physical reminder of the legacies of slavery and white supremacy that historian Annette Gordon-Reed (2018) and others have called "America's original sin."

Newsome and Tyson were both arrested and charged with defacing a public monument. This act of **civil disobedience** catapulted them to the epicenter of a longstanding debate over the place of racial imagery in America's political consciousness. The targeted execution of nine Black parishioners of Charleston's historic Mother Emanuel Church by Dylan Roof compelled Newsome to act: "A white man had just entered a Black church and massacred people as they prayed. He had assassinated a civil rights leader. This was not a page in a textbook I was reading nor an inscription on a monument I was visiting. This was now. This was real. This was – this is – still happening."[2]

One of those killed, Reverend Clementa Pinckney, spent eighteen years as a state legislator working in the very statehouse where the flag Bree Newsome removed loomed overhead. The country's first Black president, Barack Obama, delivered the eulogy for Pinckney in a state that just five years earlier had elected Nikki Haley as the second Indian American governor in the United States. President Obama linked race, faith, history, and a perceived call to action:

> Removing the flag from this state's capital would not be an act of political correctness. It would not be an insult to the valor of Confederate soldiers. It would simply be acknowledgement that the cause for which they fought, the cause of slavery, was wrong.
> The imposition of Jim Crow after the Civil War, the resistance to civil rights for all people was wrong.

Mourners gather to pay tribute to the nine victims killed at the Mother Emanuel A.M.E. Church in Charleston, South Carolina. Founded in 1816, the church has historic ties to civil rights and racial justice.

It would be one step in an honest accounting of America's history, a modest but meaningful balm for so many unhealed wounds.

It would be an expression of the amazing changes that have transformed this state and this country for the better because of the work of so many people of goodwill, people of all races, striving to form a more perfect union.

By taking down that flag, we express God's grace.[3]

The controversy over South Carolina's prominent display of the flag had lingered for decades. In the years preceding Newsome's move, the National Association for the Advancement of Colored People (NAACP) led an economic boycott of the state to draw attention to its history of racial conflict. Founded in 1909 as a multiracial, multiethnic, interfaith coalition of civil rights leaders, the NAACP focuses on political, educational, and economic equality. However, the loss of revenue did little to prompt state legislators to remove the controversial symbol.

The link between race, faith, and action was apparent in Newsome's response to demands that she let the flag stand. As state troopers shouted for her to come down, Newsome invoked her religious convictions in response: "You come against me with hatred, oppression, and violence; I come against you in the name of God. This flag comes down today."[4] In the wake of the act of domestic terrorism at Mother Emanuel Church, the shooting death of unarmed motorist Walter Scott by a state trooper, and protracted debates over the safety of South Carolina's Black residents, Bree Newsome descended to the ground by poignantly asking, "Whom shall I fear?"[5]

The Confederate battle flag was restored to the South Carolina Statehouse just hours after Newsome removed it. Following weeks of contentious debates and public outcry, members of the South Carolina Highway Patrol Honor Guard solemnly lowered the flag from its perch one final time. A bill signed by Governor Haley ordered the flag be transferred to the Confederate relic room of the State Museum. Removing the flag was a monumentally symbolic act that foreshadowed a national battle over the tension between historical exclusions and contemporary realities.

Pride or Prejudice

A 2017 poll conducted by YouGov found sharp racial differences in public perceptions of what the flag represents. As figure 4.1 illustrates, African American respondents were more likely than white respondents to view the flag as a symbol of racism. The intersection of race and geography reveals an even wider gap, with 62 percent of Southern whites compared to just 28 percent of Southern Blacks saying the flag is a symbol of Southern pride. Likewise, 68 percent of Southern Blacks compared to 9 percent of Southern whites said

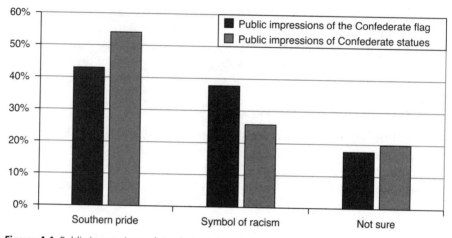

Figure 4.1 Public impressions of Confederate symbols
Source: Frankovic (2017).

they believe the flag is a racist symbol. That same poll found a political effect, as respondents who supported Donald Trump in the 2016 presidential election were significantly less likely to see the flag as racist than those who voted for Hillary Clinton (Frankovic 2017). That debate over the flag as a symbol of heritage or hate reflects longstanding tensions over the relationship between race, citizenship, and political standing.

Remembrance versus Reverence

What is the proper way to recognize history while addressing its troubling elements? That question was fiercely debated in 2017 by residents in numerous towns across the United States while reviewing the public imprint of controversial figures in history. According to a study conducted by the Southern Poverty Law Center (2018), public monuments of the confederacy were erected across the United States during two major time periods as a result of increased private funding from organizations such as the United Daughters of the Confederacy.[6] The first era (1900–1920s) accompanied state efforts to disenfranchise Blacks and cement racial segregation in the wake of federal efforts to promote integration and full citizenship. These markers were created to honor Confederate soldiers as heroes while also creating a physical reminder of Southern history. The second era (1950s–1970) coincided with efforts to secure widespread civil rights protections of equity, citizenship, and political representation (Landrieu 2018; Cox 2003). In the 1980s, groups such as the Sons of the Confederacy renewed efforts to restore existing markers while building new monuments.

Just two years after the Charleston church massacre, residents in New Orleans, Memphis, Alexandria, and Baltimore came together to remove Confederate markers and monuments while renaming schools and public spaces honoring Confederate heroes. They were often met with fierce resistance from those who saw the changes as an effort to erase history. Mitch Landrieu, the sixty-first mayor of New Orleans, addressed his critics following the decision to relocate the city's five remaining Confederate monuments:

> We have not erased history; we are becoming part of the city's history by righting the wrong image these monuments represent and crafting a better, more complete future for all our children and for future generations. And unlike when these Confederate monuments were first erected as symbols of white supremacy, we now have a chance to create not only new symbols, but to do it together, as one people. In our blessed land we all come to the table of democracy as equals. We have to reaffirm our commitment to a future where each citizen is guaranteed the uniquely American gifts of life, liberty and the pursuit of happiness.
> That is what really makes America great, and today it is more important than ever to hold fast to these values and together say a self-evident truth that out of many we are one. That is why today we reclaim these spaces for the United States of America. Because we are one nation, not two; indivisible with liberty and justice for all . . . not some. We all are part of one nation, all pledging allegiance to one flag, the flag of the United States of America. And New Orleanians are in . . . all of the way. It is in this union and in this truth that real patriotism is rooted and flourishes.[7]

In a city with a contentious history around racial identity marked by a landmark Supreme Court case (*Plessy v. Ferguson*), mass displacement after natural disasters (Hurricanes Katrina and Rita), and ongoing questions regarding demographic shifts, New Orleans was well suited to address the task of defining what Landrieu (2018) called "the difference between remembrance of history and reverence of it." The city's decision to remove the statues set the context for a violent battle hundreds of miles away in Virginia.

Race and Resistance in Charlottesville

In the picturesque college town of Charlottesville, Virginia, the local city council voted to rename a park honoring Confederate General Robert E. Lee. The park and its accompanying statue were gifted to the city by a wealthy benefactor, Paul G. McIntire, who was an ardent supporter of the "lost cause" view of the Civil War – a view built on the notion that, although they lost the Civil War, Confederates succeeded in defending the soul, independence, and character of the nation. The naming of public places, the erection of monuments, and the creation of cultural artifacts such as the 1915 *Birth of a Nation* film helped promote this view and sustain support for the confederacy (Simpson 1975).

In August 2017, hundreds of avowed white nationalists and Nazi supporters descended on the campus of the University of Virginia (UVA) wielding tiki torches and chanting slogans such as "Jews will not replace us," "White lives matter," and "Our blood, our soil, our streets" to protest the renaming as an erasure of white identity.[8]

UVA was founded by Thomas Jefferson forty-five years after he penned the eloquent words to the Declaration of Independence (1776): "We hold these truths to be self-evident: that all men are created equal; that they are endowed by their Creator with certain unalienable rights; that among these are life, liberty, and the pursuit of happiness." Two years earlier Jefferson released *Notes on the State of Virginia*, which argued that slavery was necessary to protect Blacks who lacked the mental capacity necessary for survival:

> I advance it therefore as suspicion only, that the blacks, whether originally a distinct race, or made distinct by time and circumstances, are inferior to the whites in the endowments both of body and mind. It is not against experience to suppose, that different species of the same genus, or varieties of the same species, may possess different qualifications. This unfortunate difference of color, and perhaps of faculty, is a powerful obstacle to the emancipation of these people. The slave, when made free, might mix with, without staining the blood of his master. But with us a second is necessary, unknown to history. When freed, he is to be removed beyond the reach of mixture.[9]

The decision to host the fiery rally on the grounds of "Mr Jefferson's University" highlighted a longstanding gap between the principle and practice of democratic equality. Just steps away from where **alt-right** supporters gathered in "Make America Great Again" hats and khaki trousers, an interfaith, interethnic worship service was held at the St Paul's Memorial Church. The city's mayor awaited word as to whether he had the legal authority to move the rally to another part of the city.[10] As the church's rector William Peyton prayed for divine intervention, the fear, uncertainty, and foreboding of what was to come was amplified outside.

The following day the "Unite the Right" rally organized by Jason Kessler and Richard Spencer drew violent clashes between thousands of protesters and counterprotesters. To many, the images of chaos in Charlottesville were shocking and horrifying. To others, it affirmed that racial hostility persisted in the United States despite decades of efforts to eliminate it. By the conclusion of the rally over thirty people were injured, two state troopers had perished in a helicopter crash, and Heather Heyer was killed after James Fields rammed his

Protesters clash at the 2017 "Unite the Right" rally in Charlottesville, Virginia.

car into a crowd of counterprotesters.[11] A video of an African American man named DeAndre Harris being savagely beaten by six white nationalists in a parking garage went viral and prompted demands for the federal government to intervene and restore order.

In the wake of the violence, President Donald J. Trump weighed in to hold "both sides" accountable:

> I think there is blame on both sides . . . what about the alt-left that came charging at, as you say, the alt-right? Do they have any semblance of guilt? . . . What about the fact that they came charging with clubs in their hands, swinging clubs? Do they have any problem? I think they do . . . you had a group on one side that was bad, and you had a group on the other side that was also very violent. And nobody wants to say that, but I'll say it right now.[12]

The president's remarks drew immediate criticism from those who felt he was equating the actions of white nationalists with those of the counterprotesters. In a subsequent press conference he tried to clarify his remarks to emphasize the need to gather complete information before condemning "either side." However, given the racially polarized environment in the United States that was amplified during the 2016 election and its aftermath, this rebuttal did little to assure those who felt the country was on the brink of a second civil war. According to data from the Southern Poverty Law Center (2018), the number of hate groups in the United States has risen by 17 percent since 2014, with the greatest increase in the number of groups targeting Muslims (a 300 percent increase). Figure 4.2, based on data from the FBI's Uniform Crime Reports, shows that the number of racially motivated hate crimes has also surged during that same time frame.

BOX 4.1 The price of justice

Awards shows are usually opportunities to gawk at celebrities who give awkward speeches in expensive attire. In 2017, however, the MTV Video Music Awards highlighted the price many face for tackling racial injustice. The Reverend Robert Lee IV is the great nephew of Confederate General Robert E. Lee. In the wake of the violence in Charlottesville and broader national debates, Lee was a vocal critic of individuals and organizations promoting violence and hatred in the name of Southern pride:

> My name is Robert Lee IV, I'm a descendant of Robert E. Lee, the Civil War general whose statue was at the center of violence in Charlottesville. We have made my ancestor an idol of white supremacy, racism, and hate. As a pastor, it is my moral duty to speak out against racism, America's original sin.
>
> Today, I call on all of us with privilege and power to answer God's call to confront racism and white supremacy head-on. We can find inspiration in the Black Lives Matter movement, the women who marched in the Women's March in January, and, especially, Heather Heyer, who died fighting for her beliefs in Charlottesville.

Lee was joined onstage by Heyer's mother, Susan Bro, who eulogized her daughter by saying, "They tried to kill my child to shut her up. Well, guess what? You just magnified her." Days after the awards show Lee was forced to resign his position as pastor of Bethany United Church of Christ after some congregants expressed concern that his support of the Black Lives Matter movement and the Women's March were divisive. Bro currently runs a foundation in her daughter's honor that promotes social justice via scholarships and youth development. She continues to receive hate mail and threats from those on the far right.

Pride and Prejudice: The Context

Issues of race and racial identity have long dominated US politics. These contemporary struggles, however, mirror longstanding debates over the compatibility of racial identity and citizenship claims. To some, the Confederate flag and accompanying monuments represent a fierce sense of independence from federal oversight and a commitment to protecting states' rights. Throughout

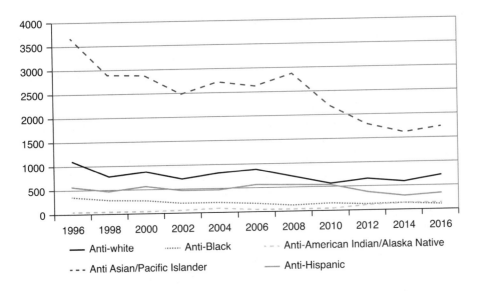

Figure 4.2 Reported racially motivated hate crimes, 1996–2016
SOURCE: FBI Uniform Crime Reports.

American history, however, the debate over federalism and states' rights often surfaces in opposition to federal efforts to promote equality and inclusion. Historically, states have played a major role in structuring the relationship between majority power and minority interests (Kluger 1979; Huckfeldt and Kohfeld 1989). For example, state institutions were at the forefront of efforts to impede federal demands to integrate public schools following the monumental *Brown* v. *Board of Education of Topeka* decision in 1954.[13]

The battle over flags and monuments, and the aftermath of the "Unite the Right" rally, connect to longstanding tensions surrounding racial identity in the United States. Race has been a central organizing identity within American political development since the first Africans arrived on the continent's shores in 1619. The initial requirements for US citizenship limited

Table 4.1 Demographic profile of racial groups

Racial group	Percentage of population	Median income	Percentage in poverty
White (alone)	76.6	$65,041	8.7
Black/African American (alone)	13.4	$39,490	22.0
American Indian/Alaska Native	1.3	$38,530	26.6
Asian (alone)	5.8	$81,431	13.8
Native Hawaiian or Pacific Islander	0.2	$57,112	

SOURCE: Based on data from the US Census Bureau and the Henry J. Kaiser Family Foundation, 2018.

inclusion to white, property-owning males. Throughout much of US history, African Americans have been excluded from many of the formal arenas of political influence, such as voting, political parties, interest groups, and office-holding (Barker et al. 1999; Harding 1981). As Walton and Smith (2000) suggest, African Americans have only been included as full participants in the process for less than fifty years.

Racial identity – like all politicized identities – is dynamic. Its meaning is constantly subject to historical time period, institutional domain, and popular understanding. The construction, meaning, and fluidity of racial identity reflects a broader negotiation of power within the scope of US politics. For example, Barack Obama's election as the forty-fourth president of the United States led some to claim that the country was effectively entering a *post-racial* phase where issues of racism and prejudice were no longer defining features of society. Others argued that Obama's election drew attention to broader divisions over identity and affinity (Cobb 2010; Harris 2012; Price 2016; Coates 2015; Hannah-Jones 2016). As table 4.1 illustrates, the differing demographic profiles of various racial groups shape the potential for political influence.

In the same electoral season that sent the Obamas to the White House, California voters approved a controversial measure to deny legally protected marriage rights to same-sex couples. Proposition 8 (Prop 8) was a ballot initiative to legally define marriage as being only between one man and one woman. Over $83 million was spent to influence voters on both sides of the issue. Prop 8 passed with 52 percent of the vote and set in motion ardent public debates over the scope of constitutional protections related to identities other than race (Abrajano 2010; Wadsworth 2011). Two months later, America's first Black president chose controversial Pastor Rick Warren to deliver the invocation for his inauguration. The move upset many LGBTQI voters, who believed Warren was hostile to their interests at best, homophobic at worst (Cole 2008). It also challenged the limits of political coalitions built by groups with shared identities and differing policy priorities.

In this chapter I examine three key domains for understanding the relationship between racial identities and US politics: 1) race and political institutions, 2) race and citizenship, and 3) race and voting rights. Capturing the whole of race and politics is beyond its scope. Indeed, entire volumes have been devoted to examining the complex ways issues of race have shaped what Philip Klinkner and Rogers Smith (1999) call the "unsteady march" of racial equality in the US. Instead, I pay particular attention to landmark Supreme Court cases, legislative decisions, and political movements that determine the quality and substance of citizenship based on racial identities. As we will see in the following sections, a change in laws doesn't necessarily translate to substantive changes in political standing.

Race and Political Institutions

Institutions both create and manage political conflicts via the policies, laws, and regulations they produce. For African Americans and other underrepresented groups, institutions have played a key role in shaping access to key areas of public life. Even as three Civil War Amendments (Thirteenth, Fourteenth, and Fifteenth) sought to carve out Blacks' political presence, extralegal methods of violence, intimidation, and suppression effectively locked them out of the political process. The uniquely US concept of federalism allowed states to pursue their interests while still upholding the Constitution that, in theory, eliminated racial distinctions. As Kousser writes:

> Institutions and institutional rules – not customs, ideas, culture, or private behavior – have primarily shaped race relations in America. The most important and longest lasting influence of course, has been that of the "peculiar institution" of slavery – conditioned by law, sustained by law and, after being devastated by war, finally dispatched and interred by law ... But other institutions and rules have also had profound impacts on the struggles for and against racial equality: the Constitution, the methods for aggregating voters into legislative seats, the structure and internal organization of political bodies, the regulations issued by the executive branch of government, the actions of political parties, and the pronouncements of the judiciary ... While liberty may arrive or depart in a moment, equality requires not only eternal vigilance but also consensus and incremental improvement. Institutional stability – with the right kind of institutions – is a prerequisite for minority success. (1999: 1)

The work of early scholars such as Alexis de Tocqueville (1835), V. O. Key (1949), Gunnar Myrdal (1944), and E. E. Schattschneider (1960) suggests that there was a concerted effort on the part of the national political parties and elected officials to keep issues of racial identity off the *national* agenda. Recognizing the divisive nature of these issues, national political actors attempted to maintain consensus politics by relegating racial disparities to the local level, particularly in the South. In light of this "agreement," the Supreme Court led the retreat from racial equality by suggesting that the Fourteenth Amendment did not place all rights under federal protection. The Court ruled against the protection of civil rights in a series of cases, including the **Slaughterhouse Cases** (1873), the Civil Rights Cases (1883), and *Plessy* v. *Ferguson* (1896). Box 3.2 (see p. 50) gives further detail of the Civil War constitutional amendments.

Race and Citizenship

One of the biggest challenges related to racial identity in the United States has been the task of defining the boundaries, entitlements, and privileges of citizenship. The courts have played a formidable role as arbitrator. As legislators and citizens debated how to accommodate people seeking entry into the country, the Supreme Court issued a resounding statement on those who were already here via its ruling in *Dred Scott v. Sandford* (1857):

> The question then arises, whether the provisions of the Constitution, in relation to the personal rights and privileges to which the citizen of a State should be entitled, embraced the negro African race, at that time in this country, or who might afterwards be imported, who had then or should afterwards be made free in any State; and to put it in the power of a single State to make him a citizen of the United States, and endue him with the full rights of citizenship in every other State without their consent? Does the Constitution of the United States act upon him whenever he shall be made free under the laws of a State, and raised there to the rank of a citizen, and immediately clothe him with all the privileges of a citizen in every other State, and in its own courts? . . . It becomes necessary, therefore, to determine who were citizens of the several States when the Constitution was adopted. (60 US 393)

Although the focus of this original case was on whether Scott could be considered a free man, the decision was used to justify the wholesale disenfranchisement of Blacks and, by extension, the total denial of citizenship (Stanley 1987). In his book *Freedom is Not Enough*, Ronald W. Walters (2005) writes that Blacks in the United States saw full citizenship as the primary goal. Central to that citizenship, he argues, was obtaining the right to vote as a fundamental badge of political membership.

Federalism, Freedom, and the Franchise

In 1906, noted sociologist and civil rights activist W. E. B. DuBois convened members of the budding Niagara movement in Harper's Ferry, West Virginia. Harper's Ferry was the site of John Brown's raid against slavery and one of the few schools that offered African Americans access to secondary education. In his "Address to the Country," DuBois outlined why movement leaders believed voting rights were essential to securing American freedom: "First, we would vote; with the right to vote goes everything: Freedom, manhood, the honor of your wives, the chastity of your daughters, the right to work, and the chance to rise, and let no man listen to those who deny this. We want full manhood suffrage, and we want it now, henceforth and forever."[14]

Pursuing full citizenship by acquiring the vote varied across region and territory in the United States. While 69 percent of the original thirteen states allowed free men of color to vote during the colonial period, the increasing size of the free Black population, coupled with the new political structure created by the Articles of Confederation, significantly reversed this trend. When these original colonies became states, only four allowed free men of color to vote. The intersection of race, gender, and class as a marker of citizenship spread across the United States as Black voting rights were revoked in New Jersey (1807), Connecticut (1818), North Carolina (1834), and Pennsylvania (1838) (Brown-Dean 2003).

Despite the tremendous structural changes resulting from the US Constitution, states retained a great deal of discretion in setting the requirements for participation and, in turn, the benefits of citizenship. This discretion gave way to a great deal of regional variation. Many of the new states in the West had substantially lower wealth requirements, while many of the earlier states sought to guarantee their power by moving toward universal white male suffrage. These efforts solidified the importance of the vote and stimulated dual efforts both to expand and to limit the electorate.

Some observers attributed the gradual extension of suffrage rights to increasing support for equality, liberalism, and egalitarianism (Bullock and Gaddie 2009; Valelly 2004). The diffusion of these views drew attention to inequities in standing and sparked efforts to create a more equal distribution of citizenship. However, this belief in egalitarianism as the impetus for suffrage ignores the competing pressures that were highly prevalent during that time. Faced with Black populations increasing in size, the collapse of slavery, and growing discontent among poor whites, ruling elites had to consider how altering election rules that helped certain groups would assist them to achieve their own political ends. In changing the standards for inclusion and defining access to the political process, those in power can better determine the outputs and beneficiaries of that process. As a result, defining the requirements for participation becomes critical both for sustaining hierarchies in standing and for limiting opportunities to challenge them. The increased tension between federal and state governments combined with partisan battles for national dominance that sparked efforts to concentrate power. Table 4.2 documents changes in white male turnout in presidential elections in select states: overall, we see a dramatic increase in turnout across this time period. Easing the institutional barriers helped solidify whites' position in both the social hierarchy and the political process. However, the strength of this position would be tested by rapid changes at the federal level.

Race, the Constitution, and the Courts

The US Constitution and the efforts to implement its protections helped assert the supremacy of the national government. These efforts would be important for altering the structure of government in general and the relationship between

Table 4.2 White male voter turnout in selected states (percentages)

State	1824	1828	1832	1836	1840	1844
New Hampshire	35.6	71.0	68.8	69.2	80.4	87.2
New Jersey	35.6	71.0	68.8	69.2	80.4	87.2
Virginia	11.6	27.7	31.1	35.2	54.7	54.2
North Carolina	41.8	56.9	31.3	53.0	2.4	78.8
Tennessee	25.4	70.0	74.0	61.1	74.3	80.7
Mississippi	41.3	56.6	28.0	64.4	88.2	86.1
Alabama	49.1	54.6	33.3	64.9	89.7	80.3
United States	26.9	57.6	55.4	57.8	80.2	78.9

SOURCE: Based on data from Silbey et al. (1978).

Blacks and government in particular. In the nineteenth century, state and local governments played a more expansive role in determining the level of rights and protections that Blacks could enjoy. The limited reach of the national government granted states a great deal of autonomy and nearly unchecked power to define these rights. One of the most important powers retained by states was their ability to set the time, place, and manner of elections (Article I, Section 4; Article II, Section 1). The right to vote was a state-created and, at times, state-sanctioned right that could be denied or abridged at their will.[15] Federalism limited the ability of federal officials to compel state action. This is best personified by the hollow promise of the *Emancipation Proclamation* issued by President Abraham Lincoln in 1863. The purpose was to free enslaved Africans living in territories that rebelled against the federal government. However, the lack of federal enforcement power meant that very few enslaved people were actually freed. In turn, the federal government's role in protecting this right wasn't formally articulated until the passage of later amendments. The full realization of emancipation was contingent upon state action.

Debates over slavery and the supremacy of the national government filtered into discussions of citizenship and immigration. The Thirteenth Amendment (1865) forbade slavery and therefore secured a minimal degree of citizenship for Blacks. The 1868 adoption of the Fourteenth Amendment prohibited states from making or enforcing laws that abridged the privileges and immunities of citizenship regardless of race, class, or gender. Its substance – citizenship, due process, and equal protection – has caused the Fourteenth Amendment to be the subject of more Supreme Court cases than any other provision of the Constitution. Congress then added a Citizenship Clause that included people of African descent in naturalization provisions. However, neither of these provided a definitive, universal statement of citizenship.

Although the Fourteenth Amendment granted citizenship to all persons "born or naturalized in the United States," it failed to explicitly prohibit vote discrimination on racial grounds.[16] The Fifteenth Amendment (1870) stated that the "rights of citizens of the United States to vote shall not be denied or abridged by the US or by any state on account of race, color, or previous condition of servitude" and gave explicit constitutional protection to the voting rights of Blacks in the North and South.[17] The Fourteenth and Fifteenth Amendments highlighted the unique role of the federal government in establishing and sustaining the full realization of US democracy. Taken together, these three amendments were critical for gradually extending protection of the franchise to African American men. Yet, most importantly, fears over their potential consequences gave rise to a tremendous backlash that personifies the nature of politics during this time.

The adoption of these Civil War amendments demonstrates the inherent contradiction between the United States' professed commitment to egalitarian principles and its desire to impose restrictions on the ability of certain groups to pursue these same goals. On the surface, it appeared that the "progressive" politicians of the North supported these extensions because they promoted fairness and justice for African Americans (even though voting rights applied only to African American men). However, the nature of partisan competition during this time significantly influenced efforts to secure Blacks' voting rights. By supporting Black enfranchisement, many Republicans hoped to gain control of national political offices, particularly the White House. The issue of Black suffrage became a part of the Reconstruction agenda only *after* radicals in Congress saw it as a useful means of widening their base of support and containing the South's influence. Although these new amendments represented incremental changes in Blacks' formal citizenship status, in practice they did very little to transform their political status. Further, the modest gains derived from these changes were quickly eroded.

Building upon the imperatives of the Thirteenth Amendment, the **Reconstruction Act of 1867** was critical for attempting to transform race and citizenship permanently. It dissolved state governments in the South and established a formal military presence in the region. Perhaps most importantly, it required Southern states to hold constitutional conventions with delegates elected by male citizens of "whatever race, color, or previous condition." Southern state governments could only be established after these conventions were held.

Race and Region

Before the Civil War, all states except Maine, Massachusetts, New Hampshire, Rhode Island, and Vermont included Black disenfranchisement provisions in their constitutions. Although suffrage was available in these states in theory, in practice full voting participation was still an elusive goal. Of those that joined the Union after 1800, Maine was the only state that allowed Blacks to vote in general elections. In the decade preceding the Reconstruction Act of 1867, Maine, Massachusetts, New Hampshire, Rhode Island, and Vermont continued to be the only states that allowed Blacks to vote on the same terms as whites (Keyssar 2009). Thus, the Reconstruction Act attempted to address race and citizenship by enfranchising Blacks in the North.

These changes at the federal level dramatically changed the makeup of the Southern electorate. In the South's Black Belt region, Blacks constituted the numerical majority of the electorate. This numerical presence, combined with a federal presence, led to the election of nearly 800 Black candidates across the South (Harding 1981). The resulting elections helped Republicans extend their power and influence in the South. This shift in the balance of power expanded Congress's control over making laws and shaping the face of Reconstruction.[18]

Although Congress passed numerous laws aimed at establishing Blacks' citizenship status, President Andrew Johnson attempted to obstruct their full implementation. Johnson was impeached in 1868 as a direct result of these efforts. Other actors at the state and national levels followed Johnson's lead and significantly reversed congressional efforts to affirm Black citizenship. Guided by a common fear of Black dominance and contempt for Northern influence, many Southern whites worked earnestly to regain their political rights and status (Kousser 1999). As a result, the marginal gains of Black enfranchisement served as a catalyst for massive countermobilization efforts on the part of whites that relied on both legal and illegal tactics.

While the passage of these laws provided Blacks with modest political rights, they did nothing to alter their social and economic status. In turn, Southern white elites were able to use their control over social and economic institutions both to discourage and to undermine Black participation. Key classifies the formal disenfranchisement measures as "the roof rather than the foundation of the Southern political system" (1949: 533). The rise and prominence of the Ku Klux Klan during this time effectively threatened the formal changes in Blacks' citizenship status (Harding 1981; Foner 1988; Gates 2000; Packard 2002).[19] Violence in the form of kidnappings, fire-bombings, and lynchings were effective at "scaring" Blacks away from the polls by instilling a persistent sense of fear and vulnerability. Table 4.3 documents the tremendous rise in lynchings that coincided with key organized efforts to challenge Black political exclusion.

Violence as Political Instrument

Lynching and similar acts of racial violence were most concentrated during the periods of greatest political turmoil.[20] Although African Americans accounted for only 44 percent of the lynching victims in the 1880s, their representation

Table 4.3 Reported illegal lynchings by era and alleged offense, 1880–1960

	1880s	1900s	1920s	1940s	1960s
Homicide	537	372	100	5	0
Rape	259	154	70	0	0
Attempted rape	9	99	22	6	0
Insult(s) to a white person	5	11	17	2	1
Total	810	636	209	13	1
% of victims who were Black	44	72	89	94	100

SOURCE: Calahan and Parsons (1986).

increased to 72 percent in the 1900s and 89 percent in the 1920s. Lynchings based on allegations of raping and/or insulting a white person also rose dramatically. These attacks reflect a decidedly regional character. For example, 83 percent of the reported cases in the South involved a Black victim compared to 67 percent in the Northeast, 36 percent in the North Central region, and 5 percent in the West. In every state except Oklahoma and California, more than 85 percent of the reported cases involved an African American victim (Gonzales-Day 2006). These illegal tactics sustain the civic and social inequality that could not be achieved via legal means.

BOX 4.2 Lynching and racial violence

Lynching has long been used as one of the most inhumane and violent means of reinforcing racial/ethnic boundaries in the United States.

Between 1882 and 1968, over 5,000 acts of lynching were recorded. This number is likely much higher, as some incidents were either not reported or misclassified based on fear and intimidation. The overwhelming majority involved Black men, who were abducted, tortured, shot, and hung for infractions that ranged from accusations of being "disrespectful" to rape and murder. Lynching was an extralegal means of preserving the racial status quo and of invoking fear among those who wanted to challenge the existing social order.

Ida B. Wells-Barnett was a courageous journalist who documented lynchings across the United States while exposing how law-enforcement officers, judges, and business leaders were complicit in various crimes.

The National Memorial for Peace and Justice chronicles the use of lynching as a tool of racial *and* gendered terror throughout the South. In her book *Southern Horrors*, Crystal Feimster (2009) documents that nearly 200 women were lynched throughout the South between 1880 and 1930. In 1918 in Georgia, Mary Turner was abducted by a mob outraged by her threat to take out a warrant against those who had lynched her husband. Turner was eight months pregnant. The mob tied her to a tree upside down before burning off her clothes, cutting open her stomach, and shooting her repeatedly.

In 1891, eleven Italian immigrants were kidnapped and lynched in New Orleans for allegedly killing a beloved police chief, who identified his attackers as "dagoes." Similarly, Leo Frank was a Jewish factory owner who was abducted and lynched by a mob who accused him of raping and murdering a young worker.

Together these stories highlight the atrocious use of lynching to intimidate various groups.

Outraged by the murders of three prominent Black businessmen, journalist Ida B. Wells-Barnett led the country's most comprehensive anti-lynching crusade. Wells-Barnett worked closely with abolitionists, **suffragists**, and other leaders to promote greater awareness of lynching and encourage political leaders to condemn the practice. She viewed violence as a political tactic used to reinforce differences in social standing and keep Blacks in their (lesser) place:

> With no sacredness of the ballot there can be no sacredness of human life itself. For if the strong can take the weak man's ballot, when it suits his purpose to do so, he will take his life also. Having successfully swept aside the constitutional safeguards to the ballot, it is the smallest of small matters for the South to sweep aside its own safeguards to human life. (Wells-Barnett 1895)

Wells-Barnett invokes the historical consequences of the federal government's retreat from protecting Blacks from the whims of the South. This consequence is reflected in the aftermath of the Compromise of 1877 that led to an end to Reconstruction and an effective end to Black electoral participation. The Compromise resulted from a dispute over electoral votes in the presidential election of 1876. The votes in question came from the last three states still under federal occupation: South Carolina, Louisiana, and Florida. To resolve the dispute, party officials agreed that the contested votes would go to the Republican candidate Rutherford B. Hayes. In exchange, Republicans agreed to withdraw federal troops from the South and, in effect, end Reconstruction (Keyssar 2009). To some extent, the Compromise was simply a symbolic move to formally withdraw federal interference. However, these extralegal maneuvers were just as, if not more, effective at solidifying racial hierarchies. The illegal tactics of violence and corruption coupled with the legal imperatives of the Compromise of 1877 helped Southern whites regain their political dominance.

With the removal of federal troops, Blacks were left to the mercy of state elites, who were committed more to a return to the ante-bellum political world than to the egalitarian principles that had supposedly led to the original constitutional revisions. As a result, the country witnessed a dramatic decrease in Black electoral participation. In turn, "within 10 to 15 years after 1867 the

---

BOX 4.3 Major disenfranchisement tactics

Poll tax	Required citizens to pay a tax before being eligible to vote. Many states instituted a cumulative poll tax that assessed multiyear fees. These tactics effectively prevented Blacks and poorer whites from being able to vote in Southern elections on account of their limited income.
Literacy test	Required citizens to read, comprehend, and answer complex questions whose answers varied based on the race of the respondent. For example, the state of Georgia allowed registrars to ask potential voters the number of bubbles in a bar of soap or recite from memory an obscure passage of the state Constitution.
Grandfather clause	Allowed those who were able to vote before the Reconstruction Act of 1867 and those whose father or grandfather could vote before 1867 to skip literacy tests, poll taxes, and other requirements for voting. The clauses effectively eliminated Black voters because their grandfathers would not have been eligible to vote.
Criminal disenfranchisement	Various statutes prohibited those convicted of certain misdemeanor and felony crimes from voting in elections. In some states, disenfranchising crimes included those to which Blacks were believed to be more prone, such as stealing edible meat and loitering, and excluded those which whites were thought to commit more frequently, such as murder.
White primary	Political parties, as private organizations, were able to determine who was allowed to participate in primary elections. Much of the South was dominated by one party (Democrats) at the time, so primaries played a crucial role in determining nominees and policy priorities.

premature enfranchisement of the Negro was largely undone, and undone by a veritable revolution" (Key 1949: 536). For a detailed discussion of the major disenfranchisement tactics discussed in box 4.3, see Kousser (1974).

Courting Citizenship

Two key cases address the link between racial identity, federalism, and citizenship. In 1873, Colfax, Louisiana, was the site of violent clashes between Black and white voters following an electoral upset in the state's gubernatorial election. Over 300 white members of the KKK and other groups descended on the local courthouse armed with cannons and guns. That day over 150 Black men were killed, alongside three whites (Blee 1996). The resulting case, *United States v. Cruikshank* (1876), restricted the scope of federal statutes that were designed to prevent discrimination on account of race. The Court held that the rights the defendants were accused of violating could not be enforced: "The Government of the United States, although it is, within the scope of its powers, supreme and beyond the States, can neither grant nor secure to its citizens rights or privileges which are not expressly or by implication placed under its jurisdiction. All that cannot be so granted or secured are left to the exclusive protection of the States."[21]

United States v. Reese (1876) extended this belief by isolating the right to vote as a state-created rather than a federal right. Together, these two cases highlight the complex ways federalism has been invoked to limit the scope of government protections of citizenship. By relegating the issue of race to a regional rather than a national concern, the federal government retreated from previous efforts to protect Blacks' access to the ballot. This retreat fueled Southern efforts to guarantee their political dominance at the national level. The relocation of federal efforts to protect electoral access in pivotal Northern states sparked the rise of massive efforts to disenfranchise African Americans in the South. Although this early history suggests that race and racial concerns were always present in the United States, the Gilded Age marked a concerted effort by the national parties and elected officials to keep race off the national agenda.[22] Recognizing the potentially divisive nature of racial issues, national political actors attempted to maintain consensus politics by relegating the issue of racial disparity to the local level, particularly in the South. In light of this "agreement," the Supreme Court led the retreat from racial equality by suggesting that the Fourteenth Amendment did not place all rights under federal protection. To cement this assertion, the Court ruled against the protection of civil rights in a series of cases.

The Slaughterhouse Cases (1873) consisted of two separate cases that articulated a clear delineation between federal citizenship and state citizenship.[23] The Court held that, while the purpose of the Fourteenth Amendment was to abolish slavery and involuntary servitude, the immunities and privileges clause addressed only the rights attached to US and not state citizenship. In delivering the opinion Justice Miller wrote:

> The next observation is more important in view of the arguments of counsel in the present case. It is, that the distinction between citizenship of the United States and citizenship of a State is clearly recognized and established. . . . It is quite clear, then, that there is a citizenship of the United States, and a citizenship of a State, which are distinct from each other, and which depend upon different characteristics or circumstances in the individual. . . . We think this distinction and its explicit recognition in this amendment of great weight in this argument, because the next paragraph of this same section, which is the one mainly relied on by the plaintiffs in error, speaks only of privileges and immunities of citizens of the United States, and does not speak of those of citizens of the several States. The argument, however, in favor of the plaintiffs, rests wholly on the assumption that the citizenship is the same, and the privileges and immunities guaranteed by the clause are the same. (83 US 36, at 73)

The Court's position in the case laid the foundation for the *Civil Rights Cases* (1883), which held that the protections of the Fourteenth Amendment could apply only to the actions of government and not those of private individuals. Therefore, individuals could not sue other individuals or private entities for violating their rights. The Court's decision struck down many of the earlier measures passed by Congress to protect Black citizenship. Following this trend, Congress did not pass a single civil rights bill, after Reconstruction, until the Civil Rights Act of 1957.[24] Similarly, no president until Truman sent a civil rights program to Congress.

BOX 4.4 Major US Supreme Court cases addressing race and discrimination

Dred Scott v. *Sandford* (1857)
Civil Rights Cases (1883)
Yick Wo v. *Hopkins* (1886)
Plessy v. *Ferguson* (1896)
Powell v. *Alabama* (1932)
Korematsu v. *United States* (1944)
Shelley v. *Kraemer* (1948)
Sweatt v. *Painter* and *McLaurin* v. *Oklahoma State Regents* (1950)
Hernandez v. *Texas* (1954)
Brown v. *Board of Education of Topeka* (1954)
Heart of Atlanta Motel, Inc. v. *United States* (1964)
Loving v. *Virginia* (1967)

Regents of the University of California v. *Bakke* (1978)
Batson v. *Kentucky* (1986)
Grutter v. *Bollinger* (2003)
Ricci v. *DeStefano* (2009)
Fisher v. *University of Texas at Austin* (2016)
Evenwel v. *Abbott* (2016)

The Slaughterhouse Cases and the Civil Rights Cases led to *Plessy* v. *Ferguson* (1896). *Plessy* articulated the concept of "separate but equal" that endorsed racial segregation in private *and* public accommodations and affirmed the right of states to create differential standards for citizenship.[25] This landmark case arose after the state of Louisiana passed an ordinance in 1980 that required separate accommodations for Blacks and whites on railcars that had to be equal. Homer Plessy was a "free person of color" who sued the state of Louisiana for violating his rights under the Thirteenth and Fourteenth Amendments to the US Constitution. The high court ruled in favor of Louisiana and argued that requiring separate facilities did not imply racial inferiority. The 7 to 1 ruling was monumental because it represented the first time that racial segregation was both codified and protected by federal statute. The lone dissenter in the case, Justice John Marshall Harlan, attacked the ruling's assertion of a federally supported racial hierarchy: "But in the view of the Constitution, in the eye of the law, there is in this country no superior, dominant, ruling class of citizens. There is no caste here. Our Constitution is color-blind, and neither knows nor tolerates classes among citizens. In respect of civil rights, all citizens are equal before the law" (163 US 537).

This federal retreat from Black citizenship helped the South keep the question of suffrage off the political agenda for nearly a decade. However, as Matthews and Prothro (1966) argue, internal conflict between white factions made the issue pertinent once again. In particular, the populist rebellion of the 1890s represented a formidable threat to white supremacy. The rebellion arose from growing discontent among farmers, laborers, and other agrarian interests over declining agricultural prices and rising transportation costs. The Farmers Alliance was originally formed in Texas in 1876 to promote the interests of farmers and press for changes in state and national policies. This coalition grew in numbers and popularity across the South and eventually led to the formation of the Populist Party, which emerged in the 1890s as a direct challenge to the failure of both Democrats and Republicans to address their interests effectively. The party's platform, "The Omaha Plan," addressed a number of issues, including the need for a graduated income tax and the abolition of national banks. The growing strength of the party and its ability to capture working-class supporters in various pockets of influence posed a direct threat to the dominance of the two major parties. To counter the populist influence, Democrats and Republicans began actively courting Black voters:

> The Farmers Alliance and the Populist Party generated a dispute among whites whose outcome was of such deep concern that both factions breached the consensus to keep the blacks from the polls. Both Democrats and Populists were in a position to hold the balance of power between white factions. The degree to which Negroes actually voted *en bloc* and participated in the elections of the agrarian uprising has never been adequately investigated. . . . Nevertheless, the Populists, either alone or in combination with Republicans, threatened Democratic supremacy, and a situation emerged in which the plea for white supremacy could be made effectively. (Key 1949: 541)

Political elites soon realized that the only assured means of countering these efforts would be to adopt formal, legal barriers to voting. Although violence had successfully limited participation in the past, elites viewed this as a temporary remedy rather than a permanent solution. Instead it was necessary for state legislators to create new schemes that could survive constitutional scrutiny. These efforts often made appeals to white supremacy and solidarity to garner greater support. In areas where the Populist movement threatened to exacerbate internal cleavages among whites, these appeals highlighted the threat posed by granting Blacks full citizenship. This strategy served two major functions. First, it increased support for racial exclusion. Second, it raised hope among previously disenfranchised whites that they would eventually be included as full citizens. This strategy helped separate Blacks from poorer whites and, in turn, decreased the potential for these two groups to leverage their numerical presence and create a multiracial coalition.

This process helped reunite the South under the common goal of keeping African Americans out of the voting booth and, by extension, solidified whites' position. Keenly aware that the Fifteenth Amendment prohibited overtly racial discrimination, white politicians were forced to devise more subtle methods of racial exclusion. These politicians also had to insure that the methods meant to exclude Blacks wouldn't have the unintended consequence of disenfranchising whites as well, particularly poorer whites. Although some of this could be avoided because of the selective enforcement practices of election supervisors and registrars, legislators sought a more durable means of safeguarding the electorate in a way that could withstand judicial scrutiny.

Driven by these concerns, Mississippi's 1890 constitutional convention marked the first concerted post-Reconstruction effort to adopt legal devices aimed at disenfranchising Blacks. It was also the first to avoid ratification by popular vote. The state's population at the time was 58 percent Black, which posed a significant threat to the existing distribution of power (Pratt 2017). In referencing the potential danger of this composition, one Mississippi delegate remarked that "the avowed purpose of calling [this] convention was to restrict the negro vote."[26] In anticipation of threats to the existing political order, Mississippi became the only state to call for a constitutional convention before the outbreak of the populist revolt (Woodward 1981). In turn, the Mississippi convention set the precedent for all other Southern conventions.

Between 1891 and 1910, eleven states – Louisiana (1898), Virginia (1902), Alabama (1901), North Carolina (1900), Georgia (1908), South Carolina (1895), Tennessee (1891), Florida (1889), Texas (1902), Arkansas (1893), and Oklahoma – followed the Magnolia Plan.[27] Through these conventions, strategies such as difficult literacy tests, cumulative poll taxes, and lengthy residency requirements effectively decimated the Black electorate. States with smaller Black populations, such as Texas, Arkansas, Florida, and Tennessee, relied largely on the poll tax to achieve disenfranchisement.

Race, Class, and Disenfranchisement

Most states levied a cost of $1.50 upon those who wanted to register to vote. This fee may seem minimal by contemporary standards, but for Southern farm laborers that amount represented two full weeks' salary – even more for sharecroppers and itinerate laborers.[28] The tax was intended to prevent Blacks from voting but also eliminated a number of poorer whites, particularly farmers, who could not afford the tax. Poll taxes were cumulative, so that anyone who failed to pay the tax in one year would have that amount added to the following year's tax bill. The poll tax remained in effect until the passage of the Twenty-Fourth Amendment in 1962. At that time, Arkansas, Alabama, Mississippi, Texas, and Virginia still actively enforced the cumulative tax.[29]

States with sizeable Black populations, such as Louisiana, Virginia, Georgia, Alabama, and North Carolina, employed an array of tactics, including the grandfather clause, literacy tests, and stringent education requirements.[30] Table 4.4 documents some of the major tactics adopted during this time, while figure 4.3 illustrates their impact on political participation and representation. Many of the strategies in table 4.4. that were used to limit voting in the South originated in the North as an effort to restrict voting among white ethnic immigrants. This constant shifting of the requirements for full inclusion varied across region, race, religion, and ethnicity. The common thread, however, was a persistent commitment to defining which groups were deemed worthy of exercising the most basic feature of American democracy.

Chapter 8 details how Jim Crow segregation combined with violence and decades of migration to stimulate what Doug McAdam (1982) calls **cognitive liberation**. This belief that stigmatized groups could band together to

Table 4.4 Major disenfranchisement provisions and year of adoption

State	Poll tax	Literacy test	Grandfather clause	Criminal disenfranchisement (adopted/revised)
Alabama	1902	1902	1902	1819
Arkansas	1894	–	–	
Florida	1890	–	–	1831
Georgia	1802	1908	1908	
Louisiana	1898	1898	1898	1812/1845
Mississippi	1890	1892	–	1817
North Carolina	1900	1902	1902	
South Carolina	1896	1896	–	
Texas	1904	–	–	1834
Virginia	1904	1902	1902	1830/1850
Kentucky	–	–	–	1792/1850
Maryland	–	–	–	1851
Oklahoma	–	1912	1912	
Tennessee	1890	–	–	1842
West Virginia	–	–	–	1830/1851/1870

challenge their exclusion helped promote the development of the modern Civil Rights movement. For the remainder of this chapter, however, I focus on whether political access and representation continue to be stratified based on racial identity.

Contemporary Controversies: Race and the Politics of Punishment

The massive growth of mass incarceration in the United States has had a profound impact on the political, economic, and social standing of communities of color. According to data from the Bureau of Justice Statistics, there are 2 million people behind bars and another 6 million under other forms of criminal supervision such as parole and probation. This trend has had a disproportionate impact on communities of color. Although Blacks make up about 12 percent of the total population, Blacks and Latinos comprise 60 percent of all Americans behind bars. Though various sentencing reforms and alternatives to incarceration have led many states to gradually reduce the number of people in prison over the last ten years, the civil penalties attached to a conviction continue long after these sentences have been completed. Two key policies, felon disenfranchisement and prison-based gerrymandering, threaten to erode many of the gains made in terms of voting rights and representation.

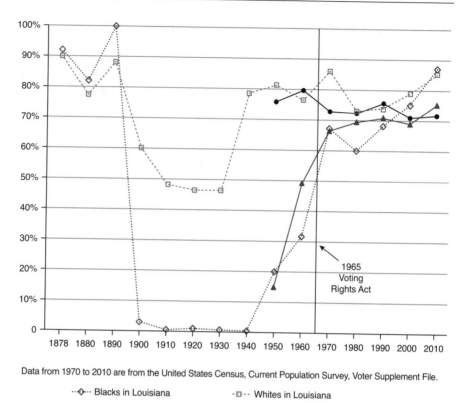

Data from 1970 to 2010 are from the United States Census, Current Population Survey, Voter Supplement File.

Figure 4.3 Black and white voter registration rates in Louisiana and former Confederate states, 1878–2010
SOURCE: Brown-Dean et al. (2015).

BOX 4.5 Race, gender, and Stand Your Ground

Marissa Alexander was a Florida resident, mother of three, and a victim of domestic violence at the hands of her estranged husband. In 2010, she fired a warning shot after he threatened to kill her and attacked her. She had no previous criminal record and invoked the Stand Your Ground defense.

Alexander was convicted of aggravated assault and sentenced to the mandatory minimum punishment of twenty years. Her conviction set off a national campaign to appeal her sentence while drawing attention to the number of women behind bars who have been victims of abuse. According to a report published by the Vera Institute of Justice (Swavola et al. 2016), 77 percent of women behind bars have experienced intimate partner violence. Ironically, Angela Corey, the same attorney who prosecuted George Zimmerman for murdering Trayvon Martin (see p. 204), also charged

Alexander. Criminal justice reform advocates organized a national campaign to draw attention to Marissa Alexander's plight and to demand that
Corey be removed from the case. Instead, during Alexander's appeal Corey
pursued an even higher sentence of sixty years. Eventually Alexander agreed
to a plea deal of three years in prison and two years of house arrest in order
to be reunited with her children. Now you determine: Should your state
adopt Stand Your Ground Laws? And, if so, how should your state define
"threat"? What measures should be in place to ensure fairness and uniform
application? Should the gender of the alleged victim and perpetrator matter
in assessing threat?

Felon Disenfranchisement

Felon disenfranchisement laws prohibit current and, in many states, former
felony offenders from voting. In forty-eight states and the District of Columbia,
inmates are barred from voting, while twelve states allow for disenfranchisement post-supervisory release. The overwhelming majority (approximately 80
percent) of America's disenfranchised population is comprised of people who
are no longer incarcerated. Together, Blacks and Latinos comprise over 40
percent of America's disenfranchised population. The impact is particularly
pronounced in states such as Virginia with sizeable minority populations.
However, even in states such as Utah with relatively small minority populations, disenfranchisement restrictions sharply constrain access to the ballot
(Brown-Dean 2016). In Iowa, for example, 27 percent of African American
men are barred from voting compared to 4.5 percent of Hispanic men and
1.5 percent of white men. The overrepresentation of communities of color
within America's criminal justice system coupled with state-level autonomy
diminishes access to the simplest tool of democracy: the vote.

The issue of felon disenfranchisement is inextricably tied to racial
politics in the United States. Due to a variety of factors, ranging from out-
right racism to national class dynamics, American Blacks face much higher
incarceration rates than the nation as a whole – 10 percent of African
Americans are under some form of supervision compared to 2 percent of
the general public. Despite Kentucky's effort in 2001 to assist some former
offenders in regaining their rights through a petition to the governor, one
in four African Americans in the state remains disenfranchised.[31] Going
beyond disproportionate impact, racial politics appears to inform the design
of these laws as well. Though many felon disenfranchisement laws date back
over a century – some before the federally mandated enfranchisement of
Blacks – a number of states have moved toward making their voting laws
more restrictive in the modern era. Several laws in the American South can

be directly traced to efforts to prevent formerly enslaved Africans from being able to exercise the franchise. However, emphasis on this history has proven to be a double-edged sword for opponents of disenfranchisement law, while knowledge of this racial history can contribute to the law's unpopularity (Wilson et al. 2015).

Various legal challenges, such as *Farrakhan v. Washington* (2003), have raised the question of whether felon disenfranchisement laws violate Section 2 of the Voting Rights Act of 1965.[32] The majority opinion of the Ninth Circuit Court stated that "felon disenfranchisement is a voting qualification, and Section 2 is clear that *any* voting qualification that denies citizens the right to vote in a discriminatory manner violates the VRA [Voting Rights Act]" (*Farrakhan v. Washington*, 10139). Under the guidelines set forth by the Court's decision in the monumental *Hunter v. Underwood* (1985) case from Alabama, previous plaintiffs focused on the "intent requirement" to show a discriminatory denial of the franchise.[33] However, *Farrakhan* eased this burden by requiring that future plaintiffs "show, based on the *totality of the circumstances*, that the challenged voting practice results in discrimination on account of race," including evidence of discrimination in the justice system (*Farrakhan v. Washington*, 10142–4). This ruling has not been echoed in similar cases across the country.

The Eleventh Circuit Court rejected the federal constitutional claims raised in *Johnson v. Bush* (2002) by noting a provision in the Fourteenth Amendment allowing for the exclusion of felons from the vote and similarly rejected appeals to the Voting Rights Act of 1965. The court noted that "the case for rejecting the plaintiffs' reading of the statute is particularly strong here, where Congress has expressed its intent to *exclude* felon disenfranchisement provisions from Voting Rights Act scrutiny" (Eleventh circuit, en banc). While the court reaffirmed that disenfranchisement laws may not be used to intentionally discriminate on the basis of race, the justices claimed no clear evidence on the question of intent and stated clearly that "federal courts cannot question the wisdom" of any given state policy outside of its constitutionality (ibid., 40).

Determining whether the formerly incarcerated would vote has been challenging, given their pre-conviction socio-economic profiles and low rates of voter registration (Burch 2013). However, in understanding the relationship between disenfranchisement and electoral politics, the scope should be widened to consider not just the individual convicted of a crime but the broader community to which she or he belongs. The concentration of punishment, disenfranchisement, and civic retreat within communities of color weakens their ability to promote their policy interests in an increasingly competitive political space. This confluence of declining political and socio-economic conditions and facially neutral policies with a disparate racial impact heightens the sense of *civic death* (Brown-Dean 2016).

Prison Gerrymandering and Urban Political Representation

While current and former felons may be denied access to the ballot, their procedural impact on representation and congressional apportionment cannot be erased. Inmates in the United States are counted as residents of the town where they are incarcerated as opposed to their place of legal residence before conviction. Though most inmates come from urban communities, the overwhelming majority of prisons in this country are sited in rural and suburban areas. In turn, areas with larger prison populations receive a disproportionate share of valuable resources, such as legislative districts and funds for the delivery of social service programs (Ebenstein 2018; Kelly 2012). More than $175 billion in federally funded programs is allocated based on census data. These programs target some of the most vulnerable populations: the poor, the elderly, children, the unemployed, and those battling addictions. For example, over 20 percent of children nationwide live below the poverty line, the majority of whom are concentrated in urban and rural rather than in suburban areas. The distribution of these resources directly shapes the status of these communities.

Counting inmates as residents of the prison in which they are held rather than their former communities while simultaneously denying them the vote can function as a "representation drain," where high-crime communities lose legislative representation to communities hosting prisons. This has been a persistent challenge in states such as New York, with distinct patterns of residential segregation between urban and suburban areas (See *Hayden v. Pataki* 2006). As cited by the Prison Policy Initiative, "rural white counties with additional population based on the presence of disenfranchised prisoners in upstate prisons" gained representation while "diminish[ing] the voting strength of non-incarcerated persons of color in the prisoners' home communities."[34] This representation calculus is used for both state and federal apportionment, thus diminishing the ability of poor and minority communities to receive adequate representation relative to their size. One cannot help but draw a parallel between this system and the since amended three-fifths clause of the US Constitution allowing slave societies to draw apportionment power from their slaves held in bondage while preventing them from obtaining the franchise.

The relatively smaller size of state legislative districts increases the possibility that enumerating inmates where they are incarcerated can skew both representation and resources. For example, prison overcrowding has forced many states to send their inmates to other states to be housed.[35] Exporting inmates also means that states export resources. For example, Wisconsin houses approximately 10,000 inmates in Oklahoma, Tennessee, and Texas. Faced with the threat of losing a congressional seat, Congressman Mark Green (R-WI) introduced a bill that would allow states to count state and federal prisoners exported to other states as residents of their pre-conviction place of residence. The bill failed, and Wisconsin lost a congressional seat. It should be noted that the state's total population loss was greater than its number of out-of-state inmates. However, Green argued the issue would become increasingly important given Wisconsin's incarceration projections for the next ten years.

Conclusion: Racial Identity as Intersectional Construction

Efforts to build a more perfect union in the United States have often been hampered by challenges, controversies, and inequities related to racial identities. At times, racial inequality has been sanctioned by the very political institutions to which groups turn for redress. These formal statements issued by Congress, the Supreme Court, and other entities both shape and are shaped by mass acts of political expression via voting, lobbying, violence, and protest.

Over time, groups have formed meaningful coalitions to protest their exclusion or to reinforce the exclusion of other groups. While the Civil Rights movement illustrated the potential of using the political process to secure changes in laws and public policies, subsequent debates over issues such as police accountability, monuments, and Confederate markers make it clear that changes in legal standing don't translate neatly into changes in social standing. Further, the practices of and actors within political institutions help define the meaning and presence of other identity-based groups demanding political representation. Growing rates of immigration across the United States from diverse countries of origin also challenge many of the longstanding views on racial identity and political representation (Lee et al. 2007).

Controversy box: Starbucks, BBQ Becky, Permit Patty, & Foul Shot Freddy

In April 2018, Donte Robinson and Rashon Nelson chatted about real estate in a Philadelphia Starbucks while waiting for a third friend to arrive. Moments later, two Philadelphia police officers responded to a call from the store manager that the two men were trespassing and refusing to leave. Robinson and Nelson – who hadn't made a purchase – insisted they had done nothing wrong and were simply replicating a practice that plays out every day in the popular coffee chain. For many years Starbucks has marketed itself as a "third space" (after home and office) for workers and creatives to gather. This mission of creating an inviting space for everyone was consistent with the belief of company founder Howard Schultz that Starbucks could play an integral role in building a stronger sense of community: "We strive to create a welcoming environment for all of our customers. We do not have any time limits for being in our stores, and continue to focus on making the Third Place experience for every Starbucks customer" (Needleman 2009). The two men alleged that the manager had singled them out as a potential threat simply because of their race and gender.

Based on the manager's statement, Robinson and Nelson were both arrested and charged with criminal trespass. Although they were released and the company declined to press charges, the encounter ignited a broader debate about race, space, and belonging. It also highlighted broader fears concerning the many instances where disproportionate contact with law enforcement results in harm for people of color: "Anytime I'm encountered by cops, I can honestly say it's a thought that runs through my mind. You never know what's going to happen" (Madej 2018).

In the days following the incident, Starbucks sent its entire senior leadership team to Philadelphia for a vigorous discussion about issues of implicit bias, cultural sensitivity, and de-escalation tactics. On May 29th the company closed over 8,000 stores for a mandatory discussion about bias that was developed in consultation with noted figures such as rapper Common, director Ava DuVernay, and criminal justice reform advocate Bryan Stevenson. Documentary filmmaker Stanley Nelson also released a short film, underwritten by Starbucks, about the historical denial of access to such public spaces as stores, restaurants, pools, and movie theaters based on race.

As the proliferation of cell phones makes it easier for recordings of incidents to go viral, creative memes abound to highlight the racial divide between whites calling the police on people of color for barbecuing in a park, swimming in a community pool, selling water to cover school expenses, and even committing a foul during a pickup basketball game. These incidents popularized names such as BBQ Becky, Permit Patty, Dog Park Diane, and Foul Shot Freddy. Although the policing of public spaces isn't new, using the internet to publicly shame and punish raises new questions regarding what should be done to protect people from harm. What do you think? Is the tendency to call the police on people of color in public spaces based on racial bias or a genuine concern for public safety? What, if anything, should be done to ensure that racial identity doesn't preclude people from being protected from harm? How can groups come together to discuss their differences in a constructive way?

Questions for Debate

- The debate over the Confederate flag and monuments raises the question of whether public spaces should be used to commemorate controversial figures and events. What are the boundaries for determining whether these symbols should be allowed in public spaces such as courthouses, parks, and schools? Who should decide?
- The Civil Rights movement helped win important policy changes related to racial identity. However, it wasn't able to eliminate issues of racism and discrimination completely. Recent groups have reignited the use of protest and disruption to draw attention to social challenges. Is protest an effective way to communicate political discontent? What about the use of social media and hashtag activism?
- Researchers have documented the exceptionally high number of American Indians killed by law-enforcement officers. However, media coverage rarely focuses on these deaths. How might the Black Lives Matter movement be used as a template for other groups fighting against brutality and lethal force?

Key Terms

- alt-right
- Civil Rights Act of 1964
- *Dred Scott* v. *Sandford*
- Voting Rights Act of 1965
- Emancipation Proclamation
- Slaughterhouse Cases
- Fourteenth Amendment
- felon disenfranchisement
- *Plessy* v. *Ferguson*
- prison gerrymandering

5

Ethnic Identity: Demography and Destiny

The Boundaries of Belonging

The large wooden door at the entrance to Junta for Progressive Action is starting to come off its hinges. For forty-nine years the door has welcomed members of the Latino community of New Haven (Connecticut) and their allies to promote economic and social well-being via civic engagement and education. There are programs for adults seeking to earn their high-school equivalency diploma. There are services for city residents trying to navigate the complex maze of federal immigration policies and assistance for those who want to become more proficient in English. The organization supports an advocacy initiative to insure the needs of its clients are known to local and state legislators pondering the balance between promoting public safety and encouraging victims of crime to engage law enforcement. In 2006, Junta worked with a coalition of local activists and organizations to convince the local police force to stop asking victims about their immigration status. A year later, the city gained national attention after instituting a controversial municipal ID card that would allow any New Haven resident, regardless of immigration status, to prove municipal residency. As a public safety measure, the cards helped vulnerable undocumented residents open bank accounts rather than carrying their earnings in cash and becoming susceptible to street robberies. To critics, however, the cards legitimized those who had come to the country illegally. Days after the resident ID cards were released, federal Immigration Control and Enforcement agents raided the homes of families who had signed up for the cards. While this move heightened tensions over the incorporation of undocumented immigrants, public reaction revealed deeper resentments toward the area's growing Latino community.

Some questioned whether a disproportionate amount of public resources was being diverted to translation programs in local schools. Of the district's 21,500 students, about 16 percent are classified as English-language learners, a growing concentration of whom are in neighborhood schools. Across the district, 14 percent of students identify as white compared to 42 percent Black, 41 percent Latino, and 2 percent Asian.[1]

Others raised public safety and public health concerns related to the burgeoning crop of unlicensed food trucks operated by Latino entrepreneurs. The public debates surrounding the city's changing demographics highlighted tensions within and between ethnic groups based on the failure to address differences in immigration status, coupled with the assumption that most Latinos were "foreign-born" (Abraham and Buchanan 2016). This conflation shaped public support for aid following the devastation of Hurricane Maria in 2017.

Contested Citizenship

Junta has long focused on promoting full inclusion for Latino communities based on shared culture, historical experience, and contemporary challenges. That commitment was amplified in 2017 as it disrupted the national narrative surrounding immigration to the United States to demand greater public attention to *migration* by US citizens. Hurricane Maria slammed into the Caribbean with winds of 155 miles per hour. The storm caused significant damage to islands such as Barbuda, Dominica, and the US Virgin Islands. The Category 4 storm was the strongest to hit the island of Puerto Rico since 1932 and caused over $100 billion in damage and displaced many of its 3 million residents (Meyer 2017). It knocked out power to the entire island and, in turn, eliminated its chief economic engines of tourism and manufacturing. The

Members of the Puerto Rico National Guard help clear road access for residents following Hurricane Maria. The storm devastated the island and caused over $100 billion in damage.

ripple effects of the devastation were felt across the mainland. For example, the Baxter Corporation is one of the United States' largest manufacturers of intravenous (IV) medical supplies. The lack of power reduced productivity at the company's three factories on the island, causing a shortage of IV fluids for major hospitals across the United States (Baxter Corporation 2017). The rolling blackouts also spurred the growth of mold, which seeped throughout homes and buildings to stimulate asthma flares. The lack of electricity coupled with the difficulty of getting supplies to the island thrust Puerto Rican residents into despair. To be sure, through a combination of declining economic instability and political uncertainty, the exodus of people had begun long before Hurricanes Irma and Maria hit.[2] However, as thousands of residents scrambled to abandon the island and move to the mainland, the aftermath of Hurricane Maria revealed the political challenges associated with defining the political status of the island's residents (Peak 2018).

The Legacy of Conquest

The **Jones–Shafroth Act of 1917** established Puerto Rico as a US territory whose residents are citizens of the United States.[3] It also established federal authority over the island's economic and political decisions. Puerto Ricans who live on the island are barred from voting in federal elections and don't have a voting member to represent their interests in the US Congress; however, those who live on the mainland (continental US) have full voting rights. In spite of this, there is tremendous ambiguity about the status of the island and its residents. The storm and its aftermath highlighted a longstanding challenge for Puerto Ricans: the extent to which they are viewed as US citizens and thus deserving of support.

A 2017 survey conducted by Morning Consult, referenced in table 5.1, revealed that nearly half of American respondents did not know that residents of Puerto Rico are US citizens. The data show that 52 percent of people without a college degree either don't believe or don't know if Puerto Ricans are US citizens, while those least likely to believe Puerto Ricans are citizens are young people between the ages of eighteen and twenty-nine, whites, women, and those who live in rural communities. Understanding the citizenship status of people on the island also shapes the level of support for government aid to support post-storm recovery. Eight in ten of respondents who believe Puerto Ricans are US citizens, and four in ten of those who don't, support recovery aid. The lack of public understanding of this question, coupled with the absence of full voting representation in the US Congress, complicated efforts to advance government support for recovery efforts. The humanitarian crisis on the island forced many residents to abandon their homes and seek refuge on the mainland. Organizations such as Junta became the front line of

Table 5.1 Are people born in Puerto Rico citizens of the United States or not? (percentages)

Demographic	Yes	No	Don't know	Total N
Gender male	62	18	20	533
female	47	26	27	578
Age 18–29	37	31	32	214
30–44	56	22	22	329
45–54	59	21	21	179
55–64	56	20	24	221
65+	64	16	20	168
Democrat	58	20	21	370
Independent	50	23	27	398
Republican	55	23	22	343
Liberal	64	18	18	328
Moderate	55	24	21	285
Conservative	57	23	21	360
Education less than college	47	24	28	771
Bachelor's degree	72	17	12	223
Post-grad	66	18	16	116
Income: under 50K	49	24	27	638
50K–100K	61	20	19	349
100K+	65	12	18	123

SOURCE: Based on data from the Morning Consult Tracking Poll, September 2017.

support for displaced US citizens struggling to affirm their presence and, by extension, deservedness. Federalism and the variation in resources available in various states help shape the places to which displaced citizens fled after the storm. As table 5.2 shows, states with existing Latino diversity were attractive locations for those seeking a place of refuge.

Ethnic Identity: The Context

Ethnic identity in the United States is shaped by a complex mix of court rulings, legislative decisions, and political practices. This mash-up shapes how groups see themselves and others. Often it is difficult to disentangle the various dimensions of ethnoracial identity that determine access to power and representation. However, the political meaning of ethnic identity – like that of other identities – reflects the tendency to collapse large diverse communities into singular groups that make it easier to define their presence and, in turn, the boundaries of belonging. To be sure, ethnic identity in the United States is also constrained by a broader process of **racialization** that moderates

Table 5.2 Number of FEMA applications for assistance for selected states, 2017–2018

State	Number of applications
Florida	5,500
New York	1,003
Pennsylvania	557
Massachusetts	527
Texas	418
Connecticut	323
Illinois	267
Georgia	190
California	159
Virginia	156
North Carolina	135
Ohio	116
Maryland	108
Arizona	61
Other	635

SOURCE: CNN Analysis; Federal Emergency Management Agency; US Postal Service.

which groups are allowed to "become white" and which groups are allowed to embrace a more nuanced sense of ethnoracial identity. This process helps us understand why groups initially branded as others (e.g. white ethnics) were eventually incorporated into the political structure. It also helps explain how differing countries of origin and proximity to the diaspora racializes groups within ethnic categories.

At times this interplay masks internal differences between groups to promote a homogenized view of group identity that may not be shared by group members. For example, Hurricane Maria hit just as the president of the United States announced aggressive plans to crack down on illegal immigration in an effort to rid the country of "rapists and murderers." Although his remarks initially referenced immigrants coming from Mexico, the stereotype of people coming to the United States and making illegitimate demands resonated with those who resist the country's changing demographics. In turn, demands for assistance to the island after the storm were met by resistance from those who feared the impact on scarce public resources. Group identities are often imposed upon diverse groups with differing priorities. In turn, the politicization of ethnic identity may exacerbate tensions among groups with a shared ethnic identity and differing countries of origin as groups struggle to differentiate themselves from negative social norms and stereotypes. Consider, then, that pan-ethnic labels such as "Asian American" and "Latinx" don't fully capture how differing countries of origin, language, citizenship status, and personal preference help order political standing. Even as individual group members prefer to distinguish themselves based on country of origin (e.g. Laotian or Cuban American) or citizenship, the construction, meaning, and fluidity of ethnic identity is nested within longstanding questions of access and power.

In this chapter I explore how ethnic identity emerges in response to complex negotiations over citizenship, power, and access. To do so, I examine three key domains for understanding the relationship between ethnic identities and US politics: 1) ethnicity and immigration policy, 2) ethnicity and political participation, and 3) ethnicity and policy controversies. The focus of this chapter isn't on how groups forge their identities. Rather, it emphasizes how public and political negotiations impose a sense of group solidarity upon diverse populations that helps shape preferences and participation.

Often these negotiations that are intended to target one group or set of groups have spillover effects that undermine the power and standing of others. As Cristina Beltrán argues, in her book *The Trouble with Unity*: "There is no sleeping giant – only political subjects whose variegated actions and intentions are obscured by this limited vision of Latino empowerment" (2010: 9). From an intersectional point of view, these assumptions of solidarity can both stifle dissent and mask internal differences in standing related to complementary identities such as gender identity, country of origin, and citizenship status. Similarly, the public politics of ethnic identity often focus on particular groups with higher visibility (e.g. Latinos) while neglecting the political challenges faced by groups with more limited political visibility (e.g. Asian Americans). This is further complicated by the process of *racialization*, which sets the terms by which certain groups can assimilate and/or have a less contentious path toward acceptance and inclusion. Recognizing this isn't an attempt to prioritize the needs of certain groups over others. Rather, it is an affirmation of how **media framing**, public opinion, and political maneuvering reinforce the boundaries of belonging. As a result, the focus of this chapter is on the institutional changes that shape group presence.

This is America

According to data from the most recent census, the size of the US population has increased by over 100 percent in the last fifty years. This rate of growth dwarfs peer countries such as the UK, Germany, and Italy. The 325 million people living in the United States are older and more diverse than ever before. Non-Hispanic whites number around 198 million, in comparison with 21.4 million Asians, 46.8 million African Americans, 57.5 million Latinos, and 2.9 million American Indian/Alaskan Natives.[4] About 9 million people in the United States self-identify as mixed race or multiracial.

Over half of the US population resides in just nine states: Texas, California, Ohio, Illinois, Pennsylvania, Michigan, Florida, New York, and Georgia. During the 2016 presidential election, four of those states (Florida, Michigan, Ohio, and Pennsylvania) were identified as battleground states where shifting demographic diversity challenged traditional political affiliations, placing the state in play for candidates. The growing ethnoracial diversity of the US results from two major factors: (1) changes in immigration policy and (2) differing rates of mortality and fertility, which vary by race, ethnicity, and geography. The size of the population, the growing diversity of that population, the concentration of diverse communities, and differing policy experiences all shape political affiliations. Across the board, ethnic groups highlight the political importance of ethnic identity.

In the next section I examine how changes in immigration policy set the context for the political importance of ethnic identity and, in turn, challenges related to representation and standing. Often policy shifts and accompanying efforts to accomplish or resist them helped fuel internal conversations about political preferences and modes of participation. At the same time, the tendency of US politics and policy to create large, diverse swaths of people as singular entities simultaneously fuels group-based assessments of risk and desirability within various spheres of public life. The politics of ethnic identity has been used both to dampen and to amplify intersecting identities.

Immigration and the Making of Ethnic Group Identity

Although the United States was formally organized as a country in 1776, Congress did not establish the first naturalization law until 1790. The Naturalization Act of 1790 (see box 3.4, p. 54) created three key requirements for citizenship, the first being a two-year period of residence, with at least one year of residence in the current state. The Act required proof of good character and restricted citizenship at the time to those who were classified as "white."

The Act codified the belief that citizenship in the United States centered on men by declaring that "children of citizens of the United States that may be born ... out of the limits of the United States shall be considered as natural born citizens." It also demanded that "the right of citizenship shall not descend to persons whose fathers have never been resident in the United States." This distinction was not removed until 1934, and then by an act of Congress rather than constitutional amendment. Supporters viewed the Naturalization Act as necessary to protect the US government from foreign influence. It also helped limit those who could legitimately access government and, in turn, make demands for redress.

A number of organizations in the United States helped advance this nativist sentiment by supporting policies and candidates that sought to limit the presence of "others." The **Know Nothing Party** was formed in 1850 as a nativist, anti-Catholic organization guided by the mantra that "Americans Must Rule America." The party successfully elected its supporters to local, state, and national office to solidify its influence over every aspect of public life. For example, members successfully lobbied the Massachusetts legislature to require that the King James Bible be read in the Commonwealth's public schools. This seemingly innocuous requirement was an effective means of limiting the number of Catholic students enrolled in the school system. This move directly targeted the increased number of Irish families in the area. By adopting the King James Bible in direct conflict with Catholic teachings, the legislature successfully forced many Irish Catholic families to not enroll their children in public schools.

Ethnicity and Economic Fears

The emphasis on whiteness as a condition for citizenship and the fear perceived by difference was reinforced with the passage of the 1882 Chinese Exclusion Act. Between 1870 and 1900, nearly 12 million immigrants arrived in the United States, pushed and pulled by a range of economic, political, and social reasons. During that same period, a massive wave of Chinese immigrants arrived, mainly on the West Coast. By 1870, Chinese residents formed 9 percent of the total population of California and constituted 25 percent of the labor force. Chinese laborers differed from European immigrants because most came to the country under contract to work as laborers building the transcontinental railroad. After the completion of the railroad, many Chinese workers decided to remain.

Many politicians feared the growing numbers of Chinese immigrants and sought to limit their numerical presence and potential political influence. In particular, Congress expressed concerns over the presence of a non-Christian, non-European group that comprised such a large share of the population. Chinese immigrants were also viewed as an economic threat because they would work for less than white males. Recall from chapter 2 that the Chinese Exclusion Act was the first time in US history that an immigration restriction had been adopted based on race and ethnic identity: "Whereas in the opinion of the Government of the United States the coming of Chinese laborers to this country endangers the good order of certain localities within the territory thereof . . . That hereafter no State court or court of the United States shall admit Chinese to citizenship; and all laws in conflict with this act are hereby repealed." Congress adopted the Exclusion Act in response to claims that Chinese laborers were to blame for economic decline in the US, particularly in places such as California, where unemployment was rising among the native-born population. Displaced workers saw Chinese immigrants as a cheap labor source that made it more difficult to compete for jobs, housing, and business licenses. The Chinese Exclusion Act barred people of Chinese descent from becoming US citizens in the hopes that it would make the country less attractive and, in turn, reduce economic competition.

In principle, the Act focused only on Chinese immigrants who were perceived as an economic threat to US workers and their families. In practice, however, the legalized ban on citizenship provided a foundation for disparate treatment of other groups based on country of origin. In 1908, an organization called the Asiatic Exclusion League was formed to promote bans on *all* immigrants from Asian countries. The group believed that Asians "come to the United States entirely ignorant of our sentiments of nativity and patriotism, and are utterly unfit and incapable of discharging the duties of American citizenship" (Asiatic Exclusion League 1908: 15). The objections derived from a combination of fears over economic security, religious beliefs, and the concern that Asian men would taint the United States by preying upon American women. These stereotypes shaped how other groups of Asian descent positioned themselves in the US. For example, the Japanese government imposed strict requirements for its citizens seeking to gain permission to live and/or work in the country. The goal was to send "morally superior" Japanese citizens who could push back against the stereotypes and, in turn, demonstrate their embrace of American cultural values (Wei 2016). This often meant not allowing single men to emigrate or allowing only those who already had families in the US to come.[5] These self-imposed limits upheld the respectability politics approach to acceptance that recognized how other Asian subgroups were perceived and working hard to achieve differentiation. Such challenges affirm the view that pan-ethnic identifiers (e.g. Asian or Asian American) often mask the complex internal calculations related to access and desirability. They also foreshadow subsequent debates over immigration as a necessary barrier to the displacement of US citizens.

Shutting the Door to White Ethnics

The United States witnessed a resurgence in immigration following World War I. The increased movement of people into the country heightened anti-immigrant sentiment and increased public desire to restrict the flow. While previous statements on immigration focused exclusively on denying a path to citizenship for non-white groups, the passage of several pieces of legislation in the 1920s offered a more complex view of "desirability" that affected white ethnics.

Congress passed the Emergency Immigration Act of 1921 to stem the tide of immigrants flooding into the United States from particular countries and regions. The consequence of the Act helped solidify the primacy of public

> ### BOX 5.1 Push and pull factors prompting immigration to the United States
>
> *Push factors*: Those social, economic, and political forces that drive people out of their home country and into other countries
> *Examples*: Poverty; religious persecution; limited economic opportunities
>
> *Pull factors*: Those social, economic, and political forces that draw people out of their home country and into countries
> *Examples*: Economic freedom; religious freedom; legal protections

categorizations over self-identity. Two cases, *Ozawa* v. *United States* (1922) and *United States* v. *Bhagat Singh Thind* (1923) tested whether groups from other countries (here Japan and India) could meet the qualifications for attaining US citizenship. Singh's application to become a naturalized citizen was rejected because the law didn't allow him to meet the requirement of being a "free white person" even though he self-identified as a white "high caste Aryan."

The **Johnson–Reed Act of 1924** solidified this by using census data to determine the origins of people already in the United States. Using these data as a baseline, Congress decided to limit entry to 3 percent of that country's current presence. The Act was significant because, for the first time in US history, it imposed numerical limits on the number of people who could immigrate. This quota system dramatically reduced the number of people coming from Southern and Eastern Europe and completely barred all immigration from Asia. Thus, in spite of efforts by Japanese officials to position themselves as a desirable immigrant class, the panic and fear about immigration wasn't restricted to Asian borders. As table 5.3 shows, the majority of immigrants to the United States after the Act was adopted came from Germany, the UK, and Ireland.

The reasons for imposing this quota system were somewhat varied. Some legislators argued that the new system would help reduce the number of unskilled workers. Others believed that this new system would promote stronger adherence to American values and accelerate the assimilation process. Concerns over the compatibility of religion (e.g. Catholics coming from Ireland and Italy), interpersonal relationships, and cultural customs helped fuel the decision to focus on certain countries. Still others embraced the quota system based on the view that Northern Europeans were a more desirable group and better able to contribute to the US population.

The basis for this view resulted from a 1916 book authored by eugenicist Milton Grant called *The Passing of the Great Race*.[6] Grant promoted the view that restricting immigration was necessary in order for the United States to purify its population. This purification could occur only via selective breeding that

Table 5.3 Immigration quotas for the 1924 Immigration Act

Northwest Europe & Scandinavia	Quota	Eastern & Southern Europe	Quota	Other countries	Quota
Germany	51,227	Poland	5,982	Africa (other than Egypt)	1,100
United Kingdom	34,007	Italy	3,845	Armenia	124
Irish Free State (Ireland)	28,567	Czechoslovakia	3,073	Australia	121
Sweden	9,561	Russia	2,248	Palestine	100
Norway	6,453	Yugoslavia	671	Syria	100
France	3,954	Romania	603	Turkey	100
Denmark	2,789	Portugal	503	Egypt	100
Switzerland	2,081	Hungary	473	New Zealand & Pacific Islands	100
Netherlands	1,648	Lithuania	344	All others	1,900
Austria	785	Latvia	142		
Belgium	512	Spain	131		
Finland	471	Estonia	124		
Free City of Danzig	228	Albania	100		
Iceland	100	Bulgaria	100		
Luxembourg	100	Greece	100		
Total (number)	142,483	*Total (number)*	18,439	*Total (number)*	3,745
Total (%)	86.5	*Total (%)*	11.2	*Total (%)*	2.3

Total annual immigrant quota: 164,667

Source: *Statistical Abstract of the United States* (Washington, DC: Government Printing Office, 1929).

would reduce the alleged spread of inferior "stock" throughout the country. Grant believed that, by opening its borders, the US had become polluted and needed to purify itself by restricting access. In particular, it was overrun by Greeks, Italians, and Jews. In support of this view, South Carolina Senator Ellison DuRant Smith had the following to say:

> It seems to me the point as to this measure – and I have been so impressed for several years – is that the time has arrived when we should shut the door. We have been called the melting pot of the world. We had an experience just a few years ago, during the great World War, when it looked as though we had allowed influences to enter our borders that were about to melt the pot in place of us being the melting pot.
>
> . . .
>
> I think we now have sufficient population in our country for us to shut the door and to breed up a pure, unadulterated American citizenship. I

recognize that there is a dangerous lack of distinction between people of a certain nationality and the breed of the dog. Who is an American? Is he an immigrant from Italy? Is he an immigrant from Germany? If you were to go abroad and some one were to meet you and say, "I met a typical American," what would flash into your mind as a typical American, the typical representative of that new Nation? Would it be the son of an Italian immigrant, the son of a German immigrant, the son of any of the breeds from the Orient, the son of the denizens of Africa? We must not get our ethnological distinctions mixed up with our anthropological distinctions. It is the breed of the dog in which I am interested.[7]

A number of coalitions and organizations sought to reverse the Act on the grounds that it was discriminatory and antithetical to America's democratic tradition. In particular, a number of politicians argued that the Act prevented Europeans seeking to flee the Nazis from finding refuge in the US. Despite this opposition, the Act remained in effect for nearly thirty years with only modest revisions.

Alien Enemies: Citizenship, Ethnicity, and National Security

With firm rules in place to privilege certain European nations over others, World War II helped define the status of ethnic groups within the United States. Whereas immigration policy defined who could come into the country, a number of executive orders shaped the status of ethnic groups who were already here. Following the bombing of Pearl Harbor in 1941, President Roosevelt issued three public proclamations drawing upon a 1798 Act concerning **alien enemies**: "all natives, citizens, denizens, or subjects of the hostile nation or government, being of the age of fourteen years and upward, who shall be within the United States and not actually naturalized, shall be liable to be apprehended, restrained, secured, and removed as alien enemies" (An Act Concerning Aliens, Section 1). The proclamations classified over 600,000 US residents as alien enemies and forced thousands out of their homes. Although the language of the proclamations was meant to apply only to non-citizens, the implementation also ensnared US citizens of Japanese and Italian descent.

BOX 5.2 Public proclamations designating alien enemy status by country of origin

Proclamation 2525	Japan
Proclamation 2526	Germany
Proclamation 2527	Italy

These proclamations laid the foundation for the issuance of **Executive Order 9066**, which authorized the forced removal of thousands of people of Japanese descent. The order made no distinction between citizens and "resident aliens." By designating the entire West Coast as a protected military area, enforcing the order had a disproportionate impact on Japanese communities. In ***Korematsu* v. *United States*** (1944), the US Supreme Court ruled against claims made by Fred Korematsu alleging that the executive order violated the Constitution. Korematsu was a native-born US citizen whose parents emigrated legally from Japan. He was arrested after refusing to comply with the order and sentenced to five years' probation after detention at a Californian **internment** camp. The justices ruled that the concerns for national security and public safety were more important than group rights. The case highlighted the precarious citizenship status of people of Japanese descent and, by extension, affirmed the link between ethnicity and legal protection.[8]

Modest revisions to US immigration policy came with the passage of the **McCarran–Walter Act of 1952**, which upheld the national origins quota system and introduced a new set of preferences based on skills, assets, and family reunification. Supporters believed that people coming to the United States should be able to have an immediate positive impact on their host country. Family reunification ensured that there were already people in the country capable of assisting them with their transition, as opposed to draining public services. Critics, however, including President Truman, feared that the law's provisions undermined the freedom of expression provisions embedded in the First Amendment.[9] The controversy surrounding the passage of the McCarran–Walter Act foreshadowed broader changes in immigration policy based on ethnicity and country of origin.

Changing the Face of US Immigration and Political Presence

Recall from chapter 4 that President Lyndon B. Johnson signed the Voting Rights Act of 1965 (VRA) to strike down decades of tactics used to restrict Black access to voting and representation. By removing grandfather clauses, white-only primaries, and poll taxes, the VRA singlehandedly transformed American politics by ushering in more African Americans as voters, candidates, and legislators (Brown-Dean et al. 2015). Yet, beyond its impact on Blacks, the VRA also elevated the political presence of American Indians, Asian Americans, and Latinos. Just two months after signing the Act into law, President Johnson eliminated national origin quotas that privileged immigrants from Northern Europe and raised the ceiling on immigration from the rest of the world to 170,000. As a result, the **Hart–Celler Immigration Act** permanently changed the face of, and formula for, immigration to the United States by transforming America's racial and ethnic makeup. As figure 5.1 illustrates, more than

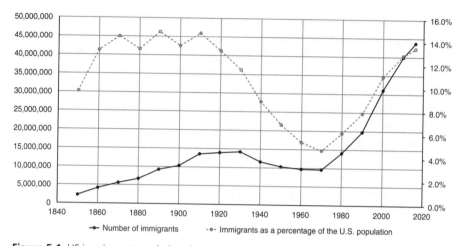

Figure 5.1 US immigrant population size and share, 1850–2016
SOURCE: Based on data from the Migration Policy Institute data hub, www.migrationpolicy.org/programs/migration-data-hub.

20 million immigrants have arrived from countries in Latin America, Asia, and the Caribbean.[10] Table 5.4 shows that immigrants from Mexico, China, India, and the Philippines comprise the bulk of new arrivals since 1965. The dramatic surge in the number of immigrants holds important political consequences.

Accommodating Difference

The increasing diversity resulting from Hart–Celler prompted the 1975 amendments to the VRA. Section 203 mandates bilingual materials and oral language assistance for certain linguistic groups. The amendments expanded **preclearance** to include jurisdictions with large numbers of language minority groups (e.g. speakers of Spanish, Asian, American Indian/Native Alaskan languages) who had English-only voting materials and low registration or turnout (McCool et al. 2007). The 1975 renewal also required language assistance

Table 5.4 Major sources of immigrants to the United States since 1965 (2016)

Country	Total number	Percentage of total
Mexico	11.6 million	25.5
China	2.7 million	4.9
India	2.4 million	4.6
Philippines	2.0 million	4.2

SOURCE: Based on data from the Migration Policy Institute.

(e.g. bilingual ballots, registration forms) in jurisdictions with large numbers of minority groups with limited English proficiency.[11] Currently, twenty-two states are required to provide bilingual ballots and oral language assistance for American Indian and Alaska Native voters. Since many Indian languages are unwritten, identified jurisdictions must provide oral assistance to Native voters. In 1982, Congress amended the Act to clarify that a discriminatory *purpose* was not required to bring a lawsuit to invalidate election procedures that *result* in discrimination. Taken together, these changes were viewed as an effective means of increasing registration and turnout rates among communities of color. However, the results have been uneven.

BOX 5.3 Section 203 coverage formula

A jurisdiction is covered under Section 203 of the Voting Rights Act of 1965 where the number of US citizens of voting age is a single language group within the jurisdiction:

- is more than 10,000 or
- is more than 5 percent of all voting age citizens, or,
- on an Indian reservation, exceeds 5 percent of all reservation residents; and
- the illiteracy rate of the group is higher than the national illiteracy rate.

Ethnicity and Language Protection

Under the 1975 amendments, a jurisdiction qualifies for language protection if (1) at least 5 percent of voting-age citizens belong to a language minority group, (2) fewer than 50 percent of the voting-age population voted in the 1972 presidential election, or (3) registration/voting materials were provided only in English. The amendments were beneficial to a number of Spanish-speaking communities, with particularly high concentrations in the Southwest. However, Hawaii was the only area where Asian Americans met the 5 percent threshold. A 1992 amendment covers areas that meet either the 5 percent standard *or* have at least 10,000 voting-age members of a single language community with limited English proficiency.

Currently, immigrants from Latin American comprise 51 percent of all new arrivals. Across the United States, more than 26 million people speak Spanish at home, and two-thirds of Asian Americans speak a language other than English at home. Some 40 million Americans are classified as possessing limited English proficiency.[12] Based on the results of the 2010 census, a total of 248 jurisdictions across the United States are now required to provide language assistance for those who speak Spanish and various American Indian,

Table 5.5 States with the greatest population diversity by total population and share of population

Group	Total population	Share of population (percentage)
Asian	California (6.6 million)	Hawaii (57.0)
American Indian/ Alaska Native	California (1.1 million)	Alaska (19.9)
Native Hawaiian and other Pacific Islanders	Hawaii (381,000)	Hawaii (26.7)
Hispanic/Latino	California (15.3 million)	New Mexico (48.5)
Black/African American	New York (3.8 million)	District of Columbia (49.4)
White	California (14.8 million)	Maine (93.5)
Mixed race	California (1.5 million)	Hawaii (23.7)

SOURCE: US Census Bureau, *2017 Report*.

Alaska Native, and Asian languages. The 2020 census will be an important tool for assessing the ethnic diversity of the country and determining what adjustments need to be made to comply with the mandates of the Voting Rights Act. Table 5.5 highlights the diversity that exists within the United States across states and ethnic groups. This diversity and the residential concentration of language minorities define which jurisdictions are affected by the VRA. For example, twenty-two counties in eleven states are required to provide assistance in Asian languages. Altogether, 32 percent of voting-age citizens live in jurisdictions covered by Section 203 (Schuit and Rogowski 2017; Marschall and Rutherford 2016; Jones-Correa 2005).

Researchers believe that the language provisions have had a positive impact on voter participation among Latinos as a whole and first-generation immigrants from particular countries. However, the results are more mixed for Asian Americans and negligible for American Indians. The utility of these language provisions is largely contingent upon proper compliance by those charged with administering and providing translated materials and other forms of assistance. The rapidly changing demographic patterns suggest the importance of evaluating the impact of various factors, such as country of origin, generational status, region, and compliance.[13]

The Political Consequences

Only in the wake of the Voting Rights Act did Black voter registration in the South begin to approach that of whites. Five years after the passage of the

Act, the racial gap in voter registration in the former Confederate states had closed to single digits. By the start of the 1970s, the Black–white registration gap across the Southern states was little more than 8 percentage points. In Louisiana, the gap between Black and white voter registration rates decreased nearly 30 percentage points from 1960 to the end of 1970s and continued to decrease over the next three decades. By 2010, Black registration in the state of Louisiana and many of the other former Confederate states had exceeded that of white registration for the first time since Reconstruction. The Voting Rights Act had delivered a Second Reconstruction. To solidify this and further to protect voting rights and representation, several civil rights groups were created, such as the Asian American Legal Defense and Education Fund, the Native American Rights Fund, the Mexican American Legal Defense and Education Fund, and the NAACP Legal Defense and Education Fund. Together these groups monitor laws, policies, and procedures that infringe upon group rights while advocating for a host of public policies and laws that challenge legislators to act on their behalf.

The Voting Rights Act enabled similar gains in African American voter turn-out. Figure 5.2 tracks self-reported turnout in presidential elections from 1956 to 2012 among Blacks and whites living in former Confederate states. At the time of the 1956 presidential election, turnout among Blacks who lived in former Confederate states was roughly 50 percentage points lower than that of whites in these states.

The registration rates of Asian and Latinx citizens, despite their being two of the fastest growing pools of eligible voters in the United States, have

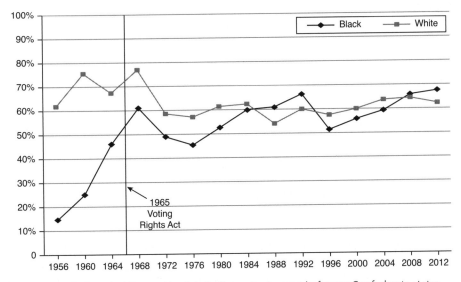

Figure 5.2 Black and white presidential election voter turnout in former Confederate states, 1965–2012

Source: Brown-Dean et al. (2015).

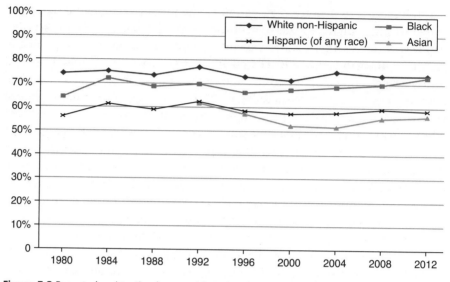

Figure 5.3 Reported registration by race, Hispanic origin, November 1980 to 2012
SOURCE: Brown-Dean et al. (2015).

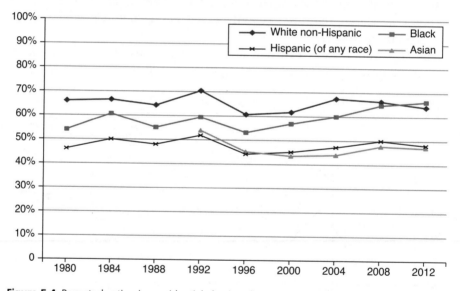

Figure 5.4 Reported voting in presidential elections by race, Hispanic origin, 1980 to 2012
SOURCE: Brown-Dean et al. (2015).

consistently lagged behind those of both Black and white Americans. For American Indian voters, that rate is even more limited. As we can see in figure 5.3, for the last thirty-five years the rates of registration among both Asian Americans and Hispanic Americans have consistently been 10 and 15 percentage points lower than that of Black Americans and 15 to 20 percentage

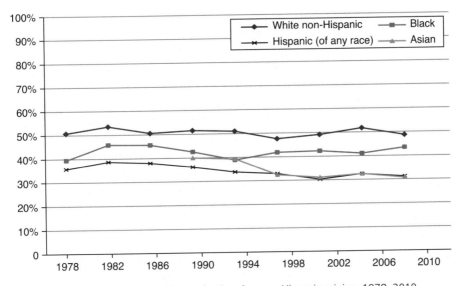

Figure 5.5 Reported voting in midterm elections by race, Hispanic origian, 1978–2010
Source: Brown-Dean et al. (2015).

points lower than that of white Americans. The lack of effective language accommodation, younger than average populations, unenthusiastic efforts at mobilization on the part of political parties and candidates, and discrimination are but a few of the many likely explanations for these differences.[14]

Similar gaps characterize the turnout behavior of Asian and Latinx voters. Figure 5.4 describes reported voting by race in presidential elections from 1980 to 2012. Here we see that the racial gap in turnout between Latinx and non-Latinx whites has for the most part held steady for the last thirty years, fluctuating between 16 and 20 percentage points. We also see that Asian American turnout exhibits similar variability. Despite there being data only from 1992 to 2012, the gap between Asian American and white turnout also varies between 16 and 23 percentage points. Figure 5.5 shows turnout by race in midterm elections from 1978 to 2010, and here we see more of the same – large turnout differences between whites, on the one hand, and Latinx and Asian citizens, on the other. The results of the 2016 presidential election further highlight these gaps.

Ethnicity and Political Incorporation

Hanna F. Pitkin (1972) offers the concept of **descriptive representation** to capture the extent to which members of legislative bodies match demographic features of their constituents. This can include a range of identities, such as partisanship, gender, religious affiliation, socio-economic class, and ethnicity.

Various scholars (Gay 2002; Brown 2014; Smooth 2006, 2011; Barreto 2007) have shown that enhancing descriptive representation can impact a range of political behaviors, among them registration, turnout, trust, and protest. The policy changes wrought by the Voting Rights Act of 1965, including the creation of **majority-minority districts** to enhance political representation, all helped diversify the US Congress. Considering changes in descriptive representation for Congress, gains for Blacks, Latinos, and Asian Americans have been substantial. When the Voting Rights Act was passed, there were only five African Americans in the US House and Senate combined. Today there are fifty-eight – fifty-five members of the House and three Senators (fifty-six Democrats and two Republicans). The growth for Latinos has been similarly impressive. Until 1980, Latinos seldom held more than five seats at the federal level, but that figure has since increased more than fivefold. In the 116th Congress there were four Hispanic Senators and forty-four Hispanic House members (thirty-four Democrats and ten Republicans, split into two partisan-oriented caucuses), as well as one nonvoting delegate from Puerto Rico.

The growth in the number of Asian American elected officials has been less robust, but it is still evident (Lien et al. 2004). Their number in the House and

Senator Tammy Duckworth represents the state of Illinois in the US Congress. She is a veteran of the Iraq War and lost both limbs as a result of combat injuries. She is also the first US Senator to give birth while in office and the first Congress member born in Thailand.

the Senate today has more than doubled: from about five in the 1970s, by the time of the 116th Congress there were fifteen Asian and Pacific Islander members of Congress – three Senators and twelve members of the House (all Democrats) – plus one nonvoting Republican delegate from American Samoa. Some members, such as Senator Kamala Harris (D-CA), joined both the Asian and Pacific Islander caucus and the Congressional Black Caucus.

In 2018, voters dramatically increased the diversity of the congressional delegation while still falling short of proportional representation. Although Hispanics comprise roughly 19 percent of the total US population, they form less than 10 percent of the US House. Two candidates, Deb Haaland of New Mexico and Sharice Davids of Kansas, became the first American Indian women ever elected to Congress. Their entry would come over 190 years after Hiram Revels of the Lumbee tribe was elected as the first African American and first American Indian to enter the legislature. The number of American Indian members of Congress doubled in the 116th Congress. Currently, there are four American Indian members: two Republicans, both representing the state of Oklahoma in the House (Markwayne Mullin and Tom Cole), and the two newly elected Democratic women.

State Growth

In terms of raw numbers, growth has been most remarkable at the state level. Over the past fifty years the nation's fifty legislatures have been transformed from institutions that were almost completely white into more diverse bodies that have begun to reflect their respective populations. Figure 5.6 plots the ethnoracial diversity of state legislatures.

The proportion of African Americans, Latinos, and Asian Americans in state legislatures still falls below their proportion in the general population. Blacks have made the greatest gains – from holding 2 percent of all state legislative seats in 1969 to about 8.5 percent of all seats in 2009. The Latino share has likewise grown, from 1 percent in 1973 to almost 5 percent today. For Asian Americans the growth has been less steady and less robust: from a low of 1 percent in the 1970s, Asian Americans still hold under 2 percent of all state legislative seats. Whites hold over 85 percent of all seats at the state level, despite accounting for just under 75 percent of all US voters and 62 percent of the total population (Brown-Dean et al. 2015).

Deval Patrick (D-MA), who left office in early 2015, was the last Black governor elected to office. In 2018, three African American candidates – Ben Jealous of Maryland, Stacy Abrams of Georgia, and Andrew Gillum of Florida – launched bids to become governor of their respective states, but all three fell short in elections clouded by allegations of voter suppression and racial bias (Lopez 2018; Thrush and Peters 2018). Latinos started from a lower base – there

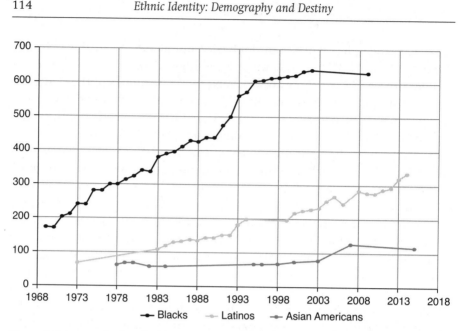

Figure 5.6 Increase in diversity in state legislatures, 1969–2015
SOURCE: Brown-Dean et al. (2015).

were only sixty-eight Hispanic state legislators in 1973 – but have experienced growth at a roughly equal pace over time. In 2018, across the fifty states, there were 334 Hispanic state legislators as well as two Latino governors, both of whom had left office by the start of 2019.

Once again, we see growth in the number of Asian American elected officials but at a slightly slower pace; there were sixty-three in 1968 and there are 116 today. In 2018, Idaho State Representative Paulette Jordan failed in her attempt to become the first governor in US history from an Indian tribe.

For underrepresented groups, developing political organizations to foster networking and training are critical for successfully navigating political terrain. For example, the National Caucus of Native American State Legislators was created to "provide research, training, and educational services to American Indian, Alaska Native, and Native Hawaiian state legislators."[15] Although there are fewer Indian legislators, the caucus has played an instrumental role in shaping state legislative debates regarding issues of potential concern to tribes, including health care, law enforcement, gaming, and natural resources.

The Ongoing Underrepresentation of Communities of Color

The fact that enormous change has occurred is incontrovertible. Rapid growth in the number of elected officials from diverse communities across the country over the past fifty years is a development that should be applauded. Each of these electoral victories is meaningful. But, viewed through a different lens, the *gains* that ethnoracial groups have made are less significant. If we compare the number of racial and ethnic groups in office to the number of whites in office, it becomes abundantly clear that the political leadership of the nation remains overwhelmingly white and that communities of color are greatly underrepresented at almost every level of government.

To be sure, addressing the "underrepresentation" of groups in elected office does not assume that voters should cast ballots only for candidates of their own group or that the ethnic composition of elected officials should match the ethnic composition of the population precisely. Instead, the share of elected offices held by people of color – when considered along with voter turnout, racially polarized voting, policy outcomes, election structures, and other variables – is one relevant factor in understanding the relationship between ethnoracial identity and US politics (Hajnal 2010).

Despite being underrepresented in Congress, these groups have forged a common identity by creating advocacy organizations within the legislature. The Congressional Black Caucus was created in 1971, followed by the Congressional Hispanic Caucus in 1976 and the Congressional Asian Pacific American Caucus in 1994. All three organizations work to network members of Congress and raise issues of mutual concern to their respective constituencies. The caucuses also create task forces to address issues such as economic development, health care, veterans' affairs, and civil rights.

Ethnicity and the Resurgence of Fear

Refugee Resettlement

In spite, and perhaps because, of the tremendous political consequences wrought by the confluence of the Hart–Celler Act and the Voting Rights Act, more recent policies represent the resurgence of fears of displacement and public safety. In the aftermath of political instability caused by the Vietnam War, Congress authorized the **Refugee Resettlement Act of 1980**, which formalized efforts to assist people fleeing political turmoil in their home country by instituting strict requirements to minimize threats to domestic security. It granted the president statutory authority to accept **refugees** while requiring annual consultation with Congress. Currently, the Act allows the US to accept 50,000 refugees per year – defined as a "person with a well-founded fear of persecution" – and includes a flexibility provision in times of international crisis.[16] Today, nearly half of those who enter the United States via refugee resettlement come from just three countries: the Democratic Republic of Congo, Syria, and Burma.

Unauthorized Immigration

The **Immigration Reform and Control Act of 1986** (IRCA) was the first major attempt to regulate unauthorized immigration to the United States. The Act punished employers who knowingly hired undocumented workers and created an opportunity for undocumented residents to apply for legal status. This approach to amnesty reflected the view, at the time, that the major villains of unauthorized immigration were the companies and employers who benefited economically from subverting US law. The IRCA created divisions within undocumented populations by conferring legal status upon seasonal agricultural workers. The more than 3 million undocumented immigrants in the country at the time had to meet the following qualifications in order to apply for amnesty:

1   to have entered the United States before January 1, 1982
2   to have resided in the US continuously
3   to prove that they were not guilty of any crimes
4   to possess a basic knowledge of US history and the English language.

The passage of the IRCA allowed 2.7 million undocumented immigrants to achieve legal status (Orrenius and Zavodny 2003). However, it did not fully eliminate concerns over immigration to the country in general, and unauthorized immigration in particular. Some questioned whether the Act went far enough in requiring employers to enforce federal immigration policy. Critics saw its emphasis on amnesty as being incompatible with its efforts to reinforce border patrol and security. In response to this debate, Congress authorized the formation of the **Jordan Commission** to evaluate and make recommendations for comprehensive immigration reform. The commission was named after the late Barbara Jordan, who was the first African American woman to represent the state of Texas in Congress. Jordan summarized the work of the commission as a recognition that "The credibility of immigration policy can be measured by a simple yardstick: people who should get in, do get in; people who should not get in are kept out; and people who are judged deportable are required to leave."[17] Although the committee recommended increasing visas for spouses and families and deregulating the visa process for skilled workers, Congress responded by passing the Illegal Immigrant Reform and Immigrant Responsibility Act (IIRIRA), which, in practice, made legal immigration more difficult while failing to significantly reduce unauthorized immigration.

Today, issues of unauthorized immigration dominate nearly every level of government involvement, from access to public education to law enforcement and public health. Federalism and the separation of powers have made it more difficult for state and local governments to determine how to carry out what is essentially a federal function. Indeed, the issue dominated debates during the 2016 presidential election, as candidates outlined plans to punish the many cities and states that have declared their desire to allocate public resources carefully. In 2017 the US Department of Justice attempted to impose new conditions upon all cities and localities applying for its grants. The proposal would require that grantees give immigration authorities access to local jails and notify the federal government at least forty-eight hours before an unauthorized immigrant could be released from a local jail. The proposal was part of a larger effort by President Donald J. Trump to make good on his campaign promise to punish cities and states economically if they provide refuge to undocumented communities. Former Attorney General Jeff Sessions justified the necessity of the provisions to counter

> policies [that] encourage illegal immigration and even human trafficking by perpetuating the lie that in certain cities, illegal aliens can live outside the law. This can have tragic consequences, like the 10 deaths we saw in San Antonio this weekend. This is what the American people should be able to expect from their cities and states, and these long overdue requirements will help us take down MS-13 and other violent transnational gangs, and make our country safer. (US Department of Justice 2017)

In 2018, a federal appeals court ruled against the injunction on the basis that it overreached federal authority (Laughland 2018).

Ethnicity and the War on Terror

On September 11, 2001, nearly 3,000 civilians were killed after twenty foreign-born terrorists orchestrated the largest act of domestic terrorism in modern US history. The men who hijacked four flights came to the United States from Saudi Arabia, Lebanon, the United Arab Emirates, and Egypt. The utter devastation of the attacks, combined with lingering concerns about vulnerability to subsequent offensives, elevated public pressure for Congress and the president to take decisive action. Following the passage of the **USA PATRIOT Act**, legislators cited the attacks of 9/11 as evidence of the deadly consequences of failing to crack down aggressively on people who overstayed visas and remained in the country illegally.[18] These concerns over homeland security, coupled with mounting public pressure to limit movement into the United States, significantly changed the political space. In fact, bipartisan support for increasing border patrol and protection helped defeat a number of congressional efforts both to enhance amnesty and to elevate enforcement. This conflation of terrorism, ethnicity, and immigration was reflected by public opinion data showing that one in three Americans supported targeted surveillance and the internment of Arab Americans.[19]

Contemporary Controversies

Voting and Representation

In 2013, the US Supreme Court effectively rolled back preclearance by striking down the coverage formula that determined which jurisdictions must preclear new election rules and plans.[20] Writing for five members of the Court (four justices dissented), Chief Justice John Roberts indicated in *Shelby* v. *Holder* (2013) that the coverage formula was outdated because flagrant discrimination no longer persisted in covered jurisdictions since the "country has changed." The Court held that "the conditions that originally justified these measures no longer characterize voting . . . these improvements are in large part because of the Voting Rights Act."

The justices believed that the Voting Rights Act of 1965 had been so effective in addressing ethnoracial discrimination that the formula used to identify covered jurisdictions was no longer necessary. Within hours of the ruling, states such as Texas and North Carolina instituted new rules that made it more difficult for citizens to vote. In 2016, the first round of national elections held post the *Shelby* decision, fourteen states adopted new restrictions on voting.[21] Researchers documented the impact of these new restrictions, including exceedingly long wait times to vote in places such as New Mexico and Arizona, massive voter purges in New York, the elimination of early voting, and the reduction or moving of polling places in states such as Ohio, South Carolina, and Wisconsin (Arthur and McCann 2018; Berman 2017). These results made it clear that the *Shelby* decision had in fact erected new barriers to voting for communities of color – particularly those in urban and rural communities. There remains a persistent gap between the numerical potential of communities of color and their political incorporation.[22]

BOX 5.4 Citizenship and the census

Since the first census was taken in 1790, the bureau has used the "usual residence rule" to identify "the place where a person lives and sleeps most of the time." Usual residence, however, is not synonymous with legal residence. In most states, legal residence is defined as the place where "you have your permanent home or principal establishment and to where, whenever you are absent, you intend to return." Usual residence is used to determine where people are counted on census day. The standard is used to count a range of groups, such as college students, military personnel, and prison inmates.

Though the Fourteenth Amendment allows states and localities to include inmate populations within their census counts, many have argued that this practice violates the one person–one vote standard. The standard derives from the Supreme Court's 1964 *Reynolds* v. *Sims* decision, in which justices agreed that state legislative districts must be "as nearly of equal population as is practicable." The one person–one vote standard requires that US congressional districts and state legislative districts be drawn so that their residents have a fair and equal share of representatives in Congress. Congressional districts must conform to an ideal size based on the formula: total state population divided by number of districts. On average, congressional districts contain approximately 645,000 people. However, current provisions make no distinction between those who are there as legal residents and those there as inmates. Overall, 52 percent of New York State's prison population is African American; Hispanics account for 30 percent. The concentration of communities of color within certain prison districts varies across geography and rural setting.

The Constitution mandates the use of census data only for apportionment. However, census data have become critically important for distributing other political and economic resources. More than $175 billion in federally funded programs was allocated based on census data. This money flows to programs that support some of the most vulnerable members of communities – children, the elderly, those with disabilities, and those fighting addiction. Thus, the census plays a critical role in determining how communities are accounted for and responded to. Accurate data take on particular importance given the rapidly diversifying makeup of the United States. In 2018, members of the Trump administration floated a proposal to ask census respondents about their citizenship status. Civil rights organizations worry that this question will deter people from participating and, in turn, lead to a severe undercount of diverse groups.

Public Education

The increasing diversity of the United States coupled with institutional protections provided underrepresented communities with the tools needed to fight against their exclusion. Much like the passage of the Voting Rights Act of 1965, policy changes meant to enhance the standing of one group may spill over to elevate the standing of other groups as well. For example, *Lau* v. *Nichols* (1974) questioned whether the failure to provide English-language learning assistance to Chinese public school students in San Francisco violated the protections of the Civil Rights Act of 1964 and the Fourteenth Amendment. Following a number of judicial decisions mandating the full integration of public schools, Chinese students with limited English proficiency were held back in the same grade for years or forced into special education classes. In a unanimous decision, the Supreme Court ruled that public school districts which receive federal funds are required to provide equal educational opportunities to all students regardless of ethnicity and language proficiency.

The *Lau* decision laid the foundation for the 1982 case **Plyer v. Doe**, which questioned whether undocumented children could be barred from attending public elementary and secondary schools. The Court struck down a Texas statute by arguing that education is a public good. However, it limited the scope of that public good to K-12 education. In 2001 Congress began debating several versions of what became known as the Development, Relief, and Education for Alien Minors Act (DREAM Act) intended to provide conditional permanent residency to certain immigrants who were brought to the United States as minors. Although the Act failed to pass at the federal level, fifteen states have passed their own versions to guarantee educational access for youth regardless of their status. Currently eighteen states allow undocumented students to qualify for in-state tuition as long as they meet certain requirements (Chávez et al. 2014). These decisions made at the state level reflect the continuing importance of federalism for determining which groups have access, representation, and standing. The link between ethnicity, citizenship, and public access shapes debates over other modes of accommodation, such as voting rights, drivers' licenses, and insurance.

Today, the achievement gap in educational outcomes remains an important focus in the area of ethnoracial identity. In spite of the 1954 *Brown v. Board of Education* ruling that separate was inherently unequal, public schools in the United States remain excessively segregated by race, ethnicity, and social class. According to data from the US Department of Education, public school students have a high likelihood of attending racially isolated schools in spite of a number of state and federal efforts to reduce such disparities. Gary Orfield and Chungmei Lee (2007) found that the average white student attends schools where 77 percent of their peers are white. The proportion of peers for other groups are 35 percent for American Indian students, 23 percent for Asian students, 55 percent for Latino students, and 52 percent for Black students. These patterns are even more pronounced when we add the layers of urbanicity, geography, and class.

BOX 5.5 Disaggregating the model minority myth

Gaining and protecting access to education has long been a primary goal for underrepresented groups in the United States. Education provides a foundation for both pursuing individual goals and accessing upward mobility, which can, at times, surpass institutional constraints based on identity. One of the major challenges, however, is determining how to address the reality that some groups who may be underrepresented in the general population may be overrepresented within school populations.

Recently, a number of states have adopted policies that allow for granular disaggregation – or the breaking up of data on Asian students based on countries of origin. Proponents in places such as California, Rhode Island, and Minnesota argue that disaggregating the data allows analysts to better understand how the achievement gap, income inequality, health outcomes, and college persistence vary across groups. In turn, these data help weaken the "model minority myth" that, supporters argue, unfairly brands Asian students as exceptional and without need of additional resources. For example, supporters of the California bill argued that South Asian students often struggled under this myth because it did not properly account for how differences in wealth and occupational status may shape education outcomes.

Opponents of disaggregation bills point to the historical use of country of origin data to separate and discriminate against certain Asian communities. For example, disaggregating census data allowed the federal government to set national origin quotas and, later, authorize the internment of Japanese citizens on the West Coast. Disaggregation is viewed by some as a way of branding Asians as non-Americans or as second-class citizens.

Other critics are concerned that, rather than addressing disparities, disaggregated data will be used to privilege certain groups while punishing others based on country of origin and relative levels of success. Many Chinese American families, for example, fear that separating out the data may constrain opportunities for their children to gain acceptance to prestigious schools out of concern that they are overrepresented within student populations.

Over the last two decades, Asian American students have launched a number of lawsuits protesting what they see as discriminatory policies that unfairly limit their educational opportunities based on country of origin. The bulk of these cases have been filed by students of Korean, Indian, and Chinese descent. An essay published in the *Harvard Law Review* criticized the Ivy League school's efforts to diversify its student body at the expense of Asian applicants: "In order to be admitted to certain selective institutions, Asian applicants needed to score – on the 1600 point scale of the 'old SAT' – 140 points higher than whites, 270 points higher than Hispanics, and 450 points higher than African Americans if other factors are held equal" (Harvard Law Review Editors 2017). These debates highlight the importance of understanding how interactions between groups can shape tensions and interactions within groups.

Environmental Justice

Across the United States, communities of color are disproportionately affected by environmental hazards such as the location of toxic waste, lead contamination, and climate change. In 2016, then President Barack Obama declared a federal emergency in the city of Flint, Michigan, after the decision by state officials to switch the city's water supply imperiled the safety of thousands of residents; 40 percent of the residents in this majority Black city live below the poverty line. Residents have long pressured the state to intervene and help address the related challenges emanating from concentrated poverty. Despite residents' pleas and concerns about water quality, city and state officials refused to respond to the brewing public health crisis. It wasn't until there were outside threats of legal and criminal action that state officials responded to the documented impact of lead poisoning on the children of Flint. The effects of lead poisoning (e.g. learning disabilities, cognitive deficiencies, and skin rashes) may last for a lifetime. Analysts refer to the neglect of the health needs of communities of color and the disproportionate impact as **environmental racism**, or the disproportionate exposure of underrepresented groups to pollution via water, air, and soil. Often this exposure results from patterns or residential segregation and economic displacement that relegates communities of color to land and neighborhoods that are either contaminated or compromised.

BOX 5.6 Battles over the border

There are nearly 2,000 miles of border separating the United States and Mexico, including 18 miles in the Pacific Ocean and 12 miles in the Gulf of Mexico. The terrain at the border is often treacherous and secured by an intricate system of electronic surveillance and members of the US Customs and Border Protection. In spite of these conditions, recent attention has focused on deterring unauthorized immigrants from crossing into the United States. These efforts have been offered by states and the federal government with varying results.

In 2010, Governor Jan Brewer of Arizona signed SB 1070 into law. At the time, it was one of the most sweeping state-level provisions for addressing unauthorized immigration to the US in general, and into a state in particular. SB 1070 made it a *state* crime for an unauthorized immigrant to be in the state without proper documentation. Likewise, it required that law-enforcement officers determine the citizenship status of anyone they suspected of being in the state illegally. Critics argued that the law encouraged a pattern of racial profiling that would unfairly target groups based on race and perceived country of origin. Supporters of the bill believed that it was a necessary step toward public safety that the federal government had failed to ensure. The US Supreme Court struck down some of the bill's major provisions on the grounds that it usurped the supremacy clause outlining the powers of the federal government to regulate and enforce immigration. In so doing, Arizona and the Court prompted broader discussions about the most effective means of discouraging unauthorized immigration.

The battle over borders reached new heights in 2018, when Attorney General Jeff Sessions announced an aggressive "zero tolerance" policy that would prosecute anyone found crossing the border. This new policy required the automatic separation of adults and the children traveling with them. Adults were processed by the federal courts while children were sent to detention facilities overseen by the Department of Health and Human Services' Office of Refugee Resettlement. Legislators, activists, and lobbyists converged on Texas to view the facilities and demand judicial intervention. Over 2,000 children were separated from their families in just one month of the policy's enactment, while various courts debated the length, conditions, and location of the separation policy. In 2019, President Donald Trump declared an unprecedented national emergency at the Mexican border in order to divert more money toward building a border wall.

The importance of land as both a source of protection and a threat was amplified during protests of the Dakota Access Pipeline project in North Dakota. Members of the Standing Rock Sioux vehemently objected to the plan to transport 570,000 barrels of crude oil per day.[23] The $4 billion project creates significant environmental hazards because of soil contamination and the potential for spills. The Standing Rock tribe protested the project because it traversed sacred tribal ground and increased the possibility of contaminating their chief water source. Beyond these direct physical and environmental hazards, the refusal to engage tribal leaders in discussions about the project highlights the failure to address notions of incorporation, sovereignty, and authentic power highlighted in chapter 2. In 2016, a coalition of tribal members and their supporters launched a number of protests designed to draw attention to the complex issues of power and environmental justice that play out not just in North Dakota but across the country. Dubbed the "Water Protectors," Standing Rock protesters were arrested in clashes with federal authorities. In the wake of the acts of civil disobedience at Standing Rock, thirty states have crafted fifty-six bills designed to restrict public protests. In spite of these efforts to limit dissent, the Standing Rock protests inspired a record number of American Indian women to run for elected office in 2018. Unlike their male predecessors, the overwhelming majority of these women ran on Democratic or Green Party tickets.[24]

Conclusion: Ethnic Identity as Intersectional Construction

Throughout this chapter I have used the term *ethnoracial* identity to highlight the difficulty of separating out racial and ethnic identity for certain groups based on both country of origin and phenotypic appearance. The adoption of early immigration policies in the United States was designed to limit the number of people coming from countries thought to be less desirable. From the wholesale denial of citizenship to Chinese aspirants to more recent debates over refugee status, the notion of desirability is often colored by perceptions of group interests. Global conflicts such as war also shape shifts in immigration for those seeking to immigrate, while defining the limits of incorporation for those who are already in the country.

In spite of these challenges, ethnic groups have made tremendous gains in the United States in terms of their numbers and presence as political actors. However, these groups remain underrepresented in every facet of political life. The path toward full political incorporation has been shaped by a collection of policies, legal decisions, and practices that limit the standing of large, diverse groups of people. At times these efforts mask important differences based on country of origin, group preferences, and policy arenas. In other instances, diverse groups have responded to their exclusion by forging their own political agenda and practices. Whether protesting the contamination of water sources or pressuring the courts to protect access to public education, ethnic groups in the US constantly challenge the boundaries of belonging. They do so by demanding not just increased descriptive representation but a determined commitment to elevating the **substantive representation** of group interests. To be sure, defining those interests has been a challenge that reveals the tremendous diversity that exists *within* groups.

Historically, that diversity is reflected in the differential responses of groups to things such as internment and the war on terror. In a contemporary sense, the complexities of intragroup diversity are evident in the crop of political hopefuls representing new interests and new constituencies. The task comes in deciding whether American politics provides space for groups to pursue their diverse varied interests on their own terms and based on their own negotiations of identity and belonging.

Controversy box: Protecting or suppressing the vote?

In 1950, South Carolina became the first state in the country to require identification to allow people to vote. Since then, a fierce debate has emerged over the motivations and consequences of state laws that require identification, particularly photo identification. Today, thirty-four states require identification, but the type of ID that is acceptable varies by state and, in many areas, jurisdiction. Some believe the requirement is an effective means of preventing fraud which taints elections and weakens democracy (Hasen 2012; Hajnal et al. 2017; Hicks et al. 2014). In 2017, President Donald Trump announced the formation of a national voter fraud commission led by Kansas Secretary of State Kris Kobach to investigate and protect election integrity. The group was short-lived, as most states refused to comply with the request for sensitive data. Various groups have protested photo ID requirements as discriminatory. For example, some jurisdictions do not accept tribal ID cards as being acceptable, even though they are issued by the federal government. Such requirements further limit the voting potential of groups with a long history of struggle accessing the ballot box.

To some groups, these contemporary photo ID requirements are reminiscent of historical efforts to limit voting based on group identity. For example, Alabama used to have a system that required applicants to have a registered voter "vouch" for them in order to be considered eligible to vote. This often rendered African Americans ineligible because they couldn't find a registered white voter willing to publicly endorse their application. You decide. Do these provisions help protect or suppress access to voting?

Questions for Debate

- A number of states have adopted policies to allow undocumented students to attend state colleges and universities at in-state tuition rates. Is everyone in the United States entitled to an education? And, if so, for how long?
- Although Latinx and Asian American communities have increased their statistical share of the US population, they haven't been able to convert that numerical presence into full political representation. Is it important for groups to have similar statistical representation within Congress and other elected offices?
- The 2016 presidential election highlighted ongoing tensions related to immigration, citizenship, and political participation. It also emphasized the ways in which partisanship varies across racial and ethnic lines. Looking ahead to future presidential elections, how might these groups work together to promote their policy preferences?

Key Terms

- *Korematsu* v. *United States*
- USA PATRIOT Act
- *Shelby* v. *Holder*
- alien enemies
- Naturalization Act of 1790
- Executive Order 9066
- Johnson–Reed Act of 1924
- Hart–Celler Immigration Act of 1965
- Chinese Exclusion Act of 1882
- environmental racism
- preclearance
- environmental justice
- descriptive representation

6

Gender, Sexual Identity, and the Challenge of Inclusion

The energy inside the Wells Fargo Center is electric. Over 50,000 people have gathered in Philadelphia for the 2016 Democratic National Convention (DNC). It is an eclectic mix of party faithfuls and upstart insurgents who come to advocate on behalf of their candidates and issues of choice. Conventions are usually massive pep rallies designed to excite the party's base with a cavalcade of celebrities, politicians with future electoral aspirations, and everyday people who connect their stories to various aspects of the party platform. This year the "Mothers of the Movement" appear on stage dressed in all black with bright red silk flowers on their lapels discussing the common pain that binds them together. They speak on behalf of their children, Sandra Bland, Eric Garner, Michael Brown, Trayvon Martin, and many others whose names are familiar to the public. Among them is Lucy McBath, whose seventeen-year-old son, Jordan Davis, was shot and killed while sitting in a car with friends. Davis was gunned down by a 45-year-old who claimed he felt threatened by the group's loud music and shot in self-defense. Inspired by the frequent pleas for common-sense gun reform and civil rights protections, McBath was elected to the United States Congress in 2018 representing a Georgia district that was previously led by Newt Gingrich.

The mayor of Tallahassee, Andrew Gillum, who would go on to become the first African American to run for governor of Florida, is there to speak, as well as survivors of the 9/11 attacks, the Pulse nightclub shooting, the Charleston massacre, and families of fallen soldiers and law-enforcement officers. Signature addresses by former First Lady Michelle Obama, Congresswoman Gabby Giffords, who survived an assassination attempt, and civil rights leader Delores Huerta were strategically timed to bind supporters across a range of identities, issues, and priorities. Even with the carefully crafted roster of speakers and performers, the tone of the 2016 convention is different. Party leaders are keenly aware of the tension felt by many at the gathering. After a contested primary battle, disgruntled voters accuse the party leadership of stacking the deck against Vermont Senator Bernie Sanders in favor of former Secretary of State Hillary Clinton. The disdain over the process and the heir apparent produces fractures within the party that are tangible and significant. With every speaker who appears at the event, ardent Sanders supporters turn their backs, hold placards decrying his loss, and jeer in an attempt to disrupt the event.

Convention roll calls are an opportunity to highlight what makes individual states unique as well as to make a political declaration. Some states emphasize products unique to their state, such as Connecticut with Pez candy, or reference links to historical milestones. New York chooses state leaders with national profiles who can command the crowd, while others take the moment to express their displeasure that their candidate of choice is no longer in the running. That cloud of discontent looms over the DNC roll call as spontaneous protests erupt throughout. Arizona's delegate count was given by Jerry Emmitt, a woman who, at 102 years old, was born six years before the **Nineteenth Amendment** granted women the ability to vote. Ohio's delegate count was announced with the declaration "Love trumps hate!" by Jim Obergefell, whose 2015 Supreme Court suit, *Obergefell v. Hodges*, struck down state bans on same-sex marriage. In taking the microphone on behalf of the state of Vermont, former candidate Bernie Sanders closed the roll call with a motion that Clinton be selected as the party's nominee. Four days of convention proceedings captured the breadth of debates over the meaning of identity and citizenship in a rapidly changing political landscape.

"I'm In": What's Next?

In 2008, Barack Obama became the first African American candidate to secure a majority party nomination for president. Some pundits argued that the United States was entering a post-racial era where issues of race would no longer constrain those seeking elected office (McWhorter 2008; Ford 2008). The message was clear: stop complaining and start running. However, the net electoral and social gains of Obama's candidacy were modest (Dawson and Bobo 2009; Lawless and Fox 2010; Tesler 2016). In 2008, thirty-nine African Americans served in the US Congress, but there were none in the Senate. Today there are fifty-five members in the House and three in the Senate. In accepting the 2016 Democratic nomination, Clinton observed the significance of her bid as historic for both men and women: "because when any barrier falls in America, for anyone, it clears the way for everyone. When there are no ceilings, the sky's the limit" (Clinton 2016). As she cracked the political glass ceiling as the country's first female nominee, the question arose as to who would be left to clean up the pieces.

According to data from the Center for American Women and Politics (CAWP 2017), women now comprise 52 percent of the voting-age population. Women of color, particularly African American women, were crucial to Barack Obama's victories in 2008 and 2012, with a 70 percent voter turnout rate that topped

Table 6.1 Gender and sex disparities in governing (as of 4/2019)

	Percentage of population	Percentage of elected officials
Women	51	29
Men	49	71
Women of color	24	4
Men of color	23	7
LGBTQI	4.5	0.1

SOURCE: Center for American Women and Politics; Joint Center for Political and Economic Studies; US Census Bureau; Gallup Daily Tracking.

that of all other demographic groups. Converting that electoral strength into office-holding has been a more arduous task. One hundred years after the Nineteenth Amendment first granted the vote, women hold 19 percent of the seats in Congress and 25 percent in state legislatures; they form 12 percent of US governors. As table 6.1 illustrates, women remain one of the most under-represented groups in American politics: just thirty-three of the 104 women in Congress and two of the six women serving as governor identify as women of color.

Hillary Clinton's bid to become president of the United States challenged the status quo for a number of reasons. She was the first woman to secure a major party nomination, the first spouse of a former president to run for the office, and the first to run after serving in the administration of the opponent who beat her in presidential primaries. While her bid speaks directly to a number of challenges surrounding gender identity and politics, she rests as an outlier not just for women candidates but for all candidates. For many women, diffi-culty raising campaign funds, electoral structures that favor incumbents, and stereotypes regarding leadership style are persistent challenges for those seek-ing elected office (Githens and Prestage 1977; Fox 2011; Boyle and Meyer 2018; Burrell 1994). But raising money wasn't an issue for Clinton, who outraised and outspent her Republican rival nearly fivefold. Her name recognition and a long, varied record of public service also helped topple some of the barriers encountered by other candidates. Clinton faced the major hurdle of balancing the historic nature of her candidacy while rejecting attempts to pigeonhole her issue priorities:

> Our Founders embraced the enduring truth that we are stronger together.
> America is once again at a moment of reckoning. Powerful forces are threatening to pull us apart. Bonds of trust and respect are fraying. And just as with our founders, there are no guarantees. It truly is up to us. We have to decide whether we all will work together so we all can rise together. Our country's motto is e pluribus unum: out of many, we are one. Will we stay true to that motto? (Clinton 2016)

Hillary Clinton supporters gather for a rally at Arizona State University in Tempe. In 2016, the former secretary of state and US senator became the first woman in US history to secure a major party nomination for president.

Being first can be a hollow victory when identity is used as both a credential and a source of critique. Clinton's nomination speech highlighted the delicate way she and other women candidates tread the fine line between being committed to issues that disproportionately impact women (e.g. reproductive rights, pay equity, early childhood education) and not being pigeonholed based on gender norms. Protesters at the DNC responded with chants of "No more war" as Clinton spoke of her role in the assassination of Osama Bin Laden. The constant description of her as "hawkish" harkened back to longstanding critiques of women such as former Secretary of State Madeline Albright and former British Prime Minister Margaret Thatcher, who went against the gendered expectation that women should be less aggressive and more conciliatory. Clinton's candidacy was indeed historic. Yet it shouldn't be viewed as a launch pad for a post-gender era in American politics. Nor should the election be viewed solely through the lens of who was running.

Mobilizing across Markers

The significance of the 2016 election was greater than the potential to elect the country's first woman president. The long and at times bizarre nature of the election season raised a number of issues of concern to multiple identity

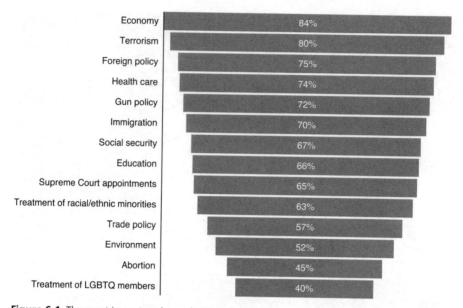

Figure 6.1 The most important issues in 2016 (percentage of voters saying the issue was very important)

SOURCE: Based on data from the Pew Research Center.

groups. Figure 6.1 provides an overview of the major policy interests of 2016 voters. After seismic shifts in legal restrictions on military service, marriage rights, pay equity, and civil rights protections, the election mobilized groups of voters who felt the country was moving in the right direction as well as those who felt the changes undermined their beliefs. That sense of being left behind rather than being empowered highlights sharp differences in how members of the public respond to claims of exclusion based on gender identity and sexual orientation.

The post-election headlines conveyed the tremendous shock felt by many that the pre-election predictions had been wrong. In spite of Clinton's capture of the popular vote, the Electoral College distribution meant that Donald Trump would become president. The election capped a year of tension over the potential challenge to protections for women and sexual minorities. In a now infamous audio recording of an *Access Hollywood* television segment that cost host Billy Bush (nephew of former President George H. W. Bush) his job, the forty-fifth president of the United States was heard bragging about grabbing a woman by her genitals. Some defended the remarks as simply "locker room banter," while other voters expressed their outrage (Nelson 2017). Even President Trump's choice of running mate engendered concern among voters who questioned his religious conservatism. As the governor of the state of Indiana, Vice President Mike Pence signed into law the Religious Freedom Restoration Act (RFRA), which allowed businesses to refuse service to individuals and groups who violated their religious beliefs (see Indiana Senate Bill 101, 2015). Advocates argued that the Act posed a tremendous threat to LGBTQI residents who could be subjected to discrimination, while a number of businesses and corporations pointed to the potential loss of revenue (Neuman 2015). A number of states pushed economic boycotts of Indiana to express their discontent with the new law. Pence's support for the RFRA, combined with his documented backing for conversion therapy and restrictions on reproductive rights, vaulted the 2016 election as a litmus test and battle between social conservatives and social justice advocates.

The exclusive focus on Clinton's loss overshadowed the very real electoral gains made during the 2016 election. Table 6.2 shows that, more than being just the opportunity to elect a president, the election ushered in a large and diverse class of candidates for national and state office. Voters selected Catherine Cortez-Masto of Nevada as the first Latina member and Iraq War veteran Tammy Duckworth of Illinois as the first woman of Asian-Pacific Islander descent to serve in the Senate. Former California Attorney General Kamala Harris made history as the second African American and first South Asian woman elected to the Senate. The House of Representatives saw six new women of color elected to serve, while a record number of openly LGBTQI candidates launched bids for Congress and state legislatures. The increase in candidacies of women, people of color, and LGBTQI individuals across the political spectrum was matched by increases in registration and turnout, captured in table 6.3. Together, these contextual factors highlight the importance of examining multiple layers of group identity and their relationship to the battle for full inclusion.

Gender Identity and Sexual Orientation: The Context

Gender identity is socially constructed based on a set of prevailing norms, conditions, expectations, and experiences. It is fluid and distinct from our understanding of sex as two discrete categories based on biological differences. This is not to say that gender identity is simply a choice made through personal preference. To be sure, the category we are assigned at birth (e.g. boy

Table 6.2 Number of women candidates for elected office, 2016 and 2018

	2016	2018
House of Representatives	167	234
Senate	18	22
State legislatures	2600	3379
Statewide offices	70	132

Source: Based on data from the Center for American Women and Politics, Eagleton Institute, Rutgers University.

Table 6.3 Gender gap in registration and voting based on race and ethnicity

	Percentage of eligible voting population		Number who reported voting (millions)	
2016	*Women*	*Men*	*Women*	*Men*
Asian/Pacific Islander	48.4	49.7	2.7	2.4
Black	63.7	54.2	10.1	7.0
Hispanic	50.0	45.0	6.9	5.8
White, non-Hispanic	66.8	63.7	53.1	47.8
2012	*Women*	*Men*	*Women*	*Men*
Asian/Pacific Islander	48.5	46.0	2.1	1.8
Black	70.1	61.4	10.4	7.4
Hispanic	49.8	46.0	6.0	5.2
White, non-Hispanic	65.6	62.6	51.8	46.3

SOURCE: CAWP (2017).

or girl; male or female) may or may not be consistent with the identity we develop into or express as we grow older. A newborn, for example, has little ability to choose or confirm its gender identity. Sex is assigned based on a set of common parameters such as chromosomes, hormones, and reproductive organs (American Medical Association 2018). Consider the recent surge in "gender reveal" celebrations. Expectant parents announce an impending birth via extravagant balloon drops, decorative cakes, and themed parties. In Arizona, an elaborate gender reveal plan sparked a 47,000 acre wildfire that caused $8 million in damage. Although parents may look forward to sharing the sex of their unborn child via the reveals, some critics argue that this approach introduces and reinforces gendered stereotypes (Appiah 2018). From clothing choices to colors (pink for girls, blue for boys), toys, games, and activities, our collective notions of gender heighten the distinctions between self-identity and social identity.

Gender identity captures the myriad ways we are socialized to associate certain behaviors, characteristics, and traits as masculine or feminine and what it means to embrace those qualities in a consistent way. These negotiations shape the qualities we prefer in political candidates, the policies we embrace as relevant, and our approaches to navigating political conflict. Although the ways we conceive of and express our gender identity may vary, within the realm of politics our options are often prescribed for us. For example, drivers' licenses in most states allow people to choose only between "male" and "female." Census forms, birth certificates, passport applications, and the photo IDs we use to vote all conflate sex and gender.[1] Publicly financed colleges and universities maintain single-sex dorm rooms, and correctional institutions are still segregated by sex. In a number of states, transgender inmates are assigned to correctional facilities based on their assigned sex rather than their gender identity. Trans inmates are often held in solitary confinement to protect their safety.[2] Gender and sexual identity shape our relationship to and experience with the institutions, agents, and decisions of government.

Unlike gender identity, sexual identity is not a social construct. However, our collective understanding of, reaction to, and regulation of sexual orientation is socially constructed. Gender and sexual identity are inextricably linked. For the bulk of American political development, efforts to politically define sexual orientation have rested on a "gay" versus "straight" dichotomy. This limited understanding of sexual orientation as group identity has shaped access to employment, protections against discrimination in housing, and the ability to adopt, make medical decisions, and inherit property.

BOX 6.1 The spectrum of sexual identity

Asexual	People who do not experience sexual/romantic attraction toward anyone.
Graysexual	People who rarely experience sexual/romantic attraction toward anyone.
Demisexual	People who experience sexual/romantic attraction toward someone only after developing a strong bond.
Heterosexual	People who experience sexual/romantic attraction toward genders other than their own.
Homosexual	People who experience romantic/sexual attraction toward the same gender as their own.
Bisexual	People who experience romantic/sexual attraction toward the same gender as well as other gender(s) than their own.
Pansexual	People who experience romantic/sexual attraction toward all, regardless of gender.
Polysexual	People who experience romantic/sexual attraction toward multiple (but not necessarily all) genders.

Consider, for example, the plight of Charlie Baker, who applied for a job with the federal government as a typist in 1971. Baker received a letter from the Civil Service Commission delaying his employment because, "In view of the above described immoral, infamous, scandalous and notoriously disgraceful conduct, you are invited to show cause why you should not be disqualified from Federal Employment." Baker was required to prove to the commission that he was not a gay man in order to gain employment.

Today there are over fifteen categories of sexual identity, which highlight a wide range in how groups conceive of their identities. In spite of this diversity in self-identification, the social identification imposed by various arenas of political influence are much more restrictive yet no less significant. Baker sued the federal government for discrimination and lost his suit. This judicial decision allowed for federal investigations and termination of the employment contracts of people based on their sexual orientation until 2014, when President Barack Obama issued Executive Orders 13672 and 13673, which included gender and sexual identity as protected categories. To accompany these orders, members of the Senate introduced, yet failed to pass, a federal Employment Non-Discrimination Act (ENDA) banning discrimination in employment on the bases of gender identity and sexual orientation. Some version of the Act has been introduced in Congress every year since 1994 but has yet to pass. In March of 2017, Executive Order 13673 was rescinded, leaving some more vulnerable to workplace discrimination based on group identity.

Scholars have long observed the seemingly intractable nature of debates over racial or ethnic identity and US politics (Blumer 1958; Bobo and Gilliam 1990; Alexander 2010; Bell 1973; Parker and Barreto 2013; Anderson 2017). However, American political development has heightened the intersection of gender and sexual identity to frame the path toward universal freedom and inclusion (Sherrill 1993; Murib 2018; Engel 2015). This chapter explores challenges to (1) citizenship, (2) political representation, and (3) mobilization through the intersectional lens of gender and sexual identity. Its focus isn't on how individuals formulate their identity. Efforts to combat, and in many instances reinforce, the boundaries of inclusion based on gender and sexuality highlight the tremendous diversity that exists within and across identity groups.

Early Challenges to Exclusion

Early appeals to gender equality were intimately tied to appeals for racial equality. As abolitionists such as Harriett Tubman, Frederick Douglass, Henry Highland Garnett, and Robert Hamilton cultivated support for abolishing slavery, they gradually built a coalition of support among white women who viewed the abolition of slavery as a necessary first step toward eroding institutional barriers to universal freedom. In 1840, over 350 delegates from across the world gathered in London's Exeter Hall for the World Anti-Slavery Convention. Although women were allowed to attend the event, they were not allowed to speak, vote, or serve as official delegates (Maynard 1960). Women were even forced to sit in separate sections away from the main decision-making. The task for women, according to the event's supporters, was to provide resources to help men pursue their abolition goals. Elizabeth Cady Stanton registered her disgust at the treatment of women attendees: "My experience at the World's Antislavery Convention, all I had read of the legal status of women, and the oppression I saw everywhere, together swept across my soul, intensified now by many personal experiences."[3]

The 1848 **Seneca Falls Convention** was organized to combat women's exclusion from the World Anti-Slavery Convention and discuss the "social, civil, and religious condition and rights of women."[4] It was initiated by women for women; attendees included suffragists Elizabeth Cady Stanton and Lucretia Mott and abolitionist Frederick Douglass. Of the many issues discussed at the meeting to advance the interests of women, the one major issue they could not agree upon was fighting for universal suffrage on the basis of gender. Less than a third of the delegates in attendance voted to prioritize women's suffrage. The convention endorsed the passage of thirteen resolutions, though not for one calling for universal voting rights. This tension led to the formation of the National Women's Suffrage Association (NWSA), which distanced itself from the struggle for racial equality and focused exclusively on advancing voting rights for women. NWSA president Anna Howard Shaw captured the outrage of white women who felt overlooked by admonishing members of Congress, who "put the ballot in the hands of your black men, thus making them political superiors of white women. Never before in the history of the world have men made former slaves the political masters of their former mistresses!" (Shaw 1915). Rather than attacking white supremacy as a system that diminished the citizenship of *all* women by ordaining white men as leaders, NWSA supporters saw racial equality as a threat to the political standing of white women.

Membership in the NWSA was limited to women, while the rival American Woman Suffrage Association (AWSA) invited the support of men and women. Federalism as a governing principle sharply divided the two organizations. Leaders Susan B. Anthony and Elizabeth Cady Stanton believed that the NWSA should demand a constitutional amendment that would provide federal protection for women's citizenship and secure the franchise. In contrast, AWSA leaders Julia Ward Howe and Henry Blackwell preferred a more targeted state-by-state approach that would gradually build national support for extending the vote to women.

The end of the Civil War and the passage of three constitutional amendments abolished slavery, established the Equal Protection Clause, and extended the franchise to Black men. It simultaneously heightened tension between coalition partners and stimulated efforts to expand access to political freedom to women. To be sure, securing access to the franchise was the key goal for suffragists. However, a number of activists and their allies advocated for the overall protection of women's rights. The passage of the Fifteenth Amendment caused a permanent rift in the coalition between those concerned with racial equality and those fighting for gender equality. The amendment marked the first time that the word "male" appeared in the US Constitution. Some allies believed men were endowed with the inherent right and enhanced ability to make important political decisions. Others adopted a more incremental approach to political change that encouraged women's rights advocates to "wait their turn" until full protections for Black men were secured. What began as a strong coalition to promote freedom was eroded over an interplay of racism and sexism that would mark decades of subsequent efforts to pursue gender equality within a limited political framework.

In 1890, the two competing women's suffrage organizations merged to form the **National American Woman Suffrage Association** (NAWSA). NAWSA's new leader, Carrie Chapman Catt, crafted a strategy that cultivated both state and federal pressure to help women gain the ability to vote. In 1916, Montana residents elected Jeanette Rankin to serve in the US Congress just two years after she convinced state legislators to adopt a provision that lifted restrictions on women voting. As the first woman in the country ever to hold federal office, Rankin helped draft the initial legislation for what would become the Nineteenth Amendment. These early battles over freedom highlight intersectional notions of freedom and inclusion. By equating racial leadership with Black men and appeals to gendered leadership with white women, the quest to dismantle the politics of exclusion shaped authentic power.

BOX 6.2 Mabel Ping-Hua Lee

Mabel Ping-Hua Lee was born in Guangzhou, China, in 1896 and later earned a visa to study in the United States. After moving to New York City and being reunited with her father, a Christian missionary, Lee became enamored of the growing Feminist movement and its emphasis on women having full access to education, equal protection, and voting. At just sixteen years old she became a leading voice in New York City's Suffrage movement and helped lead the 1912 parade for women's voting rights.

Lee used her time as a student at Barnard College to pen essays on voting and women's equality as a means to expand democracy in the United States and to secure its superiority vis-à-vis the rest of the world. Her most widely circulated essay was titled "The Meaning of Woman Suffrage" and helped launch her commitment to mobilizing members of the Chinese community to demand equal rights for women and girls in all aspects of public life. Her activism coupled with her literary eloquence helped secure women's suffrage in the state of New York in 1917. Three years later, the passage of the Nineteenth Amendment gave federal protection to women's access to the ballot. In spite of her committed efforts in securing political freedom for all women, Mabel Lee was still barred from voting because the Chinese Exclusion Act prohibited those of Chinese descent from becoming US citizens and, in turn, being eligible to vote. This restriction lasted until 1943. Mabel Ping-Hua Lee is but one of many Chinese women across the United States who recognized that the promise of universal suffrage embedded in the Nineteenth Amendment still excluded large swaths of women.

To Vote or Not to Vote

One of the major challenges associated with group identity is the assumption that individual group members share a common view of citizenship and freedom. While members of the NWSA pushed universal suffrage as the key means for advancing women's interests, others saw the pursuit of voting as an undesirable challenge to their social standing and well-being. Opposition to women's suffrage varied across markers of geography, class, and race. Anti-suffragists in the South, for example, "were generally planter class, [whose] resistance was also tied more explicitly to worries about disruption of the racial order."[5] Some feared that promoting universal suffrage would erase racial hierarchies and place white women on equal footing with women of color (McConnaughy 2013). Others saw the push for full citizenship as a challenge to traditional gender roles, which promoted business and public affairs as the domain of men and the home and community as the domain of women.

Members of the National Association Opposed to Women's Suffrage believed that politics was corrupt and dishonest. Their opposition rested on a desire to protect women from being exploited and to refocus their attention on acts of charity within their local communities. It distributed pamphlets to women across the country that combined household hints for stain removal and food preparation with reasons to oppose women's suffrage. Guided by the belief that "Votes of Women can accomplish no more than votes of Men. Why waste time, energy, and money without results," anti-suffragists penned op-eds, raised money for candidates who opposed suffrage, and generally declared universal citizenship a threat to the sanctity of the home (Dodge 1915). This tension between voting as central to freedom versus a luxury significantly slowed the pace of increasing electoral participation based on gender identity. Over time, however, women have emerged as one of the most consistent voting blocs in US elections.

BOX 6.3 The 2017 Alabama Senate race and intersectional voting

"Black women saved America."

Those words peppered post-election analysis of the highly contested 2017 Alabama Senate race. It also sparked the praise of the chair of the Democratic National Committee, Tom Perez, who credited the record-breaking voter turnout of Black women in what was initially expected to be an obscure race. The election was held to fill the US Senate seat vacated by Jeff Sessions, who had been appointed US Attorney General. The special election pitted former Alabama Supreme Court Justice Roy Moore against former US Attorney for Alabama Doug Jones. What some thought would be an obscure race captured national interest and became a litmus test for the boundaries of contesting discrimination. The campaign was clouded by allegations of anti-Semitism, racism and sexual misconduct. As more women came forward alleging that Moore had assaulted them, and as remarks by Moore and his wife promoted stereotypes about Jews, it became increasingly clear that the Republican hold over the state was no longer secure.

Efforts by organizations such as the Black Women's Roundtable to mobilize voters at the grassroots focused on increasing voter registration and turnout among Black women regardless of their income and class status. Black voters comprise a sizeable share of the population across most Alabama counties and have a long history of battling for voter rights. The state was the site of bloody protests over the right of African Americans and other groups to exercise their constitutionally protected right to vote. However, felon disenfranchisement laws prohibit one in thirteen Black Alabamians from voting.

Black women's turnout in the 2017 Alabama special election topped that of all demographic groups across the markers of race, gender, and education. Black women cast 98 percent of their ballots for Doug Jones, in comparison with 35 percent of white women and 93 percent of Black men.

The Intersectional Gender Gap

Political scientists use the term *gender gap* to capture the persistent differences between men and women in reference to voting behavior, partisanship, policy preferences, political opportunities, and political ambitions.[6] However, it is most commonly used to reflect differences in voter turnout between men and women while studying the underlying causes of this difference. Today, women comprise slightly more than half of the voting-age population in the United States but have exceeded the vote share of men in *every* presidential election since 1980 (CAWP 2017). The data represented in figure 6.2 show how the number of women voters has exceeded the number of men voters in every presidential election since 1964.

Women vote more often and in greater proportion to their share of the population than men at every level of government. The gender gap is particularly pronounced within and across communities defined by racial and ethnic identity. As table 6.4 illustrates, the widest gender gap in voting rests within Black communities, and there is a growing gender gap among the Hispanic electorate. Asian and Pacific Islander voters exhibit the greatest gender parity, while the gap across white communities remains fairly consistent. A recent study by Ansolabehere and Hersh (2013) found that African American women not only vote in higher proportions but also register at a higher rate than

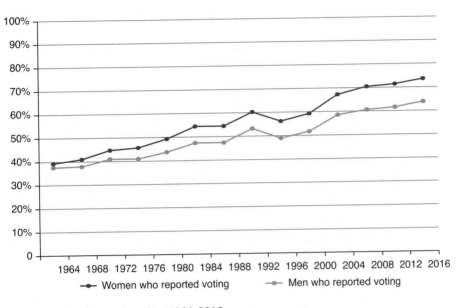

Figure 6.2 Gender gap in voting, 1964–2016
SOURCE: CAWP (2017).

Table 6.4 Gaps in registration and voting based on gender, race, and citizenship, 2008

	Male (%)	Female (%)
Citizen registration		
White	86.2	89.1
Black	75.1	90.9
Hispanic	67.4	81.4
Asian	50.7	52.6
Voting among registrants		
White	70.9	72.7
Black	61.0	69.0
Hispanic	59.0	64.3
Asian	61.0	64.1
Voting among citizens		
White	61.1	64.7
Black	45.9	62.7
Hispanic	39.8	52.3
Asian	30.9	33.8

SOURCE: Based on data from Ansolabehere and Hersh (2013).

white males, even after controlling for demographic factors such as age, income, and urbanicity.

Much of this intersectional variation results from structural barriers such as the existence of felon disenfranchisement laws that bar individuals with a felony conviction from voting in certain states. The most severe restrictions exist in states with larger concentrations of communities of color, such as Mississippi, Virginia, Florida, Louisiana, and Kentucky. The disproportionate share of men of color involved with the criminal justice system in these states heightens the legal challenges to voter participation; it may also foster a sense of concentrated punishment in communities with excessive rates of surveillance, incarceration, and disenfranchisement. The generational consequences of depressed civic engagement across intersecting identities are magnified by other socio-economic indicators, such as income, residential mobility, education, and political efficacy. The intersectional gender gap holds important electoral consequences (Hardy-Fanta et al. 2016; Carroll and Fox 2018).

Not Yet Just, Not Yet Free

In 1968, Shirley Chisholm entered the hallowed halls of the United States Congress as the first Black woman elected in its 192-year history. Her election came nearly 100 years after the first African American man, Hiram Revels of Mississippi, was elected to the US Senate and four years after Patsy Mink of Hawaii was elected the first woman of color to serve in Congress. Chisholm reached another milestone in 1972 when she became the first African American to seek a major party nomination to run for the presidency. Chisholm was a woman, Black, the daughter of immigrants, and had been elected to represent economically depressed communities largely overlooked by mainstream society. In reflecting on her accomplishments, she remarked:

> I was the first American citizen to be elected to Congress in spite of the double drawback of being female and having skin darkened by melanin. When you put it that way it sounds like a foolish reason for fame. In a just and free society it would be foolish. That I am a national figure because I was the first person in 192 years to be at once a congressman, black, and a woman proves, I think, that our society is not yet either just or free. (Chisholm 1970)

Table 6.5 illustrates just how much has changed in the fifty years since Chisholm's election. Americans have elected over seventy women of color to Congress, including four to the Senate. Forty-one women have been elected as governors, and far more have captured city halls in communities as diverse as Compton, Omaha, Dallas, Newark, Denver, and New Haven. In 2009 Sonia Sotamayor became the first Latinx Supreme Court Justice, and in 2017 six trans

Table 6.5 Number of women of color who have served in Congress, 1965–2019

African American	45
Hispanic/Latina	14
Asian and Pacific Islander	13
American Indian	2

SOURCE: Based on data from the United States House of Representatives, History, Art, and Archives.

activists won elections for state legislatures, school boards, and city councils. In 2018, Christine Hallquist ran for governor of New Hampshire as the first openly trans candidate in US history, while Arizona's Kyrsten Sinema become the first openly bisexual member of the Senate. The first two American Indian women entered Congress in 2019 and challenged the traditional gendered and partisan profiles of Indian representation. Likewise, the number of South Asian women running for office in diverse districts grew exponentially. The significance of these historic milestones indicates the persistence of political underrepresentation based on gender and sexual identity.

Tables 6.6 and 6.7 use data from Gallup Daily Tracking to show that the percentage of Americans who self-identify as LGBT increased from 3.5 percent in 2012 to 4.1 percent in 2017. However, less than 0.1 percent of elected officials identify as such. Similarly, men comprise 49 percent of the total US population and 71 percent of elected office-holders. Even though the percentage of women of color in the total population (24 percent) is only slightly higher than that of men of color (23 percent), those women vote in significantly higher proportions. Yet women of color comprise just 4 percent of all elected officials. Social class and education level can also be significant barriers to successful candidacies. As money continues to flood into US elections, the gap between class profiles of candidates and the voters who choose them widens

Table 6.6 Percentage of US adults identifying as LGBT by gender and race/ethnicity, 2012–2017

	2012	2013	2014	2015	2016	2017
Gender						
Male	3.4	3.5	3.6	3.7	3.7	3.9
Female	3.5	3.6	3.9	4.1	4.4	5.1
Race/ethnicity						
White (non-Hispanic)	3.2	3.3	3.4	3.5	3.6	4.0
Black (non-Hispanic)	4.4	4.0	4.6	4.5	4.6	5.0
Hispanic	4.3	4.7	4.9	5.1	5.4	6.1
Asian (non-Hispanic)	3.5	3.3	4.2	4.9	4.9	4.9

SOURCE: Based on data from Gallup Daily Tracking, 2018.

Table 6.7 Percentage of US adults identifying as LGBT by annual household income and educational attainment, 2012–2017

	2012	2013	2014	2015	2016	2017
Less than $36,000	4.7	4.5	4.9	5.1	5.5	6.2
$36,000 to <$90,000	3.1	3.4	3.5	3.9	4.0	4.7
$90,000 or more	3.0	3.5	3.6	3.6	3.7	3.9
High school or less	3.5	3.5	3.9	4.1	4.1	4.5
Some college	3.8	3.9	3.9	3.9	4.1	4.7
College graduate	2.9	3.3	3.5	3.6	4.1	4.4
Postgraduate	3.3	3.6	3.7	3.9	3.9	4.3

SOURCE: Based on data from Gallup Daily Tracking, 2018.

(Ladson-Billings 2006). The median wealth of members of Congress is approximately $1 million, while the median household income for Latino families is $13,000 per year. Even as observers tout the burgeoning political profile of diverse candidates at all levels of government, these stark differences in the profiles of elected officials and the citizens they serve highlight the myriad ways identity matters at every level of political engagement.

Substantive representation addresses the question of whether the composition of voters and elected officials shapes the resulting votes and policy preferences of those in power (Fenno 1978; Swain 1993; Brown 2014; Dittmar et al. 2018). Cultural critic Ta-Nehisi Coates (2015) notes that, in the same electoral season that sent the Obamas to the White House, California voters approved a controversial measure to deny legally protected marriage rights to same-sex couples. Converting numerical strength into electoral power has been a persistent challenge for underrepresented groups. Yet, beyond elections, organizing around gender and sexual identity raises important critiques regarding leadership and representation.

Regulating Intimacy

States play a key role in moderating the relationship between political inclusion and identities of gender and sexuality. For example, nearly every state had provisions that criminalized sodomy. Although the wording of the laws made this form of intimacy illegal regardless of gender and sexual identity, men who engaged in same-sex intimacy were frequently targeted. This was meant to embarrass gay men, who were viewed as violating socially constructed norms of masculinity, and to brand them as "perverts" who posed a threat to public safety (Sherrill and Yang 2000). In turn, key institutions of government stigmatized the identity of gay men and treated them as social pariahs.

In 1950, Harry Hay created the Mattachine Society as one of the country's first gay rights organizations. The Mattachine focused exclusively on affirming and protecting the rights of gay men by fighting against discriminatory laws. Members harnessed their resources to help identify supportive businesses, track raids and legislative changes, and provide access to social welfare services. The formation of the Mattachine Society helped launch concerted political efforts to demand inclusion and to draw attention to a web of state and local policies that limited access to universal freedom based on identity.

Gender, Sexual Identity, and Civil Liberties Protections

The Fourteenth Amendment grants equal protection under the law. However, federalism allows states to craft laws under the guise of criminalizing behaviors rather than targeting groups. Civil liberty is defined as the legally protected freedom to act or not to act, whether that be the choice of marriage partner, the decision over whether to bear or beget a child, or the ability to name a guardian for one's child. Courts have consistently reviewed cases that question whether state-level interventions increase opportunities to discriminate against identity groups thought to violate social norms. Central to those evaluations have been efforts to define the boundary between self-determination and government interference. Thus, in regulating intimacy, government institutions and actors also define the limits of group inclusion.

The Third, Fourth, Eighth, and Ninth Amendments create an implied right to privacy for citizens to make private choices about their actions, preferences, and affiliations. One of the earliest tests of this right was the 1965 Supreme Court case *Griswold v. Connecticut*. At issue was whether state laws that made it illegal to discuss, encourage, or use contraceptives violated individual rights of privacy. Estelle Griswold, executive director of Planned Parenthood, was arrested for providing information about contraception to married couples. The Court struck down the restrictions on the basis that they violated the fundamental privacy rights of *married* couples, which are "of such a character that [they] cannot be denied without violating those fundamental

---

BOX 6.4 Connecticut statute at issue in *Griswold* v. *Connecticut*

"Any person who uses any drug, medicinal article or instrument for the purpose of preventing conception shall be fined not less than fifty dollars or imprisoned not less than sixty days nor more than one year or be both fined and imprisoned." (General Statutes of Connecticut, Section 53-32, 1958 rev.)

principles of liberty and justice which lie at the base of our civil and political institutions" (381 US 479).

Although the scope of *Griswold* was limited to married heterosexual couples, it helped pave the way for subsequent efforts to protect civil liberties without regard to group identity. In 1972 the Supreme Court extended the right to discuss, possess, and use contraception to unmarried couples (*Eisenstadt v. Baird*). The precedent established by *Griswold* and *Eisenstadt* fueled the 1973 **Roe v. Wade** decision that upheld a woman's right to choose whether to "bear or beget a child." *Roe* was a landmark case because it addressed federalism as the lynchpin for setting the boundaries of individual rights and government's authority to define the universe of choices available to citizens. As with voting qualifications, states retained the right to determine access to abortion. As a result, state rules vary regarding the age of consent, gestational viability, and the location of facilities. The battle between "states' rights" and civil liberties fueled more than forty years of debates over abortion as an arena for political conflict.

In writing the majority opinion for *Roe*, Justice Harry Blackmun observed: "If this suggestion of personhood is established, [Roe's] case, of course, collapses, for the fetus' right to life would then be guaranteed specifically by the [14th] Amendment" (410 US 113). Since that initial ruling, states such as Arkansas, Mississippi, Missouri, and Colorado have considered "personhood amendments" that would establish personhood status from the moment of conception. This designation would make any attempt to prevent birth or to cause injury to an unborn fetus a criminal act. Thus states would be able to criminalize abortion while still upholding the tenets of *Roe* that legalize abortion at the behest of state regulation.

In its 2015 *Young* v. *United Parcel Service* (UPS) decision, the Court ruled on the company's refusal to accommodate a pregnant employee seeking a temporary light duty assignment. The case tested the **1978 Pregnancy Discrimination Act**, which prohibited discrimination in employment and accommodation based on pregnancy, childbirth, or related medical conditions. In this respect, the Act was intended to prevent, and so penalize, sex-based discrimination as a violation of the 1964 Civil Rights Act. Although lower courts ruled that UPS's refusal to reassign Young was gender-neutral, the Supreme Court ruled that, in fact, sex-based discrimination was at play.

Regulating Behavior, Stigmatizing Identity

Although there have been fewer federal statements explicitly limiting rights based on sexual identity, states have played an active role in regulating intimacy and enforcing the boundaries of exclusion. These formal statements help solidify and legitimize informal efforts to police citizenship and freedom. Until 1961, every state criminalized consensual intimacy between same-sex couples. In 1962, Illinois led a small group of states which gradually decriminalized this form of intimacy in spite of broader pressures to adopt stricter provisions. The passage of the Civil Rights Act of 1964 raised hopes that the federal government would outlaw all forms of identity-based discrimination in public accommodations. However, the language of the Act covered sex but not gender and sexual identity. This omission allowed government entities such as the New York Police Department, for example, to organize a specialized investigative unit to surveil and target bars, restaurants, rooming houses, and other spaces where gay men were known to gather. The state made it illegal not to dress in "gender appropriate clothing," to show affection toward members of the same "sex," or to gather socially in large groups based on gender identity.[7]

BOX 6.5 Key provisions of the Civil Rights Act of 1964

The Civil Rights Act of 1964 bars discrimination in employment on the basis of race, color, religion, sex, or national origin. It does not directly address discrimination based on gender identity or sexual orientation.

- Titles II and III: Outlawed discrimination in hotels, motels, restaurants, theaters, and all other public accommodations engaged in interstate commerce; exempted private clubs;
- Title V: Established the Civil Rights Commission;
- Title VI: Authorized withdrawal of federal funds from programs that practiced discrimination;
- Title VII: Outlawed discrimination in employment in any business exceeding twenty-five people and created the Equal Employment Opportunities Commission to review complaints.

Criminalizing various forms of human interaction and expression made city residents especially vulnerable based on their identity. Many New York establishments that catered to marginalized groups were owned by mafia organizations which bribed law-enforcement officials to stay in business. Those locations were still raided and its patrons subject to assault, arrest, and prosecution. This process heightened fears based on sexual identity while further stigmatizing groups already marginalized in society. This tension between incremental state change and localized targeting helped fuel the frustration felt by many who saw the state-sanctioned discrimination as antithetical to American freedom.

Fed up with the continued targeting of gay establishments, and determined to resist discrimination, activists converged on the Stonewall Inn in Greenwich

Village following a routine police raid. The crowds grew as word spread of the confrontation that would become known as the **Stonewall Riots**. No longer willing to accept the targeting or the risks to their well-being, patrons and supporters engaged in six days of violent clashes with the police. In spite of the tremendous physical injuries and property damage, the Stonewall uprising became a pivotal organizing force for LGBTQI members across the United States who sought to transform their stigmatized status and demand full inclusion.

Adjudicating Difference

A handful of states such as Wisconsin passed state ordinances barring discrimination based on gender and sexual identity. However, the lack of a federal statement made many citizens vulnerable to targeted discrimination. One of the most significant cases for highlighting this tension was the 1986 Supreme Court ruling in *Bowers* v. *Hardwick*. The case challenged whether Georgia's ban on sodomy violated the rights of gay adults to engage in consensual private acts. The Georgia law criminalized consensual sodomy for all couples regardless of their sexual identity. However, law-enforcement officers most often enforced the ban against homosexual couples (Stein 2012). The defendant, Michael Hardwick, was charged with violating the statute after a police officer entered a bedroom in a private residence and found him engaged in a consensual act with his partner. The Court ruled against Hardwick, deciding that "no connection between family, marriage, or procreation on the one hand and homosexual activity on the other has been demonstrated" (478 US 186). In essence, the Court decided that the right to engage in private intimate acts was constitutionally protected only for heterosexual couples who fit traditional notions of marriage and the ability to procreate. The *Bowers* decision emboldened state efforts to criminalize same-sex intimacy and, in turn, diminish the citizenship standing of LGBTQI members. The ruling remained until 2003, when the Court struck down a Texas "Homosexual Conduct" statute that determined a Texan commits a criminal offense "if he engages in deviate sexual intercourse with another individual of the same sex." The ruling in *Lawrence* v. *Texas* helped invalidate state provisions that differentiated between acts of intimacy based on the gender identity of those involved. Further, it established the principle that the right to engage in consensual private acts should not be bound by gender and sexual identity.

Military Service and the Pursuit of Full Citizenship

For many identity groups, military service has been a key means of proving allegiance to the United States and pursuing full membership in the polity. For Irish immigrants facing discrimination and crippling stereotypes, military service, whether voluntary or conscripted, helped emphasize "Americanness" and challenged the outsider status of immigrants. President Truman's Executive Order 9981 integrated the armed forces by prohibiting discrimination based on "race, color, religion or national origin." The timing of the order was critical given the increased number of Black and Latino youth serving in the military. Rather than erasing group distinctions, military service actually deepened government-sanctioned discrimination via disparate treatment, harsher punishments for minor infractions, discriminatory assignments, and neglected opportunities post-discharge (Parker 2009). A number of veterans, such as Jimmie Lee Jackson of Alabama, expressed their frustration that they were sent to fight for democracy abroad, only to return home and be reminded that they were still not viewed as citizens. In regard to gendered and sexual identity, military service has helped reinforce key barriers to full inclusion.

Challenging Exclusion

The US military explicitly barred gay, lesbian, and bisexual personnel based on the belief that they undermined trust and effectiveness.[8] Those who did serve were forced either to lie about or to reject their identity. Leonard Matlovich was a Vietnam veteran who earned both a Purple Heart and a Bronze Star for his service. In 1975 he submitted a letter to his superiors that read:

> After some years of uncertainty, I have arrived at the conclusion that my sexual preferences are homosexual asposed [sic] to heterosexual. I have also concluded that my sexual preferences will in no way interfer [sic] with my Air Force duties, as my preferences are now open. It is therefore requested that those provisions in AFM 39-12 relating to the discharge of homosexuals be waived in my case. (Hippler 1989)

Matlovich outed himself to his superiors because he believed his outstanding military record could directly challenge the belief that gender identity was a divisive force that weakened national security. He planned to stay in the military and continue to serve his country. By proving that one could be both gay and a decorated staff sergeant, he thought military leaders would change their views and modify the exclusionary policy. Matlovich was dishonorably discharged, and the constitutional question of gender identity and military service was never addressed. Instead, as a concession, the Air Force offered him compensatory damages and an honorable discharge. Leonard Matlovich died in 1988 and chose to have his tombstone inscribed with "A Gay Vietnam Veteran. When I was in the military they gave me a medal for killing two men and a discharge for loving one."

Leonard Matlovich was a Vietnam veteran who was dishonorably discharged for being gay. The etching on his headstone highlights his fight against military policies that prohibited LGBTQ service members.

Compromising on Exclusion

As table 6.8 shows, 58 percent of Americans support allowing gays and lesbians to serve in the US military. That level of support is significantly lower for older Americans, white Evangelicals, and Republicans. This variation holds important consequences that shape the electoral strategies of parties and candidates. In 1980, members of the Democratic National Convention adopted a resolution that "All groups must be protected from discrimination based on race, color, religion, national origin, language, age, sex or sexual orientation."[9] Although the official bylaws and platform expressed a commitment to gender equality, landslide losses in subsequent elections prompted some party leaders to organize around a different set of interests. The Democratic Leadership Council (DLC) emerged as a concerted effort to move the party closer to centrist positions on issues such as welfare reform, capitalism, and being tough on crime. The logic was simple: in order to win elections, the party needed to court groups of voters it hadn't already captured. One of the key leaders of the DLC was the governor of Arkansas, Bill Clinton, who in 1992 was elected president of the United States.

In 1994 President Clinton signed into law **Don't Ask, Don't Tell** (DADT), which allowed lesbian, gay, and bisexual personnel to serve in the military

Table 6.8 Support for gay and lesbian military service (percentages)

	Favor	Oppose
Total	58	27
White, non-Hispanic	60	26
Black, non-Hispanic	53	39
18–29	68	21
30–49	56	29
50–64	61	27
65+	44	28
College graduate plus	67	19
Some college	55	30
High school graduate or less	54	30
Republican	40	44
Democrat	70	18
Independent	62	23
Protestant	49	34
White evangelical	34	48
Black Protestant	52	29
Catholic	63	21
Unaffiliated	71	17
Attend services:		
Weekly or more	40	40
Monthly or yearly	66	20
Seldom or never	71	19

Source: Based on data from Pew Research Center (2010).

as long as they didn't disclose their sexual identity. Clinton saw it as a compromise between gay rights activists demanding full inclusion and members of the Joint Chiefs of Staff, who vehemently defended the need to restrict service. Even with the adoption of DADT, some service members were still surveilled and questioned about their associations or denied promotions based on assumptions about their sexual identity (Robinson 2017). Some activists considered the directive as a moral compromise, while others viewed it as an important incremental step toward universal inclusion.

Two years after Don't Ask, Don't Tell, President Clinton signed the federal **Defense of Marriage Act** (DOMA), which defined marriage as being between one man and one woman and mirrored state-level provisions that recognized only heterosexual unions. By creating a federal definition of marriage, DOMA allowed states to refuse to recognize same-sex marriages that occurred in other states. It also meant that same-sex couples were not entitled to the same type of survivor benefits, health-care coverage, tax breaks, and child-care exemptions as heterosexual couples. A number of states adopted stringent laws that rejected same-sex couples' efforts to adopt children, serve as medical executors, or access private records. Federalism shaped the level of access that same-sex couples had to various features of private and public life by determining whether to permit and recognize marriage equality.

Three Steps Forward, Three Steps Back

For nearly two decades, Don't Ask, Don't Tell and the Defense of Marriage Act weakened citizenship standing based on gender and sexual identity. In 2010, President Barack Obama signed a repeal of Don't Ask, Don't Tell. By this time, over 14,000 US service members had been ousted from the military after being outed as gay, lesbian, or bisexual. In 2015, the Supreme Court struck down the Defense of Marriage Act. Although the Court's ruling in *Obergefell* v. *Hodges* invalidated state-level restrictions on marriage equality based on gender and sexual identity, a number of state officials refused to comply, alleging that it violated their personal beliefs. This tension between federal commands and state compliance reflects a longstanding challenge to the full realization of freedom in the United States based on federalism.

A year after *Obergefell*, the Obama administration announced that the lifelong ban on transgender military service would be lifted beginning in 2017. The move was short-lived, as his successor, President Donald J. Trump, announced his intention to rescind the ban based on the cost of providing health-care benefits to trans people. The move to reverse trans military inclusion has been slowed by a number of pending court decisions. However, challenges to inclusion based on identity remain a persistent concern. For example, the Justice Department filed an amicus brief in 2017 arguing that the Civil Rights Act of 1964 does not protect gay and bisexual workers and, therefore, that firing an employee based on sexual identity should be legal.[10] The Justice Department's views on exclusion based on gender and sexual identity hold increasing significance as various states battle over issues related to equity in health care, primary education, employment opportunities, and civil rights protections based on trans identity.[11]

Identity and Intersectional Feminism

In 1966, a group of men and women convened in Washington, DC, to form the National Organization for Women (NOW). It adopted as its mission the belief that:

Former California Attorney General Kamala Harris was elected to the US Senate in 2016, becoming the second woman of African American and second woman of Asian American descent to serve. She appears here at a rally for health-care coverage.

> We, men and women who hereby constitute ourselves as the National Organization for Women, believe that the time has come for a new movement toward true equality for all women in America, and toward a fully equal partnership of the sexes, as part of the world-wide revolution of human rights now taking place within and beyond our national borders.
>
> . . .
>
> NOW is dedicated to the proposition that women, first and foremost, are human beings, who, like all other people in our society, must have the chance to develop their fullest human potential. We believe that women can achieve such equality only by accepting to the full the challenges and responsibilities they share with all other people in our society, as part of the decision-making mainstream of American political, economic and social life.[12]

NOW positioned itself as an organization dedicated to promoting the full incorporation of women by enhancing civil rights protections. Critics took issue with the lack of diversity among the group's leadership and alleged that it weakened the stated goal of inclusion. One notable exception was Dr Pauli Murray, who was rejected from Harvard Law School because of her gender. Murray went on to become the first African American to receive a JD from Yale Law School and dedicated much of her life to pursuing full inclusion for all women. She believed it was necessary to create a "NAACP for women" to pursue a multi-pronged attack on discrimination. The lack of diversity within NOW's leadership as well as the broader Women's movement prompted key critiques of its ability to advocate effectively on behalf of all women.

To challenge the multiple ways in which discrimination weakened the standing of women, the **Combahee River Collective** released a statement in 1974. The collective, named after a raid in Combahee, South Carolina, in 1853 that freed 300 enslaved Africans, was comprised of Black queer women who worked to advance the standing of marginalized women across a range of identities. The Combahee raid, led by Harriet Tubman, was a deliberate calling for Black women to lead movements for freedom and liberation. For the collective, heeding that call meant resisting discrimination based on race, class, gender and sexual identity, and ability. Its founders believed that any credible effort to address sex discrimination had to do so in the context of multiple overlapping identities that fuel group standing and exclusion. Their statement reads:

> We are a collective of Black feminists who have been meeting together since 1974. During that time we have been involved in the process of defining and clarifying our politics, while at the same time doing political work within our own group and in coalition with other progressive organizations and movements. The most general statement of our politics at the present time would be that we are actively committed to struggling against racial, sexual, heterosexual, and class oppression, and see as our particular task the development of integrated analysis and practice based upon the fact that the major systems of oppression are interlocking. The synthesis of these oppressions creates the conditions of our lives. As Black women we see Black feminism as the logical political movement to combat the manifold and simultaneous oppressions that all women of color face.

BOX 6.6 Two Spirit identity

The National Council of American Indians (NCAI) is the oldest and largest advocacy organization for American Indian and Alaska Native communities in North America. For over eighty years it has addressed the delicate balance between affirming sovereignty and demanding that Indian peoples not be denied access to and the protections of various laws governing the country as a whole. It promotes economic development, tribal governance, and the overall health and well-being of its member nations.

Two Spirit is a "contemporary umbrella term that refers to the historical and current First Nations people whose individual spirits were a blend of female and male spirits. This term has been reclaimed by Native American LGBT communities in order to honor their heritage and provide an alternative to the Western labels of gay, lesbian, or transgender."[13] In 2016, the NCAI issued a statement calling for increased attention to and support for Two Spirit people across the country. It reads:

> NOW THEREFORE BE IT RESOLVED, that the National Council of American Indians does hereby establish a Two Spirit Task Force to assist in the coordination, collaboration, and outreach to Indian Country on Two Spirit issues; and to develop and share approaches and solutions to policy issues that affect Two Spirit/ LGBTQ community members in a manner consistent with the Indian self-determination.

Affirming gender and sexual fluidity within Indian communities helps address the disproportionate rates of physical and sexual violence, disease contraction rates, and mental health access for groups who are often underserved as a result of stigma.

NCAI and its allies developed the Two Spirit Task Force based on the belief that any effort to protect sovereignty and self-determination had to directly address the myriad factors affecting disparities in access to justice, health, housing, employment, and safety. For example, 65 percent of Two Spirit people report having been harassed, assaulted, or bullied based on their gender identity. The Task Force placed a particular emphasis on the experiences of young people and the need for inclusion as a public health concern as well as a moral imperative.

The statement addressed challenges between groups and addressed the tensions created *within* communities by traditional notions of feminism. Positioning women's liberation as intimately tied to universal freedom was a direct rebuke of the breakdown of the earlier coalition between abolitionists and suffragists and the resulting centuries of mistrust that had built between white women and women of color. Recognizing these tensions, writer Alice Walker penned the term **womanism** to explicitly reference the meaning of feminism and freedom for women of color who exist in spaces marked by multiple interlocking forms of oppression (hooks 1981). This backdrop of historical tensions based on definition, access, and membership provides the context for current struggles to mobilize around gender and sexual identity.

Conclusion: Gender and Sexual Identity as Intersectional Constructions

The political salience of gender and sexual identity rests on socially constructed notions of worth and belonging rather than biologically determined attributes. From the earliest efforts to restrict the citizenship rights of women, to contemporary movements designed to combat sexual violence across a range of identities, groups have upheld their power by blocking the path to universal freedom. The last decade has given rise to a diverse and expanding cadre of political candidates who seek to challenge the longstanding under-representation of their communities of interests. These candidates affirm the need to evaluate differences in political standing that exist between and within groups. While the bulk of women running for public office do so as Democrats, an emerging class of Republican lawmakers is rejecting the monolithic view of "women's interests."

Following the 2016 presidential election, women organized at the grassroots level and within traditional political structures to express their discontent. The 2017–18 election gave rise to a record number of people from underrep-resented identity groups running for political office. For example, Christine Hallquist made history as the first openly transgender candidate, while Stacey Abrams entered as the first African American woman to run for governor of a US state. Colorado voters elected Jared Polis as the nation's first openly gay governor as a record 150 LGBTQI candidates captured elected office. Rashida Tlaib of Michigan and Ilhan Omar of Minnesota became the first Muslim women elected to Congress.

Beyond these electoral gains, a host of policies and promises illuminated the longstanding challenges groups face in gaining full inclusion in the polity. In some instances, our evolving understanding of gender and sexual identity prompts increased efforts to align law and public policy. In others, socially constructed notions of masculinity and gender roles have fueled efforts to rescind or restrict access to universal freedom and equality. Gender and sexual identity are necessarily and inherently intersectional.

Controversy box: Separate but (un)equal: do gender specific organizations undermine gender equality?

The Greek system remains an important staple of student life on many college campuses. Members believe that fraternities and sororities promote student engagement and leadership, build community, and bind students to longstanding traditions. Over the years a number of high-profile hazing deaths following initiation ceremonies, allegations of sexual assault, and complaints of excessive drinking have led many colleges and universities to reconsider the presence of single-gender organizations.

In 2014, Wesleyan University President Michael Roth issued an order that Greek organizations with on-campus housing would be required to become co-ed within three years. The edict shocked members of the school's three fraternities with on-campus facilities. Although the requirement was meant to promote gender equality, fraternity members believed it actually discriminated against them, as no sororities had on-campus housing and, in turn, weren't required to integrate. Others questioned the fairness of the university demanding a reversal of the organizations' long history of existence as fraternal bodies meant only for men. For example, Delta Kappa Epsilon was founded at Yale University in 1844 and counts among its notable alumni members financier J. P. Morgan and former presidents Theodore Roosevelt, George W. Bush, and George H. W. Bush.

While acknowledging this history, Wesleyan joined other institutions of higher education such as Trinity College and Harvard University in barring single-gender organizations that promote exclusion rather than inclusion. Roth wrote a blog post detailing his position:

> The presence of single-sex fraternities raises questions about our commitment to gender equity. And although it is obvious that not all sexual assaults happen in fraternities, there are strong questions raised about fraternity culture and what researchers call "proclivity" to discrimination and violence. While the fraternities have made it clear that they wish to be part of the solution, it's also clear that many students see fraternity houses as spaces where women enter with a different status than in any other building on campus, sometimes with terrible consequences. (Roth 2014)

Some see the demand to go co-ed as punishing women and non-binary conforming students, who may view single-gender organizations as a source of encouragement and refuge on campuses that often feel hostile to their interests. A joint statement issued by Harvard sororities Kappa Alpha Theta, Alpha Phi, and Delta Gamma defends their existence: "While Harvard's sanctions claim to support women's right to make their own decisions, these sanctions actually force women to choose between the opportunity to have supportive, empowering women-only spaces and external leadership opportunities" (Kahangi 2018).

You decide. Do single-gender fraternities and sororities promote gender inequality? And, if so, should colleges and universities recognize only co-ed student groups?

Questions for Debate

- A number of states have introduced referenda to define "sex" based on the identity that appears on a person's birth certificate and to restrict access to public restrooms based on this designation. Advocates argue the provisions purposely discriminate against trans residents, while others see it as a way of protecting public safety. Should states be able to determine sexual identity and limit access accordingly?

- Feminism is based on the belief in equality between the sexes. In practice, feminism has been an ideology that bound together women committed to fighting for equality in various sectors of public life. Can men be feminists?
- The Civil Rights Act of 1964 prohibits discrimination in employment and public accommodations on the basis of race, color, religion, sex, or national origin. Should the Act be amended to include gender and sexual identity?

Key Terms

- Religious Freedom Restoration Act
- Don't Ask, Don't Tell
- gender identity
- Nineteenth Amendment
- sexual identity
- Civil Rights Act of 1964
- Executive Order 13672
- womanism
- substantive representation
- *Griswold* v. *Connecticut*
- Employment Non-Discrimination Act
- Defense of Marriage Act
- Seneca Falls Convention
- *Obergefell* v. *Hodges*

7

Religious Identity and Political Presence

The Question Is: What Do You Believe?

Emmy Award-winning director Amardeep Kaleka seems like an unlikely candidate for national political office. Kaleka was born in India and later moved with his family to a Milwaukee neighborhood nicknamed "Little Beirut" because of its extreme poverty and random acts of violence. He built a successful company documenting American life after receiving a Master's in Fine Arts from the Savannah College of Art and Design. Just as Kaleka's career in entertainment began to take off, in 2014 a tragic crime prompted him to launch a bid for the House of Representatives. His platform focused on promoting responsible gun ownership and protecting the civil rights of all Americans.[1]

Amardeep's father, Satwant Singh Kaleka, and five other Americans were killed during a violent rampage in Wisconsin on August 5, 2012. The elder Kaleka risked his life to protect those around him, using a fruit knife against a gun-wielding attacker so that others could flee and take cover. In the aftermath of the shooting, analysts speculated that Wade Michael Page stormed the Oak Creek **gurdwara** because of his extreme white supremacist beliefs and disdain for Muslims (Umhoefer and Barton 2012). However, Kaleka and his fellow Oak Creek parishioners were Sikh, not Muslim.

According to data from the Pew Research Center (Rosentiel 2012), an estimated 500,000 Sikhs live in the United States, and there are nearly 25 million worldwide. Sikhism is the fifth largest religion in the world and focuses on principles of equality and service to others. Most Sikh men have long beards and wear turbans, which often cause them to be mistaken for Arabs and Muslims. This confusion has led to a sharp increase in violent attacks against Sikhs since the terrorist attacks on September 11, 2001.[2] Columbia University Professor Prabhjot Singh, who was brutally beaten in New York City, offers the following:

> Indeed, the first documented race riot targeting American Sikhs occurred in 1907 in Bellingham, Wash. Their distinct religious identity (uncut hair, turban, beard) has historically marked Sikhs, particularly men, as targets for discrimination, both in their homeland in South Asia and in the various communities of the Sikh diaspora. And of course, 9/11

Supporters gather for a prayer vigil following the shooting of Sikh parishioners at the Oak Creek gurdwara in Wisconsin.

brought about a surge in fear and persecution directed at Sikhs, Muslims and other minorities with ties to the Middle East and South Asia.[3]

Whether Satwant Kaleka was killed because he was mistaken for Muslim or because Page hated non-Christians will never be known (Michaelis and Kaleka 2018). Some Sikh activists, such as Valarie Kaur, argue it doesn't really matter, because "It seems to make very little difference if the brown, bearded man with the turban calls himself a Sikh and not a Muslim because they read us as un-American" (Parvini 2017). What is clear is that the motive behind the Oak Creek massacre was hatred based on religious identity. Throughout US history, religious identity has been used as a proxy for American identity and the protections of citizenship.

Amardeep Kaleka lost his quest to become a member of Congress. However, the death of his father, coupled with increased xenophobia in his father's adopted country, reinforced his commitment to making the United States safer for everyone. He and his brother Pardeep penned an essay, "The American Dream," to condemn religious intolerance as antithetical to the very principles that make America, America:

> Our Father flew an American flag in front of his house until the day he died. You really can't say that about many people. He was definitely a custom classic that they don't make anymore.
>
> My Father exemplified a good man, a strong husband, and a loving father – he was truly an American hero – a custom classic that they don't make anymore.

My immigrant father carried the American Dream on his back, and ultimately died, when his dream was fulfilled. The lunatic who murdered him and festered a nightmare was a "white supremacist" – he believed that people like my father do not belong in this country.

The question is: What do you believe?

Next time you speak about immigration, please remember the story of my father: Satwant Singh Kaleka. (Kaleka and Kaleka 2013)

Religious Identity in the United States: The Context

Religion represents a collective belief system that defines our relationship to some divine being or beings. Some people are encouraged to embrace certain religious beliefs from birth while others develop their belief system as they mature. Religious belief is not static, nor is it uniform. Table 7.1 captures the major religious traditions in the United States. It's important to note, however, that, even when people share a common label (e.g. Buddhist, Evangelical, or **Protestant**), the components of that label may vary across other identities, such as sect, geography, gender, and age. Similarly, the lack of belief in a

Table 7.1 Major religious traditions in the United States

Christian traditions (70.7%)	*Percentage of the population who identify*
Evangelical Protestant	25.4
Mainline Protestant	14.7
Historically Black Protestant	6.5
Catholic	20.8
Mormon	1.6
Orthodox Christian	0.5
Jehovah's Witness	0.8
Other Christian groups	0.4
Non-Christian traditions (6%)	*Percentage of the population who identify*
Jewish	1.9
Muslim	0.9
Buddhist	0.7
Hindu	0.7
Other world religions	0.3
Other faiths	1.5
Unaffiliated (23.3%)	*Percentage of the population who identify*
Atheist	3.1
Agnostic	4.0
Don't know	16.2

SOURCE: Based on data from the Pew Research Center (2016).

religious system is not fixed, as how people conceive of their individual power and relationship to the universe varies.

In contrast to religion as simply a belief system, *religious identity* captures the socially constructed norms, conditions, expectations, and boundaries for how we practice our beliefs and respond to the beliefs and practices of others (Grzymala-Busse 2012; Omelicheva and Ahmed 2017; Harris 2001; Wald and Calhoun-Brown 2010). The impact of religion as a social identity is broader than what scholars call **religiosity**. *Religiosity* reflects one's relationship to formal religious institutions, one's frequency of attendance, and the overall importance of religion in one's daily life. In contrast, religious identity helps define the boundaries of belonging and, in turn, opportunities to pursue or deny full democratic inclusion. Religious identity isn't formed in a vacuum. It is necessarily a response to the structure of opportunities for expression and the confluence of laws and policies that protect both the right to believe or not believe and our reaction to perceived challenges to those beliefs. Religious identity is inherently intersectional. For example, the meaning of identifying as Catholic for Hispanic communities in the Southwest may differ from that of those living in the Northeast. In addition, the legal and social barriers to expressing this identity is contextual. This is particularly true when we consider how religious identity maps onto political preferences.

I offer here an important caveat. It is impossible to express a group's religious identity unless there are beliefs and values that form the basis for that expression. I concede that the two are inextricably linked. However, I also note that the protections of the First Amendment to the Constitution focus not on the *content* of our beliefs but on the way we express them.

Beliefs versus Practices

The distinction between beliefs and practices was affirmed by the Supreme Court's decision concerning *Reynolds* v. *United States* in 1879. At issue was whether it was unconstitutional to punish members of the Church of Jesus Christ of Latter-Day Saints who were married to more than one wife, even though plural marriage was a fundamental belief for many Mormons at the time. George Reynolds protested his arrest under the **Morrill Anti-Bigamy Act**, a federal provision initiated to directly address the marriage practices of the Mormon faith. Reynolds argued that the Act was discriminatory and violated his First Amendment rights to practice key tenets of his faith. The Court ruled against Reynolds on the grounds that, while government could not regulate his right to believe in plural marriage, it had both the right and the obligation to prohibit practices that undermine public safety. Religious belief, then, could not be used as an excuse to break the law: "Can a man excuse his [illegal] practices . . . because of his religious belief? To permit this would be to make the professed doctrines of religious belief superior to the law of the land, and in effect to permit every citizen to become a law unto himself. Government could exist only in name under such circumstances" (98 US 145).

Efforts to curb expressions of religious identity often strike at the heart of civil liberties debates over "the right to be left alone." To some, public responses to religious identity often reflect fear, ignorance, and perceived threat rather than actual harm (Cacciatore et al. 2014). In other instances, government may intervene to protect people from themselves. For example, some Pentecostal adherents see the handling of snakes as the ultimate test of their faith. The practice derives from a biblical scripture that reads: "They shall take up serpents; and if they drink any deadly thing, it shall not hurt them; they shall lay hands on the sick, and they shall recover."[4] All but two states have explicitly banned the possession and handling of venomous snakes during religious services, yet the practice continues.

Although Pentecostals are a sect of evangelical Protestants, snake handling is largely restricted to a small cluster of churches in Kentucky, Virginia, Tennessee, West Virginia, Georgia, and other parts of Appalachia. Serpent handling is most popular in rural, economically depressed areas where religion is viewed as a means to overcome life's challenges. The overlap of religion, class, and race shapes the meaning of religious identity for white Southern Pentecostals defending their right both to believe and to practice snake handling. It also speaks to the challenge of retaining one's faith practice when it doesn't fit with traditional norms: "We're not a cult. We're not freaks. We're Christians."[5]

Believing, Belonging, and Behaving

Religion has been at once a central organizing force and a source of division within many countries. The various components of religious beliefs, coupled with commands to act (e.g. vote, advocate, etc.) on those components, forge an important linkage between religious identity and politics (Margolis 2018; Domke and Coe 2008; Campbell and Monson 2008). Whether that is shaping policy support (e.g. abortion, euthanasia, and capital punishment) or structuring candidate evaluations (e.g. norms about the proper role of women as leaders), religious identity continues to be a key organizing identity for Americans. However, the strength, function, and salience of religious identity varies across faith tradition, geography, generation, racial/ethnic status, and public familiarity.

In this chapter, I begin by sketching the contemporary demographic profile of religious identity in the United States. I highlight how political changes, such as shifting immigration priorities, stimulated religious diversity across the country and, in turn, created new political fault lines. From there, I address how longstanding tensions between religious freedom and government intervention privileges certain identities while stigmatizing others. What does it mean, for example, that some religious communities are excluded from participating in certain features of American life? How do changing levels of adherence to traditional religious views impact public functions such as education? This emphasis on religious identity explores the inherent tension in the Constitution's enshrinement of both a freedom of and freedom from religion.

Many scholars address the unique relationship between religious identity and politics that stretches across multiple identity markers (Lincoln and Mamiya 1990; McDaniel 2008; Harris-Lacewell 2004; Owens 2007; Green et al. 2013; Leal et al. 2016; Dana et al. 2017; Wald and Calhoun-Brown 2018; Campbell et al. 2014). This chapter builds upon that research to explore challenges to (1) citizenship, (2) political representation, and (3) public policy through the intersectional lens of religious identity. Its focus isn't on the content of groups' religious beliefs. Rather, it traces how efforts to combat, and in many instances reinforce, the boundaries of inclusion based on religious identity challenge notions of citizenship and democratic inclusion.

The Myth of Religious Freedom

It may seem odd to a casual observer that a country founded upon religious freedom would contend with such sharp tensions based on religion. However, religious identity has been a key fault line since the founding of the United States. Schools across the country teach students that early settlers came to the New World to escape religious persecution in England. This experience with discrimination, the story goes, fueled the colonists' commitment to creating a new nation where religious freedom would form the cornerstone of development. However, the experience across the various colonies highlighted the deep-seated tensions derived from differences in religious identity. Each of the thirteen colonies had provisions that established an official religion. This variation included the Church of England in Maryland, Virginia, and New York and the Congregational Church in Massachusetts (Davis 2010). Pennsylvania and Rhode Island opted not to adopt an official religion, though exclusions were still placed on certain groups based on their affiliation (Rasor and Bond 2011). As a result, religious identity shaped the experiences of all inhabitants.

Religious Identity as a Barrier to Democracy

The beliefs, norms, values, and behaviors that constitute religious identity shape how we view ourselves and others. This is particularly true when certain groups are perceived to violate our beliefs or challenge our identity. Much like other identity markers, religious identity is forged as both an affirmation of and in opposition to the rights enshrined in our governing documents. Religious identity, even in the context of variation across the colonies and later states, was often used as an indicator for determining which groups were worthy of the full benefits and protections of citizenship. The very narrow definition of desirable identities was inherently built on exclusion. In a number of places, state statutes barred Catholics from holding office while usurping the unique spiritual traditions of Indian tribes. The creation of Indian reservations and boarding schools was intended to force conformity by disregarding Indian autonomy (Prucha 1973). This clash between Christian missionaries who thought they were civilizing barbaric tribes and Indian communities who wanted to retain their centuries-old traditions highlighted the intricate ways "religious freedom" became synonymous with "Christian freedom."

Forcing assimilation by imposing religious beliefs on less desirable groups also drove efforts to strip enslaved Africans of their spiritual traditions, which themselves varied based on the regions of origin of their adherents. Some embraced polytheistic beliefs while others were guided by Islam (McCloud 1995). The diversity of traditions that constituted Christianity were built on a Eurocentric worldview. From symbols, to practices, to methods of worship, this often stood in direct opposition to the syncretic traditions of Africans and the ancestral traditions of Indian tribes. In turn, Christian identity as a prerequisite for inclusion challenged the standing of other groups.

BOX 7.1 Major religious traditions of Islam and Judaism

Islam	Judaism
Sunni	Reform
Shia	Conservative
Nation of Islam	Orthodox
Non-specific	

The Case of Aaron Lopez

Aaron Lopez, born Duarte Lopez, was an affluent merchant from Portugal. He and his family were *conversos* – people who openly practiced Catholicism in public while practicing their Jewish faith secretly in private. The spread of anti-Semitism across Spain and other countries forced many people to denounce their religious identity to survive. Lopez amassed his wealth as a trader and eventually owned over thirty ships.[6] After moving to Newport,

Rhode Island, the family reclaimed their Jewish identity. Lopez changed his name from Duarte to Aaron, began openly practicing his faith, and financed charities that provided aid to Jewish refugees.

In 1761, after having established himself as an astute businessman and community leader, Aaron Lopez applied for American citizenship. His petition and subsequent appeals were denied because of his religious identity and a Rhode Island statute that limited citizenship to Christians: "the free and quiet enjoyment of the Christian religion and a desire of propagating the same were the principal views with which this colony was settled, and by a law made and passed in the year 1663, no person who does not profess the Christian religion can be admitted free [that is, as a voter or office holder] to this colony."[7] The following year, Aaron Lopez and his family moved temporarily to Massachusetts, became naturalized citizens, and then returned to Rhode Island. The newly elected President George Washington responded to the pleas of Newport's Jewish community for full citizenship rights in Rhode Island by writing: "All possess alike liberty of conscience and immunity of citizenship. . . . For happily the Government of the United States, which gives to bigotry no sanction, to persecution no assistance[,] requires only that they who live under its protection should demean themselves as good citizens."[8]

Defining and Protecting Religious Freedom

The Establishment Clause

Religious tension in the form of forced resettlements, enslavement, violence, and the total denial or partial weakening of citizenship threatened to rip apart the fabric of the budding nation. For the Framers, guarding against future tensions caused by state-sanctioned religion became a key motivating force. The First Amendment to the Constitution contains an **Establishment Clause** that prohibits Congress from establishing an official religion or favoring one religion over another. However, the language is intentionally vague as to what it means to establish or favor a religion. A day after the amendment was adopted, members of Congress organized a national day of prayer.

For example, new members of the United States Supreme Court take their oaths of office by swearing on a Bible, while some members of the 116th Congress took their oaths by swearing on a Quran or the Constitution. In times of crisis, presidents close their address to the country with the phrase "God bless the United States," and the words "In God We Trust" appear on the US currency. Article VI prohibits the use of a religious test as a qualification for public office. Yet, to date, the United States has never had an (openly) atheist or agnostic president, and public opinion data show continued skepticism about electing candidates who do not identify as religious (Lipka 2014). This gap, between the principle of religious freedom and the reality of American political development, set in motion centuries of battles to define how religious identity could be used to challenge the power and political standing of others.

The Free Exercise Clause

In addition to the Establishment Clause, the First Amendment contains a Free Exercise Clause that allows citizens to practice their religious beliefs as long as they do not trigger a compelling government interest. The passage of the Patient Protection and Affordable Care Act (ACA) in 2010 required that employment-based health plans include contraceptives in its list of covered items. Although the Act offered exemptions for non-profit institutions and religious employers, it didn't excuse for-profit corporations. The owners of a national craft store chain, Hobby Lobby, sued on the grounds that the Affordable Care Act mandate violated their freedom not to fund procedures, medications, and devices that were inconsistent with their evangelical Christian beliefs. The company defied the ACA and dropped its coverage of the "morning after pill" and other forms of contraception. The federal government sued the company in *Burwell* v. *Hobby Lobby*, based on the question of whether the **Religious Freedom Restoration Act of 1993** (RFRA) protected the rights of a for-profit organization to discriminate against its employees. The original RFRA was signed into law after two American Indian employees of a rehab facility were fired for ingesting peyote. Despite the men's claim

Figure 7.1 Religious freedom laws by state
SOURCE: Griffin (2017).

that peyote was an essential part of practicing their religion, the Court ruled against creating an exemption based on religious belief.[9]

In a split 5–4 decision, the Court ruled that Hobby Lobby's rights had indeed been violated by imposing the coverage provision. In so doing, the door was opened for a number of state-level religious freedom acts that sought to protect individuals and business. As illustrated in figure 7.1, nineteen states have RFRAs. However, most of those new laws have been adopted in response to pressures to conform Christian views to public realities.[10] In 2015, Kim Davis, a clerk in Rowan County, Kentucky, refused to issue marriage licenses to same-sex couples in spite of the Supreme Court's ruling in *Obergefell* v. *Hodges*, which struck down state bans on marriage equality. Davis argued that her religious beliefs did not support same-sex marriage and therefore she shouldn't be compelled to affix her signature to a certificate and grant a tacit endorsement of such marriages. She continues to defend her right of refusal even after a Court ruled against her: "To issue a marriage license which conflicts with God's definition of marriage, with my name affixed to the certificate, would violate my conscience."[11] In 2018, David Ermold sought the Democratic nomination to run against Davis after she denied him a marriage certificate. She was voted out of office that year.

Adjudicating Religious Identity

The question of what constitutes favoring (a) religion by government has spawned a number of important legal cases. In *Engel* v. *Vitale* (1962), the Court struck down a New York provision that started the school day with a nondenominational prayer written by the state. Although supporters argued that the nondenominational prayer did not advance any particular religion, the justices ruled that mandating prayer in public schools violated the separation of church and state (370 US 421). The most definitive ruling was the 1971 *Lemon* v. *Kurtzman* decision. At issue were statutes in Pennsylvania and Rhode Island that used public funds to reimburse the cost of instructional materials and teacher salaries at private schools, including Catholic schools. In evaluating the case, the justices devised a three-pronged test to determine whether a provision violates the Establishment Clause. The **Lemon test** provides that government can assist religion only if:

1 the primary purpose of the assistance is secular,
2 the assistance must neither promote nor inhibit religion, and
3 there is no excessive entanglement between church and state.[12]

In the end the Court struck down the funding statutes on the grounds that using public funds to advance religious education violated at least two prongs of the Lemon test.

Assessing the Adjudicators

Many entities petition the Supreme Court to adjudicate disputes over religious expression. Relatedly, some scholars study how the religious identity of the justices themselves may influence their decision-making (Gans 2016; Strother 2017; Bailey and Maltzman 2011). Increasingly, courts review cases related to reproductive rights, religious freedom, and LGBTQI protections that are deeply tied to religious beliefs. Judges are expected to preside over the cases before them without regard to their own partisan, ideological, and ethnoracial preferences. In essence, members of the court are required to do what humans cannot: completely suspend their biases to just consider the "facts" of a dispute. Whether those biases are explicitly tied to our belief systems (e.g. religious identity) or more implicitly part of our decision-making calculus, our dispositions appear in myriad ways. The current members of the Court represent the most religiously pluralistic group ever to serve in the highest court in the land.

Historically, the overwhelming majority of justices have been Protestant – a total of 91 of the 113 who have been appointed since the **Judiciary Act of 1789** established the Supreme Court (Paulson 2009). Today, Catholics comprise just 20 percent of the total US population but hold over 60 percent of the seats on the high court and 31 percent of congressional seats. To some, this distribution may be surprising when compared to the statistical presence of Protestants in the broader society. In 1916, Louis Brandeis became the first Jewish justice; in 2019 there are three Jewish members. The changing religious profile of the Supreme Court mirrors broader changes in American society. Just as the number of Protestant justices has significantly declined, so too has the size of the white Protestant population in the country. This decline often heightens the perception that group interests are being challenged or even threatened. Thus, changes in population size can also inspire efforts to maintain political influence and dominance.

Different and Diverse: Contemporary Religious Identity in the United States

Rosh Hashanah, an occasion that marks the start of the Jewish New Year, is the first of the high holy days in the Jewish faith. Adherents traditionally celebrate by spending time with family members in reverence and contemplation. On Rosh Hashanah in 2015, Vermont Senator Bernie Sanders traveled to the small town of Lynchburg, Virginia, to address over 3,000 students and staff gathered for weekly convocation at Liberty University. Founded in 1981 by the late Reverend Jerry Falwell, Sr, as a small Baptist college, Liberty has grown to become the largest evangelical university in the world, with over 110,000 students. It counts among its famous alumni former NFL players Rashad Jennings and Nick Foles. Liberty's elevation as a central influence in Christian education has drawn visits from reality show stars Michelle and Jim Bob Duggar, actor Mel Gibson, and *Duck Dynasty* star Phil Robinson, whose TV show was suspended after he made derogatory remarks about gays.

BOX 7.2 Two major origins of Jewish descent

Ashkenazim	*Sephardim*
Origins in Central and Eastern Europe	Origins in countries such as Spain and Portugal

---

Beyond students and celebrities, Liberty attracts visits from political hopefuls seeking to connect with evangelical voters who have grown substantially in both number and political influence. Ten years ago the school convinced local leaders to create a voting precinct on campus to make it easier for students to vote (Quarantotto 2010). Now, election day is recognized as a campus holiday, with classes canceled to ease barriers to voting. After encouraging students with concealed-carry permits to arm themselves and bring their weapons to campus, university president Jerry Falwell, Jr, also announced plans to open a gun range on campus: "I've always thought that if more good people had concealed-carry permits, then we could end these Muslims before they walked in . . . I just want to encourage all of you to get a permit. Let's teach them a lesson if they ever show up here" (Bailey 2015).

In 2012, Liberty chose the first Mormon candidate for president, Mitt Romney, as its commencement speaker. Bobby Jindal, the country's first Indian American governor, used his address to graduates in 2014 to highlight his conversion to Christianity after being raised Hindu. School leaders praised Jindal's embrace of Christianity and his signing of a "Marriage and Conscience" Executive Order that protected discrimination by business owners and government employees who opposed marriage equality. Sarah Palin, the 2008 Republican nominee for vice president, has been a frequent visitor to the school, and in 2015 Senator Ted Cruz of Texas announced his campaign to become the Republican nominee for president from the campus. Some political observers were puzzled that Cruz chose a school he did not attend in a state he does not represent to announce his campaign. However, the strategic choice of location reflected his interest in courting the evangelical vote (Peterson 2015).

Bernie Sanders gave a convocation speech at Liberty after several other presidential contenders, such as Ben Carson, Jeb Bush, and Donald J. Trump, had made visits to the campus. Sanders acknowledged the vast differences between his political views and the audience gathered at Liberty by saying: "I came here today because I believe that it is important for those with different views in our country to engage in civil discourse. It is harder, but not less important, to try and communicate with those who do not agree with us and see where, if possible, we can find common ground." The swirl of praise and criticism that followed his appearance highlighted the renewed importance of religion in American political life. It also foreshadowed the myriad ways in which appeals to religious identity were embedded in the 2016 race for president. From promises to enact travel bans based on religious identity to debates over the compatibility of certain public policy preferences and religious values, the election cycle made it clear that, unlike the situation in most democratic societies, religious identity remains a prominent feature of American politics. For many voters, evaluations of the various candidates are based on the labels they promote rather than the extent to which they practice their faith. Religious identity is often used as a cognitive heuristic to help voters make sense of a complex and, at times, confusing political space (Lau and Redlawsk 2001).

Believers and Nonbelievers

According to a poll undertaken in 2016 by the Pew Research Center, 51 percent of voters said they would be less likely to vote for a candidate who does not believe in God. To date, no openly atheist or agnostic candidate has ever run for the highest office in the land. Even for candidates who do present themselves as religious, the public evaluates their desirability based on their particular faith tradition. The question is therefore more complex than simply gauging whether a candidate does or does not believe.

Table 7.2 documents the key findings of the Pew Center's "Faith and the 2016 Campaign" study. The data show that voters are less likely to vote for a candidate who identifies as Muslim (42 percent) than one who identifies as Mormon (23 percent). In regard to other identities, Muslim candidates are ranked lower than gay and lesbian candidates (26 percent) and those who had used marijuana in the past (20 percent). These findings suggest that a more nuanced view of religious identity is necessary to better capture the full religious profile of the United States. There are differences even within broad categories such as "Protestant" and "Muslim" that shape political preferences and affiliations.

The two largest denominations in the United States, evangelical Protestants and Catholics, are both part of the Christian tradition. The umbrella term *Protestant* covers a host of Christian denominations that emerged after the Reformation, the sixteenth-century movement based on

Table 7.2 Percentage of voters who would be more or less likely to support a presidential candidate

	More likely	Less likely	Wouldn't matter
Traits that are assets			
Served in the military	50	4	45
Attended a prestigious university	20	6	74
Is Catholic	16	8	75
Traits neither assets nor liabilities			
Is evangelical Christian	22	20	55
Is Jewish	8	10	80
Traits that are liabilities			
Longtime Washington experience	22	31	46
Used marijuana in the past	6	20	74
Is Mormon	5	23	69
Is gay/lesbian	4	26	69
Has personal finance problems	8	41	49
Had an extramarital affair in the past	3	37	58
Is Muslim	3	42	53
Doesn't believe in God	6	51	41

SOURCE: Based on data from Pew Research Center (2016).

differing cultural and intellectual views of the role of the Church. The result was a permanent divide between Protestantism and what we now know as the Catholic Church. Protestants view the Bible as the sole holy text and build their houses of worship, religious practices, and beliefs upon a broad set of tenets. The tremendous diversity within the category (e.g. mainline Protestant versus historically Black Protestant) recognizes the substantive ways in which interlocking identities shape the basis for religious adherence and expression. Unlike in the Catholic tradition, there is no singular unifying governing body for Protestants. Though the basis of Christian beliefs may be the same, the expression of and political connections to those beliefs vary.

Tables 7.3, 7.4, and 7.5 illustrate the tremendous diversity within and across categories of religious identity. Non-Christian traditions make up a smaller percentage of the US population. However, they also hold tremendous potential for growth and influence. Collectively, adherents to the Muslim faith have experienced the greatest and most rapid growth in the United States on account of differing rates of immigration, citizenship, births, and conversion. For example, 82 percent of Muslims in country are US citizens, and 69 percent of those born elsewhere now hold US citizenship. The ethnoracial identity of Muslims also portends important linkages (Barreto and Bozonelos 2009). Foreign-born Muslims in the United States

The meaning of religious identity varies across and within denominations. Members of various Christian traditions gather for an ecumenical prayer service in Boston.

Table 7.3 Racial and ethnic composition by religious group (percentages) (as of 12/2018)

	White (non-Hispanic)	Black (non-Hispanic)	Asian (non-Hispanic)	Other (non-Hispanic)	Hispanic
Christian	66	13	2	3	16
Protestant	69	18	1	4	8
Evangelical	76	6	2	5	11
Historically Black	2	94	0	1	3
Catholic	59	3	3	2	34
Mormon	85	1	1	5	8
Non-Christian	61	6	21	5	6
Jewish	90	2	2	2	4
Muslim	38	28	28	3	4
Buddhist	44	3	33	8	12
Hindu	4	2	91	2	1
Unaffiliated	68	5	5	4	13
Atheist	78	7	7	2	10
Agnostic	79	4	4	4	9

SOURCE: Based on data from the Pew Research Center, *Religious Landscape Study*.

Table 7.4 Religious tradition by immigrant status (percentages) (as of 12/2018)

	Immigrants	Second generation	Third generation or higher
Buddhist	26	22	52
Catholic	28	15	58
Evangelical Protestant	9	7	84
Hindu	87	9	4
Historically Black Protestant	7	3	90
Jehovah's Witness	25	8	67
Jewish	12	22	67
Mainline Protestant	7	7	87
Mormon	7	7	86
Orthodox Christian	40	23	36
Unaffiliated	13	12	75

SOURCE: Based on data from the Pew Research Center, *Religious Landscape Study*.

Table 7.5 US Muslims by ethnoracial identity (percentages)

	White	Black	Asian	Hispanic	Other/mixed
All US Muslims	41	20	28	8	3
Foreign-born	45	11	41	1	1
US-born	35	32	19	17	5
Second generation	52	7	22	17	2
Third generation	23	51	2	18	7
Overall US population	64	12	6	16	2

SOURCE: Based on data from Pew Research Center, *US Muslims Concerned about Their Place in Society*; US Census Bureau, 2016 Current Population Survey Annual Social and Economic Supplement.

are more likely to identify as Asian, while American-born Muslims are more likely to identify as Black (Pew Center 2015). African Americans represent approximately 13 percent of Muslims, yet two-thirds of Black Muslims have converted.

To be sure, the creation of the **Nation of Islam** and its particular focus on Black liberation influenced generations of Black converts. However, membership in the Nation of Islam has decreased over time. Today, nearly half of African American Muslims identify as Sunni. Recall from chapter 4 the alarming number of respondents who did not know that residents of Puerto Rico are US citizens and, in turn, opposed relief aid following the devastation of Hurricane Maria. The view that Muslims are "less politically desirable" may also be linked to differing notions of their perceived "Americanness" (Devos and Banaji 2005).

Racial Identity, Religious Identity, or Both?

Race and religion are inextricably linked in both law and public practice. Whether it was the creation of the Ku Klux Klan as a white Christian suprema-cist organization or the emergence of the **Black Church** as a liberating space of refuge, religious identity is inherently intersectional in the US. This overlap is heightened for some traditions, such as Judaism, that challenge commonly held notions about ethnoreligious identity. For example, a Louisiana magis-trate concluded that, although Judaism is a religion, Jews constitute a distinct race that should be protected against discrimination by the Civil Rights Act of 1964: "Modern sociologists and anthropologists, especially with advancements in DNA studies, debate whether Judaism is a people, a religion, or both. There is no doubt, however, that many people have and continue to view being Jewish as a racial identity" (Husain 2018). The ruling held that, because Jews are viewed as and discriminated against as a race, the law should protect them as such. However, the case was complicated because it did not distinguish between self-identity (e.g. some people who identify as Jewish are agnostic) and social identity (e.g. laws don't distinguish between people who see Judaism as a religious belief system and those who see Jewishness as an ethnic identity).

The ruling supported the 2017 claim filed by a football coach who claimed he was denied employment at a Baptist college because his Mother was Jewish. Although Joshua Bonadona was raised Jewish and converted to Christianity in college, his suit contended that the school's president explicitly referenced his "Jewish blood" in refusing to extend an offer to hire. The school justi-fied its decision by arguing that Jews are not a protected race and therefore not entitled to equal employment opportunities. Magistrate Mark Hornsby rejected this claim: "Jewish citizens have been excluded from certain clubs or neighborhoods, and they have been denied jobs and other opportunities based on the fact that they were Jewish, with no particular concern as to a given individual's religious leanings."[13] The important precedent set in this case may pave the way for discrimination claims by other groups such as Muslims, who comprise a range of racial and ethnic identities yet are often discriminated against based on a presumed identity.

The link between race and religion shapes how groups react to one another and how excluded groups forge their own identities and preferences in opposition. Scholars (Frazier 1963; Lincoln and Mamiya 1990; Grant 1989; Calhoun-Brown 1996; McDaniel and Ellison 2008; Harris-Lacewell 2004) address the unique emergence of the Black Church as both a spiritual womb for Black communities and an organizing space to develop skills and resources needed to navigate public and political life. The term *Black Church* encompasses the seven major Black Protestant denominations that evolved in response to the legal, social, economic, and political exclusion of Blacks from American life.

As a set of religious institutions and practices, it is a conduit for stimulating racial consciousness and advancing social justice. According to Lincoln and Mamiya: "A major aspect of black Christian belief is found in the importance given to the word 'freedom.' Throughout black history the term 'freedom' has found deep religious resonance in the lives and hopes of African Americans . . . In song, word, and deed freedom has always been the superlative value of the black cosmos" (1990: 3–4).

Theologian James Cone (1970) offers **Black liberation theology** as the deliberate effort to empower Blacks to love themselves in the face of a complex history of racial segregation, state-sanctioned violence, and denials of citizenship. The task lies in connecting the gospel to real-world challenges connected to both religious and racial identity. However, the emphasis on the historically Black Protestant traditions may mask the fullness of Black religious identity by neglecting adherence to other traditions, such as Catholicism, Islam, and Judaism. We will return to this point later in the chapter.

Running on, Running from Religious Identity

In 1928, Alfred E. Smith became the first Catholic nominee for the presidency. Smith was a New Yorker born to an Italian mother and an Irish father. He cultivated a strong base of support from immigrant communities in the area and eventually drew upon his Irish heritage to gain favor with the powerful Tammany Hall political machine, which helped Irish communities challenge their past exclusion from politics and public life (Erie 1988). His failed bid for the White House came after an extensive tenure as governor of New York and as a member of the State Assembly. Al Smith became a strong advocate for protecting workers' rights, immigrants' rights, and women following his response to the horrific Triangle Shirtwaist Factory fire, whose victims were mostly Jewish immigrant women and girls. Smith's willingness to advocate on their behalf and authorize investigations into workplace conditions also helped court the support of Jewish voters, who saw in him, and by extension the Democratic Party, an ally.

Smith attempted to run on a platform that avoided overemphasizing his faith. Ultimately, however, voters were reluctant to endorse a Catholic president for fear that his allegiance would be to the pope and the Vatican rather than to the American people. Smith's candidacy paved the way for John F. Kennedy, Jr, to become the first Catholic president. Rather than avoiding his religious identity, Kennedy was forced to confront it head-on in September 1960 in an address to the Greater Houston Ministerial Association. The association was comprised of Protestant ministers who questioned whether Kennedy and other Catholic candidates were capable of making national decisions independently of the Catholic Church. The irony was clear: the ministers demanded that Kennedy diminish his religious identity to protect their own.

In the now iconic speech, JFK helped reframe the importance of maintaining the separation of church and state, both to protect religious freedom and to denounce the country's pronounced history of discriminating against other faith traditions, such as Baptists and Quakers:

> I believe in an America where the separation of church and state is absolute, where no Catholic prelate would tell the president . . . how to act . . . and where no man is denied public office merely because his religion differs from the president who might appoint him or the people who might elect him.
>
> . . .
>
> Finally, I believe in an America where religious intolerance will someday end; where all men and all churches are treated as equal.

Despite winning the election, Kennedy's narrow vote margin (fewer than 100,000) over Richard Nixon highlighted the challenge of religion for candidates from underrepresented traditions.

Faith, Voting, and Election 2016

Against this landscape, the results of the 2016 election highlight the complex ways in which religious identity fuels candidate choices and policy preferences. They also emphasized how deeply divided Americans are, based on religious identity. The substance and influence of religious beliefs on individual preferences is far from uniform. As Layman (2001) and others note, the meaning of religious identity varies across and within denominations (Green and Guth 1988; Jones-Correa and Leal 2001; Wald and Calhoun-Brown 2010). Although groups may share a common religious belief, experiences within those faith traditions determine the range of benefits and resources groups derive from their affiliation (Verba et al. 1995). Differences in socio-economic standing may weaken the unifying nature of that belief and, in turn, the strength of religious identity as a defining force in shaping their relationship to the polity.

Both candidates attempted to court the votes of highly organized religious communities with a history of voter participation bound by identity. The Trump team assembled a group of Black ministers to speak on his behalf and to sway Black Christians. This outreach effort differed from past appeals by candidates to Black Protestants, which attempted to secure the backing of high-profile religious leaders such as Reverend KirbyJon Caldwell – religious advisor to George W. Bush and pastor of megachurch Windsor Village United Methodist Church in Houston. This overlap between religious leadership and candidate appeals became a key fault line in Barack Obama's primary bid in 2008 when video recordings of his former pastor, Reverend Jeremiah Wright, were released to the public. Some criticized Wright's rhetoric as anti-American and inflammatory, while those familiar with Black liberation theology praised Wright as a veteran who wanted to renew the country's commitment to social justice as a requirement of the faith (McKenzie 2011; Walker and Smithers 2012; Belcher 2016). That cloud, coupled with the accusation that Obama was in fact Muslim, shaped the general hesitance of many Black evangelical leaders to engage. As a result, Trump's Black outreach team was comprised of lesser known ministers such as Mark Burns of South Carolina and Darrel Scott of Virginia, who were not connected to the major ministerial associations or political campaigns.

Counting on Division

After a long and contentious election cycle, there were strong and discernible differences in candidate preferences in the 2016 presidential election. To be sure, these differences were reflected across denominations. Yet, perhaps most interestingly, they also highlighted key differences *within* denominations based on religious identity. Many pundits lumped all Christians together to pronounce that President Trump captured the Christian vote and that Hillary Clinton polled higher among non-Christian voters (Dias 2016). However, as tables 7.6 and 7.7 illustrate, that simplistic view doesn't properly capture the competing political evaluations that often accompany intersecting identities. Although 56 percent of white Evangelicals identify as Republican, over 80 percent voted for Donald Trump. This proportion was significantly higher than the proportion of votes cast in previous elections for Republican candidates Mitt Romney (2012), John McCain (2008), and George W. Bush (2004). The high voter turnout rates of white Evangelicals, coupled with their concentration in key

Table 7.6 2016 presidential vote choice by religious group (percentages)

	Hillary Clinton	Donald J. Trump
Black Protestant	88.1	6.0
Evangelical Protestant	18.8	80.0
Catholic	46.0	49.2
Jewish	69.0	27.0
Mormon	26.0	45.0
Muslim	82.0	15.0
Atheist/agnostic	73.0	4.0

SOURCE: Based on data from the *Cooperative Congressional Election Study*.

Table 7.7 Republican affiliation by religious identity (percentages) (as of 12/2018)

Buddhist	16
Catholic	37
Evangelical Protestant	56
Hindu	13
Historically Black Protestant	10
Jehovah's Witness	7
Jewish	26
Mainline Protestant	44
Mormon	70
Muslim	17
Orthodox Christian	34
Unaffiliated	23

SOURCE: Pew Research Center, *Religious Landscape Study*.

battleground states such as Virginia, Florida, and Pennsylvania, elevated their political influence in 2016. Whether those voters were drawn to Trump because of his policy promises (e.g. overturning *Roe* v. *Wade*) or on account of the strong ties to evangelical communities of his running mate Mike Pence, the intersections of race and religious identity overshadowed the traditional influences of class and political ideology. Although white Evangelicals are decreasing in number, their power to shape political outcomes is deeply entrenched.

The Rise of the Religious Right

Jerry Falwell was a self-professed fundamentalist Christian pastor who sharply opposed the growing involvement of religious leaders in the protest movements of the 1960s. He directly rebuked the leadership of prominent voices such as Reverend Dr Martin Luther King, Jr, and Rabbi Abraham Joshua Heschel: "Nowhere are we commissioned to reform the externals. Preachers are not called to be politicians, but soul winners" (Neuhaus 1984). Over the next decade Falwell drastically reversed course and amassed a large following as a televangelist preaching the gospel to "Christian warriors." Following the 1973 legalization of abortion and growing social unrest, Falwell launched the Moral Majority movement.

The movement was based on a hybrid blend of patriotism and evangelical tenets that condemned emerging political movements (e.g. Gay Rights movement, Women's movement, etc.) as threats to Christian principles. Falwell traveled around the country spreading his message and promoting a religious revival to restore the country's commitment to conservative Christian ideals.

His leadership helped increase the number of white Evangelicals who supported Ronald Reagan during the presidential race in 1980. Although the
Moral Majority movement was short-lived as a singular organization, it taught
conservative Evangelicals how to organize politically to impact every facet of
public life.

Rather than being a single cohesive organization, the contemporary
Religious Right refers to a broad coalition of religious conservatives composed primarily of white Evangelicals. Through the creation of think tanks,
advocacy organizations, and candidate training programs, the Religious Right
has accomplished two major goals: (1) increasing political involvement among
Evangelicals and (2) shaping public policy debates and court cases. Through
this two-pronged strategy, the Religious Right has deepened its power even as
the Evangelicals it represents have decreased in number (Wilcox 1989).

BOX 7.3 Reviving the heart of democracy

The Reverend William Barber describes himself as a "theologically conservative liberal evangelical Biblicist." It's a mouthful that sounds contradictory.
But, to Barber, it simply means an obligation to build bridges in places where
unity doesn't seem possible. As the former president of the North Carolina
State Conference of NAACP branches, Barber led the Moral Mondays movement as a coalition of believers and nonbelievers in an unlikely alliance to
protest the state's attack on voting rights and health care. Today, he works
with community leaders across the country to support the "Poor People's
Campaign: A National Call for Moral Revival." Their goal is to revive the
heart of American democracy by addressing voting rights, public education,
immigration, and workers' rights.

Organizing around political identities isn't just about the products and
outcomes of the decision-making process. Recall from chapter 5 that we call
this substantive representation. For many groups, particularly those who feel
marginalized and threatened, it may also be important to choose decision-
makers who share similar traits with the voters (descriptive representation).
Politics is about reciprocity. Politicians need to court voters who support
them. Likewise, voters derive a sense of empowerment and efficacy from
seeing people in positions of power who "look like" or "believe like" they do
(Bobo and Gilliam 1990).

Over the last two decades, various leaders aligned with the Religious Right
have sought to repeal the 1954 Johnson Amendment that provides tax-exempt
status to religious organizations that refrain from engaging in partisan activities such as collecting donations. Opponents believe the Johnson Amendment
violates their First Amendment freedom of speech protections. This approach

was buttressed by the 2010 *Citizens United* v. *Federal Election Commission* ruling that equated money to speech. In 2016 the Republican Party included repeal of the Johnson Amendment in its official party platform. Two major legislative efforts to repeal the Johnson Amendment failed to make it into Congress's overhaul of the US tax code in 2017.

Immigration and Contemporary Shifts in Religious Identity

Immigration impacts every aspect of American life, including religious identity. Chapter 4 traced how the 1965 Hart–Celler Act dramatically changed the scope, composition, and public response to the mass movement of immigrants. In increasing the number of people coming from Asia, Africa, Latin America, and the Caribbean, Hart–Celler dramatically diversified the makeup of religious communities in the United States. Though immigrants and their families may share common religious labels with native-born adherents, the political meaning of a common religious identity is contextual. The significance of common religious identities post-Hart–Celler varies across markers such as geographic location, language, and ethnicity.

The Past is Prologue

Recall from our discussion in chapter 4 the tremendous discrimination Irish immigrants faced during the second wave of mass migration to the United States. That fear of and resistance to Catholic influence stretched through the candidacies of Al Smith in 1928 and John F. Kennedy, Jr, in 1960. Although Irish Catholics were severely discriminated against, that common experience was not enough to overcome tensions that ensued after Italian immigrants began moving to the US in large numbers in the 1880s. Most Irish and Italian immigrants identified as Catholic. However, the ways they expressed and followed their faith varied. The two groups often clashed over economic interests because Italian immigrants were more willing to work in deplorable conditions and for less money than their Irish counterparts (Moses 2017). The perceived threat posed by Italian immigrants to the material and social standing of Irish immigrants heightened efforts by the groups to present themselves as separate and distinct in spite of their common religious identity.

Since 1965, the number of Latino immigrants who identify as Catholic has increased. Nearly 60 percent of Latinos – and a slightly higher percentage among those born in the US – identify as Catholic (Cox and Jones 2017). As the overall number of people who identify as Catholic has decreased, Catholic Latinos often face an impossible position. Some parishes lament their declining membership while struggling to address the best way to fully embrace and incorporate Latino members, who may bring different cultural traditions and patterns that challenge normal operating procedure. Differences in language, cultural expression, and even policy priorities highlight the dimensions that need to be considered in determining the meaning of religious identity among Catholic Latinos.

The East Haven Case

In 2012, the FBI charged three officers in the East Haven Police Department in Connecticut with conspiring to violate the civil rights of the city's Latino residents. Like many cities, East Haven experienced a sizable increase in the number of Latino residents. Some people complained that "they [Latinos] had taken over" and called on the town's mayor and police to be both the first and last bastion of defense. Officers responded by surveilling Latino-owned businesses, shutting down clubs and social gatherings with a large Latino presence, and denying attempts by Latino residents to expand their small businesses. Fear of reprisal from officers and their allies prevented many Latinos from pursuing formal avenues of redress.

After hearing many of its parishioners discuss their negative encounters with members of the East Haven Police Department, the pastor of St Rose of Lima began documenting their stories. Reverend James Manship and other church leaders believed that the hostile climate his Latino parishioners faced demanded a vigorous commitment to pursuing a social gospel that emphasizes faith and a commitment to equality and social action (McDaniel 2008). Manship was arrested and charged with interfering for videotaping East Haven officers harassing the Latino owner of a local convenience store. His arrest, coupled with the testimony of others, proved that the officer had falsified documentation while engaging in a persistent practice of violating the civil rights of Latino residents (Clear 2012).

Similar but Different

Several scholars (Leal et al. 2016; Higgins 2014; Audette 2016) document the need to move beyond the general label of "Catholic Latinos" to assess the contours of country of origin, generation, and the structure of opportunities for religious identity and expression. The meaning of a panreligious identifier such as "Catholic" may not capture the fullness of religious identity. This caution is also important in understanding religious identity among Black ethnic immigrants from the Caribbean, Latin America, and parts of Africa (Greer 2013). For many, their relationship to religion does not fit with traditional categories. Rather, some embrace *syncretic religions* that blend two or more faith traditions uniquely to honor cultural and spiritual distinctions. Recall from chapter 1 efforts by members of the Church of the Lukumi to protest a Florida ordinance banning animal sacrifice. Members of the Church of Lukumi practice Santeria, which uniquely blends elements of Catholicism, Yoruba, and a connection to the African diaspora. Similarly, Candomblé is a syncretic religion practiced by people of Afro-Brazilian descent. Organized communities who practice these syncretic traditions tend to be more prevalent in areas with strong immigrant concentrations, such as Florida and New York. However, the generational transfer of these beliefs challenges the traditional religious identity assigned to such groups based on ethnic identifiers.

Muslim Identity in a Changing US Context

Islam is one of the oldest and largest religious traditions in the world. However, research on Muslim identity and US politics often focuses on the aftermath of the September 11th terror attacks. To be sure, the tremendous hurt, anger, and outrage that followed the deaths of nearly 3,000 Americans permanently changed people's relationship to the state. The passage of the USA PATRIOT Act significantly expanded the reach of government while eroding civil liberties protections as necessary to fight the war on terror. Certainly the Muslim presence in the United States predates 9/11. The earlier discussion of Black Muslims, together with a broader historical view, shows that people who embrace Islam represent a range of identities related to citizenship, ethnicity, and sect. However, media framing of 9/11, coupled with growing demands to combat terrorism, dramatically and permanently redefined Muslim identity in America. The Department of Justice documented an exponential uptick in the number of hate crimes reported against Muslims. New security measures at airports and other public places heightened concerns about ethnic profiling that targeted Muslims and those perceived to be Muslim. The backlash prompted then President George W. Bush in 2001 to address the nation at the Islamic Center of Washington, DC: "The face of terrorism is not the true faith of Islam. That's not what Islam is all about. Islam is peace. These terrorists don't represent peace, they represent evil and war . . . When we think of Islam, we think of a faith that brings comfort to a billion people around the world . . . and that's made brothers and sisters out of every race."

Although there are tremendous differences within Muslim communities based on a range of factors (e.g. conversion, ethnic identity, country of origin), contemporary political discourse and the public policies that fuel it rarely make exceptions for these distinctions. Instead, "all Muslims" are treated as potential threats. Within his first thirty days in office, President Trump approved a number of measures targeting Muslims in the US. The first was an executive order that made good on his campaign promise to ban travel from Muslim-majority countries. The "Protecting the Nation from Foreign Terrorist Entry into the United States" order enacted a ninety-day ban on the entry of immigrant and non-immigrant nationals from Syria, Somalia, Libya, Yemen, Iraq, Iran, and Sudan. The order drastically reduced the refugee resettlement program *except* for those fleeing religious persecution in non-Muslim countries.

Opportunities to express Muslim religious identity are shaped by tradition, legal constraints, and informal public pressures based on fear and ignorance. Despite these challenges, Muslim candidates for public office have slowly made progress. In 2006, Keith Ellison of Minnesota became the first Muslim American elected to Congress, and in 2018 he was elected attorney general for the state of Minnesota. Ellison was raised Catholic and converted to Islam in college. In 2008, Indiana's André Carson was appointed as the second highest ranking Muslim elected official in the country. During his 2015 attempt to become the Republican nominee for president, former surgeon Dr Ben Carson expressed his belief that Islam was not compatible with the Constitution and that Muslims were not fit for elected office. Carson wasn't alone in his beliefs. According to data published by the Pew Research Center (Smith and Martínez 2016), 42 percent of respondents said they would be less likely to vote for a candidate who was Muslim. In 2018, a strong crop of Muslim candidates challenged that hesitance by running in a number of local, state, and national races. Just as their candidate profiles varied, so too did the districts they sought to represent. For example, Ilhan Omar represents Minnesota's Fifth Congressional District in an area where Somali immigrants have built a strong community and political presence. Across the United States, fifty-five Muslim candidates won elected office in the 2018 midterms.[14]

Conclusion: Religious Identity as Intersectional Construction

Religious identity is connected to but not synonymous with religious belief. Although individuals may embrace a common label (e.g. Protestant or unaffiliated), the meaning of and responses to that label vary across other identity markers. In spite of the commonly held belief that the United States was founded based on religious freedom, this chapter traced the complex ways in which the meaning of and access to freedom actually depended on the religious tradition in question. While some colonies explicitly refused to adopt an official religion, others used state statute to brand certain religious traditions as inferior and incompatible with the burgeoning collective identity.

Religious identity, like all social identities, is a composite construction of the norms, values, beliefs, and opportunities to which we subscribe and which are imposed upon us. Over the last fifty years, changes in the composition of immigrant communities have challenged and, in some cases, redefined how groups align their religious communities. The rise of the Religious Right elevated the political profile of evangelical Christians while weakening the standing of, and protections for, other identity groups. These parallel developments speak to the intimate connection between race and religion in the United States. Likewise, the public reframing of Muslim identity often collapses the tremendous internal diversity to make it easier to craft policies that stigmatize entire communities. Though the impact of those policies and perceptions is disproportionately felt by some groups, the constant negotiation of who does and who does not fit with American identity creates perpetual challenges for religious adherents and nonbelievers alike.

Controversy box: Religious freedom or freedom to discriminate?

There are over 430,000 children in foster-care systems across the United States waiting to find their forever home. The very social identities discussed throughout this book shape a child's likelihood of being adopted out of the system. For example, Latinos comprise slightly more than a quarter of children in state custody compared to 1 percent of Asian children. The cost to adopt a child is based on demand. Adopting African American and Latino children is significantly cheaper than adopting a white child. Similarly, white babies and children under the age of two can be the most expensive, depending on the region of the country and family circumstances.

In 1978, Congress passed the Indian Child Welfare Act to protect Indian children and families. At the time of its passage, 85 percent of Indian children who were removed from their homes were outplaced in spite of having family members capable of raising them. In 1994, the federal government adopted the Multiethnic Placement Act to prohibit discrimination on the basis of the race, color, or national origin of the prospective parent or child. Together these two acts directly addressed discrimination and mistreatment in the foster-care system based on age, race, ethnicity, and sovereignty. They did not, however, address discrimination based on religion and gender identity.

In 2017, Philadelphia's Department of Health and Human Services severed all city contracts with two private foster-care agencies who refuse to work with same-sex couples looking to adopt. The two organizations – Catholic Services and Bethany Christian Services – lost contracts under which they had operated for over twenty years. They contend that their religious beliefs define marriage as being only between one man and one woman and reject the notion that same-sex couples should be able to adopt. Further, they argue, forcing them to work with same-sex couples to place a child would amount to an implicit endorsement of homosexuality.

Earlier, the Catholic Archdiocese of Washington, DC, chose to shutter its long-serving foster-care program rather than place kids with same-sex couples. The move came after the District of Columbia legalized marriage equality and adopted a number of provisions to protect the civil rights of LGBTQI city residents. Catholic charities and Bethany Christian sued the city of Philadelphia on the grounds that it tried to deny their First Amendment rights. A judge rejected the claim that they were victims of religious discrimination and ordered the agencies to provide assessments to same-sex couples who enlisted their services. The groups have vowed to appeal the decision and hope to have a different outcome at the federal level, given judicial rulings defending a baker's refusal to make a cake for a same-sex couple and Catholic hospitals from providing contraceptives.

The US Supreme Court has long maintained that the First Amendment protects our autonomy to believe, but it doesn't always protect our autonomy to act (or not to act) on those beliefs. Now you decide. Should religious institutions and organizations be required to serve people even if they don't agree with their beliefs? Or does the First Amendment protect our right to discriminate (treat people differently) against identity groups that differ from our own?

Questions for Debate

- The Johnson Amendment prohibits all tax-exempt organizations from directly and indirectly intervening in political campaigns. Some religious organizations argue that the restriction infringes upon their First Amendment freedom of speech because it prohibits them from promoting their views and needs. Others caution that repealing the amendment would further blur the distinction between church and state. Should Congress repeal or retain the Johnson Amendment?

- Various studies document a substantial increase in the number of people who identify as atheist, agnostic, or unaffiliated. To date, however, an openly (religiously) unaffiliated candidate has never been elected to national office. Is this a problem for American democracy? Why and in what ways?

Key Terms

- Aaron Lopez
- religious identity
- Morrill Anti-Bigamy Act
- Black liberation theology
- religiosity
- Johnson Amendment
- *Lemon* v. *Kurtzman*
- Establishment Clause
- *Engel* v. *Vitale*
- Free Exercise Clause
- Judiciary Act of 1789
- *Reynolds* v. *United States*
- syncretic religion

8

Identity and Political Movements

Crowds begin to form outside Wilbur Cross High School at 6 am for a rally that isn't set to start until 1 pm. The October chill doesn't deter the thousands of people who have descended upon the school's gymnasium for a "Get Out the Vote" rally. Local and national media outlets are interspersed throughout the site as area residents hold signs that publicize their varied interests. There are labor union placards alongside catchy slogans promoting calls for universal health care. Some live in the host community while others have carpooled or piled onto church vans to reach the venue. Members of a group championing increased state support for charter schools chant in unison, while grandmothers dressed in their Sunday best patiently wait their turn to enter the gymnasium. Some public officials make their way toward a side entrance hoping to avoid the glare of constituents who have spent the last week begging them for the highly sought-after tickets. It's rare to see so much attention for a state-level race held in a non-presidential election year. But the stakes are unusually high in this Connecticut gubernatorial race.

Connecticut Governor Dannel Malloy is facing a formidable challenge in what many pundits initially thought would be an easy re-election campaign. The deeply blue state was the first in the nation to adopt a $10.10 per hour minimum wage and to protect paid sick leave for workers (Associated Press 2014). Malloy signed a repeal of the death penalty in 2012 and was honored by the National Association for the Advancement of Colored People for addressing sentencing disparities based on the race of the perpetrator and victim (Brown-Dean and Jones 2017). In spite of these policy developments, polling data showed that the race was too close to call in the weeks leading up to the election – until the surrogates were called in.[1] Across the United States, surrogates are often dispatched to close races to help push their candidates across the finish line: "It often happens when a candidate is in crisis mode or falling behind with certain demographic groups. It is viewed as a way of understanding where your blind spots are and trying to shore them up" (Brown-Dean, quoted in Lewis 2018). Political surrogates don't have to be politicians. They can be anyone with a highly visible public profile who can generate enthusiasm and mobilize voters. Their endorsements can help lesser-known candidates seem more credible while also connecting local candidates to national concerns.

At Wilbur Cross, the surrogate drawing large crowds is former First Lady Michelle Obama. The Connecticut stop is one on a long list of close races where Democrats need an extra boost. There are other visits, to Arizona, Ohio, Florida, Virginia, North Carolina, New Hampshire, and Pennsylvania, where Obama's high approval ratings draw admirers from across the political spectrum. From intimate fundraisers to arena addresses, the rallies attract attendees who demand attention to a diverse range of public policy concerns. As Obama begins to deliver a stock speech that is a blend of patriotism, partisan shade, and feel-good encouragement, a voice rings out to interrupt: "I am here with the mother of a DREAMer. She deserves administrative relief now to stay with her family" (Bass 2014). The voice belongs to Tashi Sanchez-Llaury, a local college student who is attending the rally with other members of Connecticut Students for a Dream. Some members of the crowd are audibly disgusted by the interruption and attempt to drown her out with boos and chants of "four more years." But the target of Sanchez-Llaury's disruption, Michelle Obama, acknowledges her grievance and encourages her to continue. For the activists gathered in the gym, this act of acknowledgement is a small victory in a larger battle for recognition.

Three years previously, at the very same school, Governor Malloy signed legislation making undocumented students eligible for in-state tuition if they graduated from an in-state high school. Recall from chapter 3 that a federal version of the Development, Relief, and Education for Alien Minors (DREAM) Act has failed in Congress every year since 2001. Connecticut's endorsement of the DREAM Act provided hope to students such as Sanchez-Llaury who sought to make Connecticut a model for national policy change. They also hoped that President Obama would eventually offer his support to boosting the Deferred Action for Childhood Arrivals legislation to further protect undocumented youth residing in the US.

Protecting the DREAM(ers)

The Deferred Action for Childhood Arrivals (DACA) program was created by executive order in 2012 and was intended to protect from deportation young people who arrived in the United States before their sixteenth birthday. The original provisions required that applicants earn a high school diploma or GED certificate or complete military service and, further, not be convicted of a serious misdemeanor or felony. Recall from previous chapters that military service and education have long been viewed as the primary means for non-citizens to prove their allegiance to the United States and their willingness to adopt American values and traditions. In 2016 Barack Obama announced plans to expand the DACA program to cover more young people. The backlash from members of Congress and state leaders was immediate. Twenty-six states, including those such as Texas, Arizona, and Florida with large immigrant populations, filed suit against the administration, arguing that it was an overreach of executive authority.

The use of executive orders versus legislative action has long been a source of political conflict (Branum 2002; Rosenberg 2008). Through the presidencies of both Barack Obama and Donald Trump, however, the scope of executive power related to immigration has become an even greater legal question (Graham 2018; Hanson 2016; Volpp 2016). In 2017, former US Attorney General Jeff Sessions announced that the Trump administration would rescind the 2012 DACA order and gradually phase out the program. His claim that DACA was an unconstitutional abuse of executive authority led to a flurry of lawsuits from both sides aimed at protecting or dissolving the program, which, to date, has enrolled over 700,000 undocumented youth. As figures 8.1 and 8.2 illustrate, 80 percent of DACA recipients are from Mexico and the overwhelming majority reside in just seven states. In its haste to quickly end DACA, the administration overlooked and underestimated the decade-long political organizing by immigrant youth.

In 2006, a massive wave of protests swept the United States in opposition to proposed congressional legislation (HR 4437) that sought to classify undocumented immigrants and anyone who assisted them as felons. In cities across the country, students walked out of school while their parents participated in a May Day strike called "A Day without Immigrants." The legacy of those protests helped fuel a new commitment by young people to take up the mantle of immigration reform. One of those youth organizers was Melody Klingenfuss, who had arrived in the US from Guatemala as a young child.

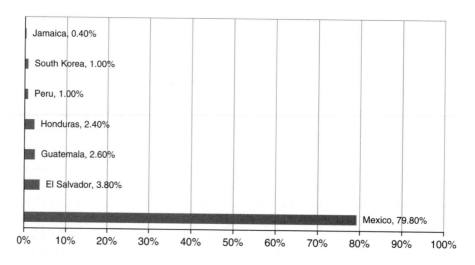

Figure 8.1 Active DACA recipients by country of origin
Source: Based on data from the US Citizenship and Immigration Services (2018).

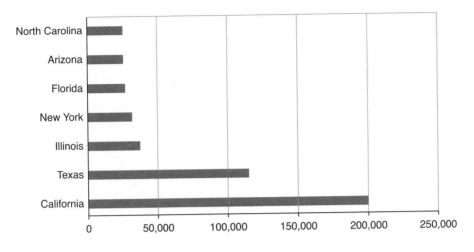

Figure 8.2 States with the highest number of DACA recipients
SOURCE: Based on data from the US Citizenship and Immigration Services (2018).

After graduating from the University of Southern California and earning a graduate degree in public policy, Klingenfuss made it her mission to advocate on behalf of other people who shared her experience of being undocumented. In 2018 she was selected by then minority leader Nancy Pelosi to accompany her to the State of the Union address in Congress. Klingenfuss implored others to support the fight to protect DACA: "In a move similar to the sit-in protests of the 1960s, allies can stand in solidarity with DACA recipients who have been targeted unfairly by peacefully disrupting and questioning what authorities are doing, instead of being complacent to actions that are not the norm and cannot become the norm. So I say, let our voices be heard by standing with us on the right side of history" (Klingenfuss 2017). What began as a small rally in 2006 grew to become one of the most visible political movements of the twenty-first century. From the absurd to the profound, political movements have been a central vehicle for channeling individual discontent into group advancement.

Political Movements in the United States: The Context

Political movements represent the pursuit of authentic power by groups who feel their interests are either ignored within or threatened by traditional nodes of political influence. Movements aren't formed in a vacuum. They are the product of broader socio-economic conditions, organizational structures, public discord, social control, and shifting political opportunities that can either enhance or suppress discontent (Orum 1974; Piven and Cloward 1979; McAdam 1982). Movements require a perfect storm of conditions that, even when met, don't guarantee groups will push for sustained acts of resistance rather than sporadic protests. Inequality and injustice are necessary but not sufficient conditions for political movements. Simply put, suffering injustices doesn't guarantee that affected groups will perceive movements as an appropriate avenue for redress.

While coming together in pursuit of a common goal can be used in positive ways, it can also amplify internal cleavages over what constitutes a "group interest" and who is included in and represented by that interest. Chapters 1 through 7 addressed the claim that identity politics is and has always been a central organizing force within US politics. They also highlighted the myriad structural challenges for groups seeking to harness authentic power in pursuit of the full rights and privileges of US citizenship. Whether women seeking to gain the vote, Evangelicals hoping to meld their faith with their policy priorities, or immigrants seeking a path to citizenship during the Civil War, groups have always faced formidable institutional barriers that often trump individual-level factors.

Rather than accepting these barriers as immutable, groups can organize at the grassroots level to exert pressure on the political process. Collective action within the context of political movements is more purposeful than simply coming together to decide what restaurant a group will choose for dinner (Olson 1971). Rather, the focus is on challenging a particular political problem or set of problems that impact group standing and inclusion. Often the focus is on securing and protecting **public goods** that are collectively created and available to everyone. Examples of public goods mentioned in earlier chapters (see the discussions of the Flint water crisis and the Standing Rock protests) are access both to clean, safe water and to a quality public education. Often groups face a **collective dilemma**, where there is a disconnect between what individuals want and what may be best for the group. For example, although individual American Indian families may have secured material success, ongoing threats to land ownership raise the importance of sovereignty for indigenous people overall.

In some cases, it may be easier or more efficient for individuals simply to benefit from the actions of other group members without actually contributing to the movement. This challenge, known as the ***free rider problem***, is a persistent one for political movements. During the 1960s, for example, college students protesting the segregation of public buses risked being expelled from their institutions of higher learning. The passage of the Civil Rights Act of 1964 eventually struck down this *de jure* segregation and made access available to all groups whether they participated in the Freedom Rides or not. This consideration of the relative costs and benefits of participation is part of a broader cognitive calculation that accompanies all political behavior (McCarthy and Zald 1973; Tarrow 1994; Baumgartner and Jones 2009). Everyone, whether a member of a stigmatized group seeking access to authentic power or a leader of a group that enjoys privilege, must gauge the weight of engaging in political action against the potential benefits and risks. When identity groups can overcome these collective action problems, political movements form a key vehicle for pursuing authentic power via meaningful social change.

From early efforts to end slavery during the Abolitionist movement to the Disability Rights movement, which led to the creation of the Individuals with Disabilities Education Act that guaranteed access to public education for differently abled children, groups have channeled their grievances into collectively pressuring a political response. Political movements can have a democratizing effect by helping groups overcome normal barriers to power, such as citizenship status, money, and language proficiency (Rule and Tilly 1975; Freeman and Johnson 1999; Tilly and Tarrow 2006). Political movements allow groups to harness their collective resources (e.g. indigenous networks and institutions) and pursue political goals.

In this chapter, I examine how contemporary political movements both affirm and challenge the meaning of identity and citizenship in the United States. Some movements, such as the DREAMer movement, are organized around an ascribed identity that seeks to remove institutional barriers to full inclusion (Keyes 2013). Recall from previous discussions about fractured citizenship that the value of belonging is both contextual and dynamic. Citizenship, then, isn't just about a formal legal standing. It also represents a particular affinity for the United States, its people, and its promise. Although the Abolitionist and Suffragist movements each prompted new constitutional affirmations of citizenship via ratification of the Fifteenth and Nineteenth Amendments, more recent efforts such as the **Black Lives Matter** movement and the Me Too movement continue to address both *de jure* and *de facto* nodes of discrimination that limit authentic power. Political movements are inherently intersectional because they highlight the gap between social identity, group identity, and perceptions of power that can both stimulate and constrain collective action. For example, the Tea Party movement and the March for Our Lives movement were both launched by groups who, to some degree, have enjoyed relative levels of privilege within the United States. However, supporters of those movements worked to bolster their ability to direct conversations about public policy and the practice of politics. In so doing, they highlight how intragroup differences can determine relative levels of support while defining the degree and duration of success (Williamson et al. 2011; Banaszak 1996).

To be sure, there are numerous organized efforts to exert pressure on the US political system and advocate for massive disruption. Covering every movement is beyond the scope of this chapter. Rather, I focus on a select group of contemporary organizing to illustrate three key points about American political movements: (1) movements exert pressure outside of the political system to influence policies, actions, and preferences within the system; (2) collective action reveals important cleavages and tensions within the broader identity group that seeks redress; and (3) measuring the success of a movement depends on both group articulation and public perception. Political movements have become the chief vehicle for stigmatized groups to resist their disenfranchisement and harness the authentic power necessary to promote full inclusion.

The Mechanics of Political Movements

Political movements occur when groups of people come together to accomplish a political goal or set of goals. Those goals can focus on acquiring and protecting rights (e.g. the right to vote or the right to marry) and/or resources (e.g. land, economic investments, or pay equity) (Hamilton 1986). Movements represent both the promise and the peril of democratic action because they emerge when members of stigmatized groups seek more effective avenues for channeling their discontent. The challenge, however, is fomenting collective action among groups for whom being disgruntled isn't enough (Tilly et al. 1975). For example, many college students complain about the growing cost of tuition alongside crippling student loan debt. Yet there is no cohesive political movement led by students to demand policy changes. Instead, intense public

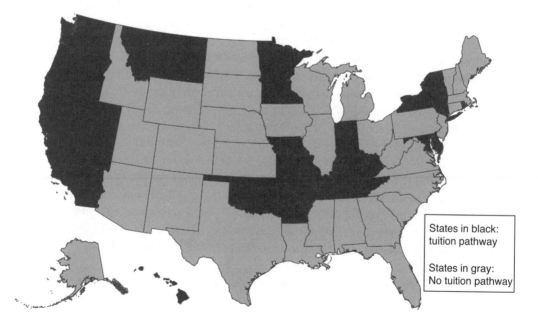

Figure 8.3 States that provide a free tuition pathway for community colleges (as of 2018)
SOURCE: Based on data from the US Department of Education.

pressure prompted some states, including California, Kentucky, and Missouri, to make community colleges tuition free (see figure 8.3). Those instances are political moments rather than a cohesive movement. So it begs the question: why movements?

From Moment to Movement

Political movements originate from seemingly diverse groups of people who feel their interests are not protected within the political process and who feel the political status quo denies them access to the full rights, privileges, responsibilities, and benefits of being in the United States. Farmers in the late 1890s blamed both Democrats and Republicans for ignoring the impact of the drought and industrialization on their financial standing. Faced with crippling debt and limited recovery options, many banded together to forge what we now know as the Populist movement. Yet, even in the face of government indifference, the Farmers' Alliance remained stratified by both race and region. The Colored Farmers' Alliance was created to represent rural Black farmers, while the National Farmers' Alliance represented white farmers across the South and Midwest (Gerteis 2007).

The leaders of the two groups eventually realized the strength of coalescing, but it was a risky union. Black citizenship wasn't fully protected at the time, and a widening economic gap made it more difficult for white farmers to risk their livelihoods in the name of movement-building. In spite of these challenges, the growth of the Populist movement was a direct rebuke of political elitism that imperiled both Black and white farmers, even if the challenge varied in degree. The movement focused directly on protecting farmers while indirectly challenging a broader structure of white supremacy that pitted the groups against each other:

> You are made to hate each other because upon that hatred is rested the keystone of the arch of financial despotism which enslaves you both. You are deceived and blinded that you may not see how this race antagonism perpetuates a monetary system that beggars both. The colored tenant is in the same boat as the white tenant, the colored laborer with the white laborer[,] and that the accident of color can make no difference in the interests of farmers, croppers, and laborers. (Tom Watson, quoted in Bell 1989: 254)

Although the movement partners were able to win some elections at the local, state, and federal level, they struggled to remain distinct from the more established Democratic Party and, eventually, the Free Silver movement that they believed would help increase crop prices and guarantee economic stability (Gaither 2005).

> ## BOX 8.1 Three key principles of political movements
>
> 1 Movements don't require unanimous consent or mutual respect for coalition partners.
> 2 Movements learn from one another.
> 3 All movements are not created equally.

The story of the Farmers' Alliance points to three key lessons from political movements. First, movements don't require unanimous consent; nor should one assume a mutual or equal level of respect for all coalition partners. They merely require a critical mass of people who perceive a greater likelihood of cultivating authentic power together than apart. By leveraging resources such as numbers and finances, stigmatized groups can draw attention to their grievances, generate public support, and, hopefully, direct political outcomes. The ability to come together in pursuit of a common goal is constrained by many of the same institutional and individual factors highlighted in the previous chapters. Identity is central to shaping how those in power solidify their standing by erecting barriers to the inclusion of others. Similarly, the relationship between identity and political power in the United States creates new opportunities for groups to resist their marginalized status via direct action.

The United States is a "movement society" where groups are constantly organizing to demand political action. Some, such as the Gay Rights movement, have been most successful pressuring policy changes at the state level, while others, such as the **American Indian movement** and the Disability Rights movement, have used local actions to challenge federal inequality. This leads to the second key point about movements: they learn from each other. Although the original Populist movement was co-opted by the Democratic Party, it inspired subsequent efforts to unite across various identity markers in pursuit of greater economic equity (Strolovitch 2008). One such example was the formation of the **National Farm Workers' movement**, championed by César Chávez and Delores Huerta. The movement was born out of the realization that farm workers, particularly those of color, were exploited and rarely protected by existing labor laws (Jenkins and Perrow 1977; Warren 2010).

The Bracero Program was an agreement between the United States and Mexico that, in theory, was meant to protect domestic workers while still addressing the US labor shortage. In practice, however, the program made it easier to pay farm workers less and subject them to deplorable work and living conditions. Workers were denied access to sanitary toilets, children were taken from schools to work long hours, and labor laws protected growers rather than workers (Garcia 2014). The strength of the Farm Workers' movement was that it positioned the protection of workers' rights as central to civil rights and economic justice.

That same principle guided the 2011 Occupy Wall Street movement, which sought a new form of populism to critique the extreme economic inequality in the United States. Supporters adopted the slogan "We are the 99 percent" to highlight the fact that 37 percent of the United States' wealth was owned by just 1 percent of the population (Lowndes and Warren 2011). The initial protests in New York's Zuccotti Park, as well as campus demonstrations across the country, pointed to the disproportionate impact of the 2007 recession on racial and ethnic minorities as evidence of the need to build a more inclusive movement.

The Occupy movement explicitly eschewed naming a singular leader or group of leaders to avoid the type of internal divisions that doomed previous movements. Organizers believed that, if the focus remained on unifying principles and priorities, they could work beyond debates about credit-claiming and leadership. But this approach drew significant criticism from those who questioned whether a movement that lacked a coherent agenda could actually succeed. To organizers, the lack of specific demands was intentional and reflected a desire to indict an entire structure that stratified access to the "American Dream" based on gender and sexual identity, region, race, ethnicity, citizenship, and class. Although the movement lasted only about a year, its existence helped identify new tools for movement-building such as social media and technology that have the potential to connect disparate members across ideology and location. The creation of hashtags allowed supporters to connect in real time, identify locations for pop-up protests, and share resources. It also highlighted the potential to connect domestic movements to international concerns.[2]

The third major point illustrated by these examples is that movements may vary in size, duration, scope, depth, level of government focus, and public support. At times, smaller movements may be better able to build consensus and coordinate action. In other instances, large numbers communicate greater political urgency and can better pressure a political response. Efforts to mobilize around a stigmatized identity may spark countermobilization when groups feel their own standing is threatened or not accounted for. For example, the creation of the "Black Lives Matter" hashtag prompted counter-slogans of "All Lives Matter" and "Blue Lives Matter."

In the remaining sections of this chapter I examine how a collection of contemporary political movements – the Black Lives Matter and Native Lives Matter movements, the Women's March and Me Too movement, DREAMers, and the Never Again movement – illustrate these three central points. Each of these has learned from, built upon, and, in many cases, challenged the movement template created by the Civil Rights movement.

Setting the Stage for the Civil Rights Movement

The Civil Rights movement is both an exemplar and an outlier of efforts to forge identity-based collective action. Recall from chapter 4 the impact of segregation and the denial of civil rights protections that African Americans and other groups experienced before the 1960s. For African Americans, the dual processes of migration and urbanization helped promote the belief that organized efforts were essential to advancing the struggle for racial equality. By constructing a comprehensive legal agenda driven by a commitment to attacking the legal system and disentangling race and diminished political standing, the National Association for the Advancement of Colored People (NAACP) became a forerunner in championing the developmental stages of the movement.

One of the organization's most significant efforts involved petitioning the Supreme Court to overturn the separate but equal doctrine in *Plessy* v. *Ferguson*. In response to these efforts, eleven Southern states filed amici briefs asking the Court to uphold its ruling. Even more monumental was the fact that President Truman filed a brief supporting the NAACP's position. This brief was historic because it was the first amicus brief filed by a president on behalf of African Americans, and also the first time since the late 1870s that the federal government had sided against the South (Lawson 2003). Though the NAACP was unsuccessful in getting the Court to overturn the case, it encouraged the formation of other civil rights groups who could engage in grassroots mobilization efforts. The Mississippi Improvement Association, the National Urban League, and the Southern Christian Leadership Conference all drew upon the experiences of the NAACP to launch the largest and most successful mass movement in the United States designed to dismantle racial barriers to full citizenship and access.

The Civil Rights Movement and Institutional Responses to Identity

The 1953 Baton Rouge bus boycott marked the beginning of massive grassroots efforts of what would become known as the modern Civil Rights movement. Drawing upon the indigenous resources of the community, such as leadership, information networks, movement centers, and the Black Church, grassroots organizers were able to mobilize non-violent **insurgency** at the local level (McAdam 1982; Morris 1984; McClerking and Philpot 2008). As the mass efforts gained momentum, the NAACP continued its lobbying and litigation efforts by successfully arguing two very important cases before the Supreme Court: *Brown I* (1954) and *Brown II* (1955). The decisions together provided for the desegregation of public schools with all deliberate speed and provided the tools civil rights leaders needed to wage a full-scale national movement. The decisions also sparked a massive white backlash designed to impede integration (Day 2014). This was particularly true in the South, where state legislatures and courts debated the constitutionality of the Supreme Court decision and its infringement upon states' rights.

In one of the most notable examples of this defiance, Arkansas Governor Orval Faubus dispatched the state's National Guard troops to Little Rock High School, where nine Black students sought to integrate the public schools under federal court order. In a now famous speech in 1958 defending his actions, Faubus warned against the "all powerful, intrusive federal government":

> To you who oppose the great majority of Arkansas people in this fight, I urge you to think – lest in your consuming desire to gain your ends, among them the destruction of Orval Faubus, you destroy also the very principles of government that enable you and all others to live as a free people, and to rear your children under the high standards of living and freedom which prevail in this state and nation.[3]

In response, President Eisenhower sent federal troops to Arkansas to protect African American children attempting to integrate the schools.[4] This conflict between the federal and state levels prompted the Supreme Court's assertion, in *Cooper* v. *Aaron* (1958), that no legislator, executive, or judicial official could undermine his or her obligation to uphold the doctrines of the Constitution. Building upon these events, President John F. Kennedy, Jr, asked Congress in 1963 to pass a bill banning discrimination in public accommodations. This request also sparked the 1963 March on Washington for Jobs and Freedom led by the Reverend Dr Martin Luther King, Jr.

Intersectionality as a Source of Conflict within Political Movements

Although the Civil Rights movement was intended to be a broad effort to liberalize American society by rejecting racial discrimination, it engendered enduring battles over the intersection(s) of race and other identity markers. The chief architect of the March on Washington was Bayard Rustin, a pacifist, a Quaker, a socialist, and an openly gay man at a time when most state laws criminalized homosexuality. Rustin believed that freedom movements had to incorporate multiple coalition partners who could capitalize on their numerical strengths while promoting a broader vision of freedom (Rustin 1965). He also realized, however, that social norms combined with legal constraints to limit the scope of that inclusion. Rustin became a trusted confidante of Dr Martin Luther King, Jr, and encouraged him to embrace the teachings of

A. Philip Randolph that emphasized the necessity of labor to freedom and independence (Long 2012). Randolph saw the push for civil rights as a means of securing political *and* economic freedom to benefit the country as a whole.

The Civil Rights movement was built on a strong coalition of multiracial, multiethnic, multifaith leaders. Indeed one of the major resources of the movement was its connection to churches as meeting spaces and centers of organizing. The religious conservatism coupled with the public profiles of many of the coalition partners led some to criticize whether Rustin was "suited" to play such a visible role in the leadership structure.[5] One of the sharpest critics was Roy Wilkins, executive secretary of the NAACP, who said of Rustin:

> I don't want you leading the march on Washington, because you know I don't give a damn about what they say, but publicly I don't want to have to defend the draft dodging . . . I know you're a Quaker, but that's not what I'll have to defend. I'll have to defend promiscuity. The question is never going to be homosexuality, it's going to be promiscuity and I can't defend that. And the fact is that you were a member of the Young Communist League. And I don't care what you say, I can't defend that. (D'Emilio 2003)

As a result of Wilkins's objections, Rustin agreed to be the deputy for the march, with Randolph being the public face of leadership. Even during the march, however, internal fractures challenged group solidarity. Most notable was the refusal to allow women to address the crowd of over 250,000 people. Leaders from the major civil rights organizations, known as the "Big Six," argued that women were excluded because they couldn't find a unifying voice to address the crowd without being divisive (Collier-Thomas and Franklin 2001).[6] The only woman to serve on the planning committee, Anna Arnold Hedgeman, addressed the hypocrisy of building a movement for inclusion predicated on the exclusion of women's voices: "In light of the role of Negro women in the struggle for freedom and especially in light of the extra burden they have carried because of the castration of our Negro men in this culture, it is incredible that no woman should appear as a speaker at the historic March on Washington Meeting at the Lincoln Memorial" (Hedgeman 1964: 189).

The March on Washington and its accompanying lobbying efforts led to the passage of the 1964 Civil Rights Act. Although the bill had the support of the president, it still faced fierce opposition within Congress. Most notably, the efforts of Senator Strom Thurmond (R-SC), via an eight-week filibuster, demonstrated the degree to which the extension of civil rights to African Americans was an incredibly divisive political issue among legislators. To circumvent this opposition, Democrats used the Commerce Clause rather than the Fourteenth Amendment to substantiate the bill's claims. This choice was important for three primary reasons. First, using the Commerce Clause allowed the bill's provisions to apply to both the public and the private domain. Second, sponsors were able to send the bill to the more liberal Commerce Committee rather than the Judiciary Committee. This was an important strategic move given that the chair of the Judiciary Committee was vehemently opposed to civil rights and could have prevented the bill from hitting the floor. Third, Democrats were able to avoid the arduous task of convincing the Supreme Court to overturn yet another precedent.

The Civil Rights Acts of 1964 prohibited discrimination in employment (under Title VII), banned segregation in public accommodations, and established the Equal Employment Opportunity Commission to investigate workplace discrimination claims. It was a monumental piece of legislation because it demonstrated that the federal government could play a role in safeguarding the rights of citizens at both state and local levels. In response, many Southern states challenged the bill as going beyond the ability of Congress to legislate under the Constitution. Despite these challenges, the bill paved the way for the Civil Rights Act of 1968 and the Voting Rights Act of 1965. Through these key pieces of legislation, many groups, not just African Americans, gained access to the tools necessary to successfully challenge discrimination in both the private and the public sector.

In 1965, John Lewis led students in a peaceful march across the Edmund Pettus Bridge in Selma, Alabama. He and the other marchers were severely beaten by those who opposed civil rights. Lewis was elected to Congress in 1987.

From Protest to Politics: The Voting Rights Act of 1965

Following the successful passage of the Civil Rights Act of 1964 and the adjudication of the *Brown* v. *Board* decision, activists heightened their commitment to voting rights as a badge of full citizenship. On March 7, 1965, state troopers attacked a group of peaceful demonstrators on the Edmund Pettus Bridge in Selma, Alabama. Television networks broadcast images of the attack around the world, attracting widespread attention and demonstrations in support of the voting rights cause. These events – as well as the deaths in Selma of activists Jimmy Lee Jackson, Viola Liuzzo, and James Reeb – produced sufficient public pressure for Congress to pass the Voting Rights Act, which President Lyndon Johnson signed into law on August 6, 1965:

> Every American citizen must have an equal right to vote . . . Yet the harsh fact is that in many places in this country men and women are kept from voting simply because they are Negroes . . . There is no constitutional issue here. The command of the Constitution is plain. There is no moral issue. It is wrong – deadly wrong – to deny any of your fellow Americans the right to vote in this country. There is no issue of states' rights or national rights. There is only the struggle for human rights.[7]

The Voting Rights Act suspended literacy and interpretation tests and allowed federal officials to register voters and monitor local elections in particular jurisdictions. The preclearance provision of the new Act required that jurisdictions with a history of discrimination submit new election rules or plans to federal officials. State and local officials could implement the proposed election rule or plan only after federal officials approved it. By shifting the burden to states and localities to prove to federal officials that changes were not discriminatory, the preclearance process avoided the delays and expenses of litigation while stopping discriminatory laws before they were used in elections. The preclearance provision applied to jurisdictions with discriminatory tests or devices and low turnout or registration in the 1964 presidential election. Although the preclearance provision was originally intended to last five years, the Voting Rights Act also included a nationwide, permanent provision that allowed private parties or the Justice Department to bring lawsuits to stop racially discriminatory election laws and electoral plans (Brown-Dean et al. 2015).

The Voting Rights Act (VRA) of 1965 had a profound impact on American elections. By extending legal protection of the franchise, the Act helped usher in a massive new class of political actors both as voters and as candidates. The number of African Americans registered to vote soared tremendously, especially in the South. This stands in sharp contrast to the regressive nature of Black registration in the period between Reconstruction and the Civil Rights movement. Similarly, the VRA helped increase the number of Black elected officials by nearly 80 percent (Brown-Dean et al. 2015). (See figure 5.6, p. 114, which illustrates the impact of passing the Voting Rights Act on diversifying the electorate as well as the candidates they chose.) In the eleven former states of the Confederacy, Black voter turnout out has matched, and in some elections exceeded, the rate of white voters (see figure 5.2, p. 109).[8]

Mobilization and Countermobilization: The Legacy of Racially Polarized Voting

An additional legacy of the movement toward increased electoral participation is the growth of racial divides along partisan lines. African Americans have increasingly favored Democrats, and recently Latinos and Asian Americans have become more loyal to the Democratic Party. However, party loyalty varies across countries of origin and generational status, with younger voters of color being more likely to split their votes than their elders. The shift to the left has been particularly pronounced for Asian Americans (Hajnal and Lee 2011). On the other side, whites have moved slowly and unevenly, but inexorably, to the Republican Party. American Indian voters are more bipartisan in nature, often supporting the Republican Party at the national level to limit government involvement in Indian affairs. In recent national contests for the presidency, the House, and the Senate, the racialized nature of the vote was very pronounced. For example, during the 2018 midterm elections,

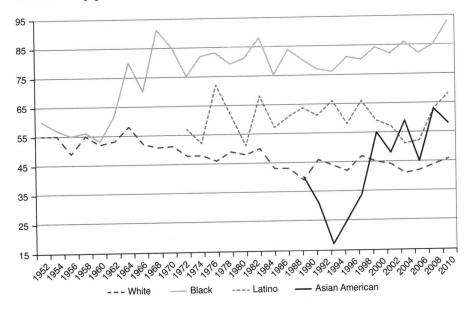

Figure 8.4 Democratic Party identification over time (percentages)
SOURCE: Brown et al. (2015).

69 percent of Latino voters, compared to 44 percent of whites and 77 percent of Asian Americans, favored Democratic candidates (Krogstad et al. 2018). This polarized voting continues a long trend of partisan divisions along racial and ethnic lines. Division is a normal and healthy part of democracy, but, when a core dividing line in a nation becomes so closely aligned with various dimensions of group identity, larger concerns about inequality, conflict, and discrimination emerge. Figure 8.4 captures the dramatic shifts in party support across groups that were solidified after the passage of the Voting Rights Act 1965 and the general opening of American politics.

One of the greatest advances of the Civil Rights movement and its accompanying policy gains was that it inculcated the belief that the electoral arena could be a viable outlet for advancing group interests (Tate 1994). Building upon this belief, many civil rights organizations and leaders organized group efforts around the power of the vote. This process led to what many term the "New Black Politics" that helped raise both the political and electoral consciousness of African Americans (Smith 1996; Walton 1985; Jennings 1992). The emphasis on full political participation helped diversify the cadre of elected officials who made use of existing resources such as political organizations and volunteers. This strategy of attempting to institutionalize racial identity was particularly successful at the local level, where the first Black mayor, Carl Stokes of Cleveland, was elected in 1967. Yet, in raising the electoral consciousness of African Americans, the Civil Rights movement simultaneously raised the racial consciousness of all Americans.

As racial barriers to engaging the political process began to shift, so too did the presentation and organizing styles of political hopefuls who sought to redefine the meaning of their racial identity to their political preferences. Andra Gillespie (2009) and her colleagues examine how the election of Barack Obama and others at the local, state, and national levels highlights a turn toward "post-racial" leadership that draws upon a broad cohesive base of support that isn't beholden to race-specific communities. This approach draws on the early work of scholars Joseph McCormick II and Charles Jones, which traces the emergence of deracialization as a political strategy that avoids making "explicit reference to race-specific issues, while at the same time emphasizing

---

BOX 8.2 Three lessons from the Civil Rights movement

1 Mobilization breeds countermobilization.
2 Political movements may advocate on behalf of one identity group but can help extend rights and resources for multiple groups.
3 Political movements can transform political culture.

those issues that are perceived as racially transcendent" (1993: 76). Where the "post-racial" concept focuses on how voters evaluate and react to candidates of color, deracialization emphasizes how candidates position themselves, their priorities, and their presentation style.

The Civil Rights movement is something of an anomaly in American politics. Few other movements have propelled such a large segment of the country toward change. However, its legacy illuminates three key lessons that have shaped the course of future identity-based action. First, mobilization breeds countermobilization. As communities across the South came together to demand full equality, other groups were prompted to mobilize in opposition. That opposition ranged from traditional methods of political participation, such as voting, to extralegal and even illegal means, such as disenfranchisement and violence. When stigmatized groups are able to harness authentic power, it automatically forces a shift in how power is dispersed. In turn, even when movements set out to focus on one particular group identity or set of identities, their acts of insurgency can help expand protections for other groups. And, finally, the Civil Rights movement teaches us that movements can transform political culture. One of its most important contributions was its ability to serve as a tool of mass socialization that empowered communities to reject complacency and demand positive social change. That transformation of both cultural and electoral consciousness has shaped a number of contemporary movements to dismantle the link between race and the criminal justice system.

The Legacy of Protest

Patrisse Khan-Cullors writes in her memoir *When They Call You a Terrorist*: "What is the impact of not being valued? How do you measure the loss of what a human being does not receive" (2018: 107–8)? That question was front and center in 2013 as crowds gathered outside the Old Courthouse in Sanford, Florida, awaiting the verdict for George Zimmerman. Zimmerman was charged with second-degree murder for killing an unarmed Black seventeen-year-old boy named Trayvon Martin. Martin was walking back to his father's home in a gated community when he encountered Zimmerman. The trial was the culmination of nearly eighteen months of heated public debate over what really happened on the night of February 26th. To some, Martin was a victim of racial profiling shot by an overzealous former neighborhood watch leader who acted on impulse rather than justified fear. To others, Zimmerman simply defended himself in a state that justified the use of deadly force under threat of injury. The details of the case and law enforcement's response heightened public scrutiny of Florida's **Stand Your Ground laws**. Signed into law by then Governor Jeb Bush, Stand Your Ground provisions protect those acting in self-defense from both criminal and civil action unless "there is probable cause that the force that was used was unlawful."[9] The high-profile nature of Martin's death prompted a number of states to limit or repeal their self-defense statutes. Currently, twenty-six states have versions of the law that allow people to use force if they feel threatened or attacked.

Deputies worked to contain the crowd that was growing in both number and frustration. The trial was an international spectacle that drew protesters and supporters from across the United States. As national media outlets descended on Seminole County, the angst loomed thicker than the Florida humidity. Protesters on both sides of the sidewalk feared that the verdict would ignite longstanding tensions over race, space, and belonging. Trayvon Martin's murder became a rallying cry for those demanding justice and accountability. Advocacy groups such as the National Action Network condemned the Sanford Police Department for waiting forty-four days after the shooting to arrest Zimmerman. Trayvon's parents, Sybrina Fulton and Tracy Martin, were initially told that no charges would be filed against the man who killed their son. Longtime media professionals from the National Association of Black Journalists refused to let the public forget about Martin while covering similar stories across the nation. The intense public pressure prompted Florida Governor Rick Scott to appoint Angela Corey to investigate. Impromptu rallies sprang up in such disparate cities as Detroit, Nashville, Los Angeles, Miami, and Lynchburg, Virginia.

Zimmerman told 911 dispatchers that Trayvon Martin was wearing a hooded sweatshirt that made him look menacing. Store footage shows the youth returning to his father's home after purchasing a bag of Skittles and an Arizona fruit beverage. Protesters carried bags of Skittles while wearing hoodies in solidarity. The hashtag #JUSTICEFORTRAYVONMARTIN became one of the most popular issues trending on Twitter, and his now iconic image was splashed across Facebook pages. Social media and access to technology played a vital role in networking people across the globe outraged by the teen's death and the justice system's seeming disinterest in pursuing his killer. The intense media coverage painted an America deeply divided.

Black Lives Matter

In the hours after Zimmerman's acquittal, the organizing efforts of three women – Patrisse Cullors, Opal Tometti, and Alicia Garza – denounced the collusion of actors, institutions, and policies that shaped the verdict and its aftermath. The phrase "Black Lives Matter" and the subsequent movement for Black lives were borne out of the frustration that the continued acquittals of people accused of killing unarmed citizens reinforced the notion that the lives of people of color were systematically deemed less valuable. The aim was to

Erica Garner speaks at a Black Lives Matter rally in New York to protest police brutality. Her father, Eric Garner, was killed by NYPD officers in 2014.

build an inclusive movement of allies and activists who would confront public indifference while demanding institutional accountability (Lebron 2017; Thurston 2018). That inclusion was buttressed by a loosely bound network of local chapters, stretching from Los Angeles to Toronto. Members famously disrupted a campaign rally by presidential hopeful Bernie Sanders to draw attention to issues of justice and race. Other leaders protested anti-trans violence that often went overlooked by media and the public. The deaths of Trayvon Martin and Michael Brown encouraged activists to build a collective effort that would address systemic challenges and not just individual experiences (Craven 2016; Taylor 2016).

Native American Lives Matter[10]

That call for systemic change resonated with Gyasi Ross, who is a poet, story-teller, attorney, and activist. Each of those titles is woven together by Ross's profound pride in and responsibility of being a member of the Blackfeet Nation, one of Northern America's oldest Indian nations. His popular podcast "Breakdances with Wolves" uses hip-hop music and culture to promote Indian pride while tackling important political issues such as mental health, poverty, and education. Ross is no stranger to taking bold stances. An article he wrote for the *Huffington Post* was a call to action for groups to cross social boundaries and demand justice:

> It's not that a black boy got shot and killed, or that a shoot-first, possible racist killed him, that should burn all of us up. Instead, we should all be angry – violently, pissed-off, scarily angry – that a child, regardless of color, was taken off this earth for no good reason and it literally could be any one of us that are feeling the pain that this mother feels today. He

didn't ask for this. She didn't ask for this – they were both minding their business, living their lives not harming anyone. This isn't about black or white or Native or Mexican or whatever. This is about life, and this is about our kids. (Ross 2012)

BOX 8.3 The Red Power movement

The American Indian movement (AIM) was founded in Minneapolis, Minnesota, in 1968 by activists who wanted to focus on the challenges facing Indians in urban areas. Chief among them were poverty, religious freedom, land rights, police brutality, and education. AIM's direct action techniques of protests drew support from groups across the country while also drawing the attention and response of government agencies such as the FBI. AIM's reach and influence sparked a number of legal battles with the federal government that led to multiple arrests and prosecutions of movement leaders.

In spite of this legal conflict, AIM's organizing efforts helped shape the broader Red Power movement, which lasted from 1969 to 1978 and used protest tactics and direct action strategies to dramatize the extreme discontent of groups whose rights were routinely ignored or subverted. One of the most notable examples was the Alcatraz Occupation by members of the Indians of All Tribes (IAT). After several attempts, over eighty American Indians landed on and seized control of Alcatraz Island in California. The group wanted to build a spiritual center, museum, and ecology center on land that, they claimed, resembled most reservations because it lacked running water or health-care facilities. The occupation's leader, Richard Oakes, penned the Alcatraz Proclamation to outline the group's demands:

> We invite the United States to acknowledge the justice of our claim. The choice now lies with the leaders of the American government – to use violence upon us as before to remove us from our Great Spirit's land, or to institute a real change in its dealing with the American Indian. We do not fear your threat to charge us with crimes on our land. We and all other oppressed peoples would welcome spectacle of proof before the world of your title by genocide. Nevertheless, we seek peace. (See Eagle 1992)

Oakes sought to build a collective Indian nation comprised of delegates from tribes across North America who could help construct a comprehensive agenda for Indian liberation. Inspired by this initial occupation and the IAT's vision for Indian self-determination, tribal members launched over seventy-four demonstrations and occupations in the following years (Wilkins and Stark 2011). But the Red Power movement revealed a persistent challenge for political movements: addressing internal cleavages while still moving forward. Noted Indian politics scholar David Wilkins (2002) points out that religious differences became an important resource for the new Red Power movement. In the past, cleavages between "traditionalists" and "Indian Christians" were a source of conflict between those who were ready to fully embrace the broader culture and those who wanted to retain the unique characteristics of Indian life. This diversity, however, helped challenge the broader monolithic view of American Indians while showing how traditional values could be compatible with contemporary demands for justice. The legacies of AIM and the Red Power movement have shaped a generation of efforts to demand justice for American Indian communities.

Critics argued that Ross glossed over the complex experiences of Native people, whose daily interactions with those in power often lead to a loss of life and/or property. Others questioned why demands for coalition-building seemed to follow only the deaths of Black victims while failing to address the reality that Native American youth are more likely than any other group to be killed by law enforcement. The critique was simple: calls for solidarity and public outrage are often conditioned upon the identities of the victim and the aggressor. According to a report published by the Centers for Disease Control, American Indians are more likely than any other demographic group in the United States to be killed by police[11] – a reality that is rarely addressed within mainstream media reports or community organizing.

As figure 8.5 illustrates, the rate of American Indian deaths at the hands of law enforcement has risen sharply. However, it's important to note that these occurrences are likely underreported due to the failure to account for people

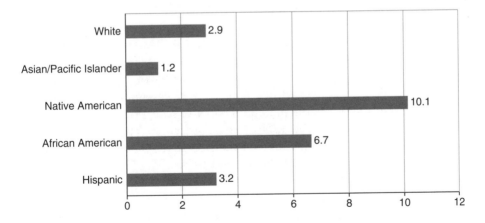

Figure 8.5 Rate of police killings per million by race/ethnicity, 2015–2016
Source: Data based on "The Counted" series from *The Guardian*, 2018.

who are mixed race. The Black Lives Matter movement and its grassroots demonstration tactics helped demand increased media coverage of the disproportionate number of Blacks killed by officers and/or dying in police custody. Political psychologists define the phenomenon of *media framing* as the process of focusing on certain events and issues and then placing them in a broader field of meaning. Schroedel and Chin (2017) find that media publications systematically fail to cover the deaths of American Indians by law enforcement with the same intensity as those of Black victims. Even in cities such as Minneapolis, with a documented history of disproportionate rates of fatal contact, the coverage tends to address Black victims more (Woodard 2016). Pointing out this difference, however, isn't an attempt to privilege the value of Black lives over Indian lives. Rather, it highlights the importance of group resources and institutional features in shaping access to power and justice via the demands of political movements. Three key points emerge:

1 Underrepresented groups must draw on community resources and institutions to promote their concerns.
2 Social institutions such as mass media can serve to moderate the relationship between stigmatized groups and public recognition.
3 Invisibility politics can impact political access, representation, and economic standing.

The organizing efforts of Black Lives Matter supporters coupled with media coverage helped elevate concerns that African Americans are at a great risk for harm. The challenge, however, is that the relative invisibility of American Indian concerns served to underestimate the scope of the problem with the lethal use of force by police.

Case and Context

Data released by the Pew Research Center (2013) illustrate that Americans were sharply divided over the amount of attention being paid to broader concerns about race and justice vis-à-vis the murder of Trayvon Martin. In table 8.1 we see that, among whites, 60 percent of respondents believed that too much attention was being placed on issues of race. White men seemed to be particularly opposed to the discussion: 66 percent of white men compared to 54 percent of white women agreed that too much focus centers on race. By comparison, 40 percent of Hispanics and 13 percent of African Americans agreed with the statement.

Together these narratives highlight the confluence of established features of the democratic process that define the limits of citizenship and the boundaries of identity. Across various institutions, actors, and policy spaces, the interaction between political decision-making, public support, and historical

Table 8.1 Race and reactions to the Zimmerman verdict (percentages)

Are you satisfied or dissatisfied with the Zimmerman verdict?	Total	White	Black	Hisp
Satisfied	39	49	5	25
Disatisfied	42	30	86	58
Dont't Know	19	21	9	17
	100	100	100	100
In this case. . .				
The issue of race is getting more attention than it deserves	52	60	13	40
Raises important issues about race that need to be discussed	36	28	78	47
Don't know	12	12	8	13
	100	100	100	100
N	1,480	1,047	153	166

SOURCE: Pew Research Center (2013).

circumstance defines the political meaning of various identities at once. This variation can impel underrepresented groups to mobilize via political movements while sparking countermobilization efforts among groups who feel their interests are challenged. Although the Black Lives Matter and Native Lives Matter movements are direct descendants of the long Civil Rights movement, the progeny of group-based demands for inclusion spans a host of identities related to gender, sexual identity, citizenship status, and policy goals that stretch across various markers.

Me Too, The Women's March, and Modern Movements for Gender Equity

The Yale Law School is an iconic space that has groomed eight members of the United States Supreme Court and numerous legal scholars who frequently testify before the US Congress. Former presidents, presidential hopefuls, and presidential advisors have walked the halls of the school, learning alongside thought leaders, ambassadors, and authors. It's also where Guggenheim Fellows and MacArthur geniuses lead sessions at the annual Rebellious Lawyering Conference on using the law as a tool of freedom. The Law School has been a key site for debating important topics of the day and strategizing a plan of action.

On a Monday afternoon in June 2018, the Yale Law School auditorium is where hundreds gather to hear from a woman who has spent the last twenty-five years of her career advocating on behalf of girls and women of color who survive sexual abuse and trauma. Tarana Burke commands the room the moment she enters. Some audience members whisper their admiration while others debate the merits of what has now become known as the Me Too movement. A small group of students from the neighboring high school clamor for seats closer to the front of the room as they prepare to hear from a woman they describe as a "warrior." They've seen her face on magazine covers, listened to her commentary on social media, and glimpsed her pressing the button to release the Waterford Crystal ball in Times Square during the New Year's Eve celebration. Some audience members attend because they feel the need to speak on behalf of "good guys" who feel lumped into a public narrative of women as victims and men as predators.

BOX 8.4 Tarana Burke, founder of the Me Too movement

"Our goal is to reframe and expand the global conversation around sexual violence to speak to the needs of a broader spectrum of survivors. Young people, queer, trans, and disabled folks, black women and girls, and all communities of color. We want perpetrators to be held accountable and we want strategies implemented to sustain long term, systemic change."

On that occasion I interviewed Burke about the increased public attention to issues of sexual violence and harassment: "There's not anything different being said right now except there's more voices saying it, so clearly the more voices raise the volume and change the frequency," according to Burke. "People keep saying women are finding their voice now, but women have had their voice for a while; they just haven't heard us. It's not that we're finding our voices, it's we've finally reached a frequency where people can hear." When asked how efforts to combat sexual violence can build inclusive constituencies that challenge past limitations, Burke urged people to first interrogate their motives. She then emphasized the need for men to commit to the movement: "This is a time for men to be allies in the workplace."

With long regal braids, Burke walks across the stage of the Yale Law School and the crowd erupts into applause. She speaks with a familiar blend of relatability and matter-of-factness that reflects her near twenty-five-year investment in advocacy work. She's clearly comfortable in front of the crowd yet keenly aware that the polite applause doesn't mean unanimous agreement with the movement she's now credited for launching. Tarana Burke launched the Me Too campaign in 2007 to draw attention to the experiences of girls and women of color. According to the Bureau of Justice Statistics, African American females experience intimate partner violence at a rate that is two and a half times greater than among women of other races. Similarly, American Indian women and Latinas experience disproportionate rates of sexual assault compared to other groups. And yet, according to Burke, the intersections of race, ethnicity, class, sexual orientation, culture, and gender identity are rarely accounted for within broader efforts to end sexual violence. She argues that this invisibility makes it even more difficult to shift the norms and behaviors that make violence so pervasive.

BOX 8.5 Movements to combat violence

In 1994, Congress passed the Violence against Women Act (VAWA) in conjunction with the Violence Crime Control and Enforcement Act. VAWA was the first federal effort to address violence against women and was the result of a sustained political movement to elevate the security of girls and women. Opponents questioned whether the provisions meant to protect women violated the due process rights of men accused of harming them. The Act created a rape shield law banning the disclosure of victims' identities, authorized federal resources to combat domestic violence and provide shelter and legal assistance to survivors, and encouraged local police departments to automatically arrest someone when called to a domestic violence situation. Later reauthorizations of the Act expanded protections for immigrant women and those with disabilities, included gender-neutral provisions to protect men who are victimized, and addressed the epidemic of sexual assault on college campuses. The 2013 extension of the Violence against Women Act created new provisions to protect women in Indian country, who are nearly three times more likely to experience sexual violence than other groups, by empowering tribal law-enforcement officials to prosecute non-tribal members and enhance resources programs on and off the reservation.

While the VAWA addresses primarily domestic violence, organizations such as the Human Rights Campaign hope to extend its coverage of trans and gender non-conforming people who are increasingly targets of violence. According to a report issued by the National Center for Transgender Equality, one in four transgender people recounts having been physically assaulted because of their identity; 102 trans people have been murdered between 2013 and 2018. In Jacksonville, Florida, for example, the rate of trans murders exceeds that for the entire country. Activists also point to the tendency of law-enforcement officials to misgender victims when describing their murders. For example, victims who now identify as women are often designated based on their identity assigned at birth.

For over a decade "Me Too" was a catchphrase Tarana Burke and her supporters used to stand in solidarity and promote empathy through empowerment: "On one side, it's a bold declarative statement that 'I'm not ashamed' and 'I'm not alone.' On the other side, it's a statement from survivor to survivor that says 'I see you, I hear you, I understand you and I'm here for you or I get it.'" In October of 2017 the ubiquitous phrase became synonymous with efforts to expose high-profile men who routinely abused their power at the expense of women. After a *New York Times* article detailed sexual assault accusations against Hollywood executive Harvey Weinstein, actress Alyssa Milano took to Twitter and encouraged survivors to tweet the hashtag "MeToo." People responded by using the hashtag over 12 million times. Many credited Milano and other celebrities with drawing attention to the prevalence of sexual violence and thrust them into the spotlight as leaders of a "new movement." However, advocates who worked with survivors of color expressed their concern that the public conversation surrounding Me Too veered far from the path Burke had established a decade earlier. Burke asserts that "Sexual violence touches every demographic but the response to it doesn't. You have to use your privilege to serve other people."

As the hashtag went viral, so too did the surge of allegations against other public figures – Matt Lauer, Kevin Spacey, Louis C. K., Bill Cosby, and even the president of the United States. Often those revelations resulted in immediate calls for firings and punishment. But in her talk at the Yale Law School Burke makes it clear: the focus on ending gender violence can't just be on punishing perpetrators. Instead, it has to be on healing survivors:

> This was not a plot to ruin his [Weinstein's] career. In fact, the women that spoke up thought their careers would be ruined. It was about every day regular people around the world . . . making a declaration and saying, "I'm a victim of sexual violence." There's never been a movement to say, "Me too, take him down." That's not what it's about. Sexual violence happens on a spectrum so accountability has to happen on a spectrum. I don't think that every single case of sexual harassment has to result in someone being fired; the consequences should vary. But we need a shift in culture so that every single instance of sexual harassment is investigated and dealt with. That's just basic common sense. (Brockes 2018)

The timing of Tarana Burke's appearance at Yale Law School capped a nearly sixteen-month cycle of public battles over the continued relationship between gender, power, and representation. Following the contested results of the 2016 presidential election, Teresa Shook of Hawaii took to Facebook to express her dismay and fear that changes in political leadership posed a threat to women's rights. Her initial request that forty of her friends join her in Washington, DC, to protest the new president's first full day in office morphed into over 2.5 million people across the world gathering for rallies and protests in places such as Washington, DC, Toronto, Berlin, and Paris. Against the backdrop of organizing for women's rights, the 2017 Women's March highlighted longstanding tensions associated with calls for gender

---

> **BOX 8.6 Four waves of the Women's movement**
>
> 1   Late nineteenth and early twentieth centuries: Focused on *voting rights and property rights*
> 2   1970s and 1980s: Focused on protecting *civil rights* of women
> 3   Early 1990s: Focused on broadening the lens to address *intersectionality*
> 4   Late 1990s–present: Focuses on increasing women's *representation* in various *political offices and policy spaces*

solidarity that ignore the diversity that exists within and across identity groups (Heaney 2018).

In chapter 1, I argued that names and labels matter for conveying notions of worth and recognition. That premise held for the call for women to gather in 2017. Organizers initially termed the effort the "Million Woman March." Almost immediately activists and observers pointed out that the choice of name co-opted marches led as early as 1997 to promote unity and cooperative development among Black women. Ironically, the proposed march in Washington to protest the results of the 2016 election marked the twentieth anniversary of the Million Woman March organized by Phile Chionesu in Philadelphia. Others took issue with the proposed leadership for the march, arguing that it whitewashed women's activism and ignored differences of race, sexual orientation, gender expression, physical ability, and class. A number of critics pointed to the tension between calls to organize in support of women's rights and the exit poll data captured in table 8.2, showing that 52 percent of white women compared to 4 percent of Black women and 25 percent of Latinas cast their ballots for the new president. The results highlighted in table 8.3 further confirm the electoral gaps across race, gender, and education level.

The challenge was clear: Any effort to represent women's interests had to be built on a commitment to diversity and inclusion that captured the breadth of policy challenges the group wanted to tackle. Linda Sarsour joined as march co-chair to diversify its leadership and to challenge participants to adopt a more intersectional approach to organizing:

> As women of color who came into this effort we came in not only to mobilize and organize but also to educate, to argue that we can't talk about women's rights, about reproductive rights, about equal pay, without also talking about race and class ... We are hoping that the conversation continues and that we can move into a different place and focus on the way that we're coming together *nonetheless*. (Traister 2017)

Critiques of the 2017 Women's March and its follow-up activities forced many to consider the foundations of representation and inclusion. While

Table 8.2 2016 election results by race and gender (percentages)

	Clinton	Trump
White men	31	62
White women	43	52
Black men	82	13
Black women	94	4
Latino men	63	32
Latinas	69	25
Others	61	31

SOURCE: Based on data from the 2016 CNN exit polls.

Table 8.3 2018 midterm election vote choice by race, gender, and education

	Republican	Democrat
All non-white voters	22	76
White men without college degree	66	32
White men with college degree	51	47
White women without college degree	56	42
White women with college degree	39	59

SOURCE: Based on data from the 2018 CNN exit polls.

The 2017 Women's March was a worldwide protest following the inauguration of President Donald J. Trump. A number of commemorative marches were canceled in 2019 because of internal disagreements over racism, anti-Semitism, and leadership.

the organizing efforts helped inspire a greater number of women to run for elected office and led pundits to declare 2017 the Year of the Woman, broader questions of accountability began to emerge. Against this backdrop the emergence of the Me Too movement that same year flamed concerns about the effort's purpose and intent. For some, it was about empowerment and rejecting stigma. For others, it was an attempt at retribution that denied men access to due process and made them uncomfortable. I asked Tarana Burke about her response to celebrity life coach Tony Robbins after a video surfaced of him denouncing Me Too as a ploy used by sexual abuse victims to "make themselves relevant." Robbins recounts a conversation he had with a powerful businessman who chose not to hire a "very pretty woman" because he couldn't "have her around because it's too big a risk." Burke responded to the controversy by saying:

> It makes my blood boil. It's such cowardice. And it's not just cowardice but callousness. You're going to watch millions of people saying, "My life has been touched by this thing," and your response is, "Aww man, now what am I supposed to do?" This is the kind of thing women are dealing with. We can't have a conversation. I'm speaking English and you're speaking Klingon.

When Tarana Burke enters the Law School to discuss her approach, the tension in the room is palpable. Results from a 2017 Harvard–Harris Poll found that, while most Americans supported the movement, there were significant divisions across gender lines regarding the best way to address allegations. Burke is clearly prepared for the whirlwind of questions she will undoubtedly face. Her opening is direct: "This movement isn't about taking down perpetrators. It's about empowering survivors" – survivors, not victims. The choice of words is intentional. As senior director of programs for Girls for Gender Equity, the Brooklyn-based organization dedicated to empowering girls and women, Burke believes it's necessary to adopt an intergenerational approach to building inclusive movements: "There are still women of all ages that have never had an opportunity to be seen and be visible. Young people will certainly have a different kind of future, and I hope that they feel hopeful about that. Even older women feel hopeful for younger people or for themselves that they will have a different reality going forward." Now she wants to shift the public focus from "MeToo" as a hashtag to "Me Too" as a movement that draws attention to the needs of those who have been harmed by sexual violence: "there is inherent strength in agency. Me Too, in a lot of ways, is about agency. It's not about giving up your agency."

Those internal conversations about agency, alignment, and agenda continue to shape contemporary movements to address gender equality. Recall from the discussion of movement preconditions that determining appropriate leadership and coalition partners rests as an important decision for any political movement. Collective action on behalf of stigmatized groups is often stronger and more effective when allies articulate their support. Likewise, the choice of allies and surrogates can provoke critique from those who conflate surrogate personalities with movement goals. The 2019 Women's March, for example, was marred by persistent allegations of anti-Semitism and calls for co-leader Tamika Mallory to step down after refusing to denounce comments made by Nation of Islam leader Minister Louis Farrakhan (Lockhart 2018). These concerns forced a number of sponsors, such as the Center for American Progress, the Human Rights Campaign, and EMILY's List, to withdraw their support.

In the Overview & Purpose of its Guiding Vision and Definition of Principles, the leaders of the Women's March write: "Recognizing that women have intersecting identities and are therefore impacted by a multitude of social justice and human rights issues, we have outlined a representative vision for a government that is based on the principles of liberty and justice for all. As Dr King said, 'We cannot walk alone. And as we walk, we must make the pledge that we shall always march ahead. We cannot turn back. Our liberation is bound in each other's.'"[12]

From Birmingham to Parkland: Political Movements and Youth Activism

Human rights leader Coretta Scott King championed the importance of young people in political movements: "Freedom is never really won. You earn it and win it with every generation" (King 1993: preface). With every generation, movements for political change have been buttressed by the energy, talent, resolve, creativity, and commitment of young people. The dedicated organizing of the Student Non-Violent Coordinating Committee in the 1950s and 1960s helped dramatize the ills of Jim Crow segregation. Young people such as Ruby Bridges, the Tougaloo Nine, Diane Nash, and children of the Birmingham March committed to a collective purpose that counted James Cheney, Mickey Schwerner, Andrew Goodman, Carole Robertson, Cynthia Wesley, Addie Mae Collins, and Denise McNair as martyrs in a movement to affirm the most basic rights of American citizenship (Luders 2010).

Young people propelled the Anti-War movement to point out the hypocrisy of fighting for democracy abroad while failing to secure and protect it in the United States (Heaney and Rojas 2015). In the 1980s, students launched divestment campaigns on college campuses across the US as a show of solidarity with the Anti-Apartheid movement in South Africa. Through vigils, protests, and film screenings, students elevated public awareness of South Africa's racial caste system while demanding that American institutions no longer finance the separation. That sense of insurgency and collective organizing drew students to the National Mall in 1995 for the Million Man March. Young people returned to their campuses and communities armed with an increased self-awareness that was reflected through various elements of pop culture and community organizing.

Students' commitment to community-building and collective action was particularly important for political movements designed to articulate the needs of Asian American communities. In fact, the very term *Asian American* was created by a student activist named Yuji Ichioka. Ichioka was born in San Francisco and was sent to an internment camp in Utah with his family. After World War II he served in the United States Army before enrolling in college. He and his partner Emma Gee created the term *Asian American* to craft a unifying label for people from countries such as India, Laos, Korea, and Cambodia who were collectively excluded from mainstream political decision-making yet didn't share a common affinity (Lee 2003; Ishizuka 2016). Ichioka's vision of the formation of a Yellow Power movement was deeply inspired by the cultural pride and nationalist identity embedded in the Black Power and Red Power movements (Pulido 2006; Ogbar 2001; Fujino 2012). Gee and Ichioka formed the Asian American Political Alliance and helped lead protests at California universities to demand the creation of Asian American Studies departments, the end to discriminatory admissions policies, and greater attention to the diverse interests of students from various Asian countries (Ichioka 2006). Along the way Ichioka and other leaders of the Yellow Power movement encountered critics who felt young people weren't fully vested in the country and therefore didn't deserve to have a say in political affairs. That same critique continues to overshadow current efforts by young people to organize and form political movements.

Keepers of the Dream

Connecticut Students for a Dream was founded in 2010 by a dedicated group of undocumented students who wanted to step out of the shadows and into the arena of public advocacy. Although their immediate focus was on the state, the leaders connected with national organizing efforts to harness the talent, energy, and engagement of young people.[13] Some boldly shared their immigration status to rebuke the shame and stigma imposed by others. Others, such as Lorella Praeli, embraced their status to empower their peers and pursue policy change: "You can talk about what undocumented people are going through or you can say 'I know this is what's happening because I myself was undocumented.'" Praeli was born in Peru and came to the United States at the age of ten for medical treatment. Her family stayed in pursuit of a better life and access to quality health care. She discovered she was undocumented while applying for financial aid during her senior year of high school (Foley 2017).

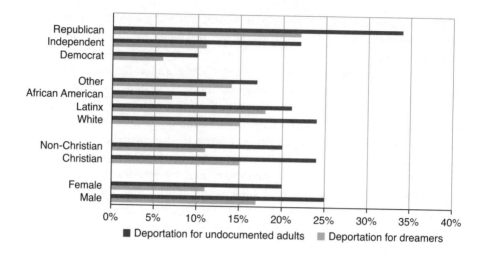

Figure 8.6 Public support for deportation for DACA versus DAPA recipients
Source: Based on data from Morning Consult poll, April 2017.

As one of the founders of Connecticut Students for a Dream, Lorella Praeli led the campaign for tuition equity in Connecticut by emphasizing the value of access to higher education for students and their families.[14] She reflected on her own experience as a stellar student who couldn't travel on school-sponsored experiential learning trips because she wasn't a citizen. Her undocumented status also prohibited her from accepting a research award and became the source of campus debate after she was selected by her peers to give a commencement address (Shear 2015). Praeli traveled across the country to meet with other student leaders and develop an action plan for pressuring policy changes at the local, state, and federal level. This emphasis on federalism and authentic power led them to reflect on the success of earlier efforts by others such as the Gay Rights movement to develop a comprehensive strategy for promoting immigration reform in general and protecting undocumented students in particular (Foley 2017).

Praeli's success as an organizer, activist, and movement builder led her to become policy director for United We Dream, which bills itself as "the largest immigrant youth-led community in the country."[15] Part of her work focused on lobbying the Obama administration and members of Congress to pass legislation that would offer deferred action for parents who were unauthorized, but whose children were either US citizens or covered by DACA. Pursuing Deferred Action for Parents of Americans and Lawful Permanent Residents (DAPA) became a contentious policy option that drew critique across the political aisle. As figure 8.6 shows, public support for DAPA and DACA varies based on race and political affiliation. For Obama, DAPA was a compromise in addressing the increasingly complex problem of undocumented immigration that exceeded the scope of US resources. In a nationally televised address to the American public, Obama made clear his distinction between amnesty and delayed deportation:

> Now here's the thing: We expect people who live in this country to play by the rules. We expect that those who cut the line will not be unfairly rewarded. So we're going to offer the following deal: If you've been in America for more than five years; if you have children who are American citizens or legal residents; if you register, pass a criminal background check, and you're willing to pay your fair share of taxes – you'll be able to apply to stay in this country temporarily without fear of deportation. You can come out of the shadows and get right with the law. That's what this deal is.
>
> Now, let's be clear about what it isn't. This deal does not apply to anyone who has come to this country recently. It does not apply to anyone who might come to America illegally in the future. It does not grant citizenship, or the right to stay here permanently, or offer the same benefits that citizens receive – only Congress can do that. All we're saying is we're not going to deport you.
>
> I know some of the critics of this action call it amnesty. Well, it's not. Amnesty is the immigration system we have today – millions of people who live here without paying their taxes or playing by the rules while politicians use the issue to scare people and whip up votes at election time. (Obama 2014)

After helping secure DACA and DAPA by executive order, Lorella Praeli became the National Director of Latino Outreach for Hillary Clinton's presidential campaign. She was featured in a lengthy video at the 2016 Democratic National Convention that traced her path from Peru to the presidential team. The young woman who had previously been ashamed of her status began her remarks to the delegation by saying: "My name is Lorella Praeli. And I am an American." Fourteen years after first arriving in the United States, Praeli became a US citizen. The naturalization ceremony was held at the National Archives in Washington, DC, and presided over by President Obama:

> Just about every nation in the world, to some extent, admits immigrants, but there's something unique about America. We don't simply welcome new immigrants, we don't simply welcome new arrivals – we are born of immigrants. That is who we are . . . It's part of what makes us exceptional. Unless your family is a Native American . . . all of our families come from someplace else. (Obama 2015)

Ironically, Barack Obama's own citizenship had been questioned by a small yet dogged group of critics who advanced the **Birther movement**. "Birthers," as they were called, believed that Obama was born in Kenya and therefore not eligible to be president. Closely aligned was the allegation that he was "a Muslim" who altered his birth name from "Barry Muhammad Obama" to

"Barack Hussein Obama" in order to deceive the American people (Tumulty 2008). The rumors first began to circulate following then Senator Obama's address to the Democratic National Convention in Boston in 2004. Shortly afterwards, a political competitor from Illinois named Andy Martin launched the allegations that Obama was, in fact, not American (Rutenberg 2008). What began as an obsolete rumor in 2004 eventually spread to become a major campaign issue.

In a now iconic moment on the campaign trail in Minnesota, Republican presidential candidate John McCain confronted a supporter who relayed her fears over a potential Obama presidency: "I can't trust Obama. I have read about him, and he's not, he's not – he's an Arab." McCain's response was hailed by many as courageous: "No ma'am. He's a decent family man, a citizen that I just happen to have disagreements with on fundamental issues, and that's what this campaign is all about" (Associated Press 2008). While defending an opponent in a tight political race is laudable, the implicit association between being "Arab" and being a "decent family man" struck many as problematic.

One of the chief proponents of the birther conspiracy was Donald J. Trump, who offered to make a $5 million donation to the charity of Obama's choice if he could produce copies of his passport and birth certificate (O'Connor 2012). The following year, at the White House correspondents' dinner, Barack Obama, the son of a Black Kenyan father and a Kansas-born white mother, made light of the critiques by sharing a clip from the opening scene of *The Lion King* as footage from his birth (C-SPAN 2011). To some it seemed silly that the citizenship of a sitting US president was still questioned three years after his initial election. Yet the voraciousness of the birther claims, coupled with their impact on voter preferences, highlighted a broader question of American identity as an affinity rather than a legal status.

The critiques of young activists as selfish, easily influenced, or incapable of fully investing in political development has an impact on how stigmatized youth see themselves and their relationship to the power structure. For some groups, that relationship can stimulate the pursuit of authentic power for themselves and others. Political movements also have the potential to force an internal reflection of power differentials related to intragroup identities such as class, skin color, and, in the case of co-ethnic organizing, racial identity (Omi and Winant 1986). Racialization can shape the meaning of difference in the home country and how groups navigate in the United States (Muñoz 2007; Zepeda-Millán and Wallace 2013; Stokes-Brown 2012). The DREAMer movement emerged from a particular set of experiences of youth who mostly identified as Latinx (Wides-Muñoz 2018). However, the disconnect between citizenship as a formal status and one that ensures safety and certain protection is relevant for a range of groups who use movement-building to raise public awareness and demand action.

The #NeverAgain Movement

The murder in 2018 of seventeen people at Marjory Stoneman Douglas High School in Parkland, Florida, is viewed by many as a watershed moment in a decades-long pattern of school-based mass shootings. From the murder of sixteen people at the University of Texas (1966), to thirteen deaths at Columbine High School (1999) and thirty-two victims at Virginia Tech (2007), the frequency and casualty count of school-based shootings have increased (Healy 2015). What has not increased, however, are substantive political reforms designed to reduce this violence and the havoc it causes (Cook and Goss 2014). While determining what qualifies as a "school shooting" is heavily debated, the disruption of peace for students, faculty, and families is indisputable.

In 2012, twenty first-graders were killed at Sandy Hook Elementary School in Newtown, Connecticut. In response, the state's legislators introduced some of the strictest gun-control laws in the country. The new laws instituted a universal background check process, banned over 100 gun models, and imposed restrictions on gun ownership among those who had been committed to mental health facilities (O'Leary 2013). The Connecticut response, however, stood as an outlier. Across the US, state legislatures passed more measures to protect gun rights than restrict them. According to data from the Giffords Law Center, states passed 600 measures to expand access compared to just 230 new restrictions (Vasilogambros 2018). Until 2018, Congress had failed to pass a single gun-control measure during that same time frame.

The survivors of the Parkland shooting began to organize almost immediately afterwards. A cadre of leaders emerged who adopted a theme and new hashtags to connect survivors across the school and, indeed, across the nation. The Never Again movement built on the tools of technology to provide a platform for students to share their experiences of violence and to demand substantive policy change. #Enough was an explicit recognition that those most affected by violence – whether in schools, theaters, churches and synagogues, or on a neighborhood street corner – had the greatest potential to effect change.

The demand for substantive policy changes post-Parkland directly addressed the legacies of power and indifference that often silenced the experiences of young people, people of color, and people living in urban areas. For example, Florida has a long tradition of youth organizing in response to violence and injustice. The Dream Defenders organization was founded to tackle Florida's Stand Your Ground law, which was used to justify the deaths of Jordan Davis and Trayvon Martin. In 2013, the group held a thirty-one-day demonstration at the state capitol to highlight ongoing concerns about racial profiling and injustice. They argued that the future of young people in the Sunshine State was contingent upon a collective commitment to protecting and affirming their worth. However, many of the youth activists involved in that effort were vilified as troublemakers rather than being considered as agents of change.

The leaders of the Never Again movement met with youth organizers from Chicago to address how they could work together to tackle the broader scourge of violence that affects young people in America's cities, suburbs, and rural communities. Tweets from Parkland student Emma González capture their recognition that identity and privilege help condition public responses to violence:

> Those who face gun violence on a level that we have only just glimpsed from our gated communities have never had their voices heard in their entire lives the way that we have in these few weeks alone. Since we all share in feeling this pain and know all too well how it feels to have to grow up at the snap of a finger, we were able to cover a lot of ground in communicating our experiences. People of color in inner-cities and everywhere have been dealing with this for a despicably long time, and the media cycles just don't cover the violence the way they did here. The platform us Parkland Students have established is to be shared with every person, black or white, gay or straight, religious or not, who has experienced gun violence, and hand in hand, side by side, We Will Make This Change Together.[16]

A young student participates in the 2018 March for Our Lives rally to demand sensible gun control following the deaths of seventeen people at Marjory Stoneman Douglas High School in Parkland, Florida.

Leaders of the Never Again movement penned editorials, encouraged millennials to register and vote, and used social media to address what they viewed as the impossibility of not politicizing an epidemic borne out of policy choices financed by groups with political interests. Thousands of students participated in the #Enough National School Walkout and lifted the names of local young people affected by violence. A month after the massacre, the Parkland survivors drew over 500,000 people to Washington, DC, for the National March for Our Lives, while companion rallies took place in 800 cities across the world. The DC rally featured speeches from an array of young people whose lives had been touched by violence in both direct and indirect ways. The focus was on finding common ground and fostering a unifying commitment to ending gun violence. Yolanda Renee King, the nine-year-old granddaughter of the Reverend Dr Martin Luther King, Jr, linked the Never Again movement to his vision for social justice: "My grandfather had a dream that his four little children will not be judged by the color of their skin, but by the content of their character. I have a dream that enough is enough."

BOX 8.7 March for Our Lives preamble

"We the Wounded of the United States, In Order to form a more perfect Future, establish Justice, ensure domestic Tranquility, provide for the common People, promote the general Welfare, and secure the Blessings of Liberty to ourselves and our Generations to Come, do ordain and establish this March for the United States of America."

Conclusion: Political Movements as Intersectional Constructions

While it may be too early to know whether the Never Again movement will last, it is clear that these young activists have learned from past movements, have incorporated new organizing tools, and have had an impact on political culture. In the months following the Parkland shooting, states adopted over fifty new gun-control measures, including new domestic violence restrictions, the expansion of background checks, urban gun violence reduction programs, and bans on bump stocks. Fourteen of the states that adopted new restrictions were led by Republican governors compared to eleven states led by Democratic governors (Vasilogambros 2018).

Political movements are inherently intersectional even if they don't intend to be. Identity-based collective action has the potential to amplify existing tensions while creating new cleavages. Every movement must consider how it will navigate the delicate terrain of building coalitions while preserving the integrity of its agenda. The threat of co-optation is particularly great for movements whose size and message challenge the political status quo. Movement leaders and their allies have a better chance of cultivating authentic power when they can harness community-based resources to create a sense of autonomy and authority to pursue meaningful social changes. However, movements must be willing to respond and adapt to a changing political environment, socio-economic context, and legal space constrained by federalism. In *NAACP v. Claiborne Hardware Co.* (1982), the US Supreme Court upheld the right to participate in economic boycotts to prove a political point. This affirmation takes on renewed significance as a number of states across the country now attempt to criminalize protest and other forms of political action. Just as identity politics is a ubiquitous feature of US politics, so too are organized efforts to mobilize underrepresented groups to demand authentic power via citizenship, equality, and justice.

Controversy box: The art of politics

Most people know Danny Glover as an actor in such iconic films as *The Color Purple*, *Beloved*, *Freedom Song*, and *Lethal Weapon*. Over the last three decades, he has also emerged as an activist, philanthropist, and artist who uses his public platform to address key domestic and international challenges. I hosted a fireside chat with him in 2018 on contemporary political movements and longstanding questions of freedom and citizenship. Glover walked through the writings of Frantz Fanon and Amilcar Cabral while exalting the understated brilliance of Paul Robeson. He weaved together the groundbreaking work of filmmaker Yance Ford and celebrated the time he and friend Harry Belafonte spent with younger artists such as Common, Usher, John Legend, and athlete Colin Kaepernick to highlight the value of intergenerational collaborations. In that hour-long conversation, Glover touched on various art forms that have been used to channel the discontent of marginalized groups into political movements such as the Abolitionist, Civil Rights, Anti-Apartheid, and Labor movements: "Art is a way of understanding, of confronting issues and confronting your own feelings – all within the realm of the capacity it represents." Art has the power to demand truth and justice that isn't bound by the markers of class, race, ethnicity, religion, region, gender identity, or tradition. Art, in all its varied manifestations, is a form of resistance.

From the creation of Jewish theater to resist anti-Semitism to the collaboration between Billie Holiday and Abel Meeropol to denounce lynching, art has been a conduit for elevating public awareness and inspiring political change. During the Civil Rights movement, for example, student activists sang freedom songs to connect their experiences to those of enslaved Africans who shared spirituals as they journeyed toward freedom. In 1970, Crosby, Stills, Nash, and Young released the song "Ohio" to condemn the shooting deaths of four unarmed students at Kent State University by members of the Ohio National Guard. The song became an anthem for broader efforts to protest the Vietnam War and support the growing Anti-War movement. However, just as some were haunted by the imagery in Holiday and Meeropol's song "Strange Fruit," many people criticized Crosby, Stills, Nash, and Young for using their art to politicize tragedy and stir up resentment.

Just as technology and social media have been used to elevate public awareness on a host of political concerns, contemporary artists use film, visual art, literature, clothing, and music to express solidarity with political movements. Hip-hop artists such as Jasiri X, Kendrick Lamar, and Maimouna Youssef have penned lyrics condemning police brutality, while songs by country artists Eric Church, Maren Morris, and Luke Bryan respond to longstanding cultural tensions. The unveiling of portraits of Barack and Michelle Obama for the Smithsonian's National Portrait Gallery by Kehinde Wiley and Amy Sherald, respectively, prompted a great deal of social reflection and critique. Although many artists may use their work to address political tensions, some, such as the Dixie Chicks, Childish Gambino, Kathy Griffin, and Joy Villa, have been criticized for blurring the line between pop culture and politics. What do you think? Should artists engage in political commentary and movement-building? Or should artists center only on entertainment and enjoyment?

Questions for Debate

1 Students have been active in a number of political movements in the United States and across the world. However, critics often question whether they possess the knowledge and investment to truly know their best political interests. How important is it for young people to be politically engaged?

2 One of the major accomplishments of the Civil Rights movement was its emphasis on protecting access to the political process via voting and office-holding. Reflecting on the data presented in the chapter on racially polarized voting and office-holding, has the United States achieved its goal of a representative democracy? And, if not, is that the result of institutional constraints or individual effort?

3 What issue, or set of issues, do you think need to be addressed via the creation of a new political movement? Considering the concept of authentic power, who should lead that movement? What should its strategy be? Possible coalition partners?

Key Terms

- political movement
- collective action
- insurgency
- free rider problem
- DACA
- DAPA
- Stand Your Ground
- cognitive liberation
- Yellow Power movement
- Red Power movement
- Violence against Women Act
- Bracero Program
- Yuji Ichioka
- Populist movement
- March for Our Lives

9

The Inescapability of Identity Politics

Long Division

Protracted debates over issues such as immigration, educational access, marriage equality, sovereignty, economic well-being, and public safety make it clear that finding middle ground seems elusive in US politics. The 2016 presidential election will be remembered by many observers as one of the most negative, contentious fights in contemporary political history. To some, it emboldened groups who long felt silenced and ignored within the political process. Others took to the ballot box to express their concerns that the changing demographic shifts hailed by analysts would introduce new demands for political and socio-economic resources that would shift the status quo. For many others, the aftermath of the election revealed the continuing failure to address the most basic notions of citizenship, civil rights, and inclusion.

On the eve of my completing this book, the US government entered into what would become the longest government shutdown in history. The stalemate rested on the president's demand that Congress provide $5 billion in funding to build a wall on the US–Mexico border (Jackson 2019). Over 800,000 federal government employees, including corrections officers, security screeners, park rangers, and Coast Guard staff, went without pay as the two publicly fought. DACA recipients were caught in the middle of the political tug of war as the president's administration promised to protect them if Congress would authorize the funding for border security. The human costs of the gridlock were staggering. Yet, for all of the uncertainty felt across the political spectrum, these current controversies are anchored in an historical context that shapes the entire course of American political development. The United States has long been divided by conflict based on group identity. The labels may change (e.g. Federalists versus Anti-federalists; Quakers versus Puritans; citizen versus undocumented), but the dynamic of ascribing political power to large diverse clusters of people remains. At the core of US politics is a persistent struggle to define the boundaries of influence based on deciding which groups are most "like us."

Politics is in Everything – and Everything is in Politics

I began this book by arguing that democracy in the United States is built upon the battle of ideas related to how we see ourselves, how we see others, and the mechanisms available to reinforce these distinctions. Recognizing difference and organizing around shared identities isn't inherently bad. Rather, the focus should be on addressing the judgements we attach to that difference and the negative behaviors we adopt in response. In the context of politics, group identities are socially constructed to convey values, norms, and expectations that determine standing. Group identity in the context of US politics has no biological value. However, it bestows tremendous **social capital** that structures political negotiations across a range of spheres of influence, from formal arenas of political conflict, such as elections and legislatures, to seemingly apolitical spaces buttressed by group dynamics – most notably, sports.

In chapter 2, I discussed how the seven stages of assimilation are supposed to provide a prescription for gaining acceptance in the broader national community. This includes casting off religious and cultural markers that differ from those of the dominant society in favor of more common traditions. In 2001, major league baseball player Shawn Green was criticized because he refused to play on Yom Kippur, just as legends Sandy Koufax and Hank Greenberg had before him. Some saw Green's refusal to participate in "America's pastime" because of a religious holiday as unpatriotic and disrespectful. This was the same type of rhetoric used by those who questioned whether certain groups were unfit for public office based on their faith traditions. Public perceptions of which groups were worthy of the full protections of American citizenship sparked the draft riots by Irish immigrants in 1863 and inspired the etching on Leonard Matlovich's headstone. Even as groups are allowed to enter the polity, the protections they are afforded are not absolute. At the core of these battles over identity, whether in regard to historical context or contemporary controversy, is a fight for recognition.

Athletes from underrepresented groups have long used their public platform to make political statements. Many find that it is on the field or on the court that they are able to gain respect denied to them in other facets of life (Leonard 2017). One of the most notable examples involves boxer Muhammad Ali, who famously defended his refusal to enlist during the Vietnam War: "The real enemy of my people is right here. I will not disgrace my religion, my people, or myself by becoming a tool to enslave those who are fighting for their own justice, freedom, and equality" (quoted in Zirin 2005). The move cost Ali his title as heavyweight champion of the world and his freedom. However, it inspired other athletes such as track stars John Carlos and Tommie Smith, who raised gloved fists during the medal ceremony of the 1968 Olympics in Mexico City to protest human rights violations around the world.[1] Carlos and

An installation at the National Museum of African American History and Culture in Washington, DC, honors the actions of John Carlos and Tommie Smith at the 1968 Olympics in Mexico City. The two men were stripped of their medals for protesting racism and poverty. They represent a long history of athletes engaging in political protest.

Smith stood in solidarity with poor people, indigenous people, and victims of state-sanctioned violence. Both men were expelled from the Olympic Games and criticized for politicizing sports. Like Ali, Branch Rickey, Jackie Robinson, and Jesse Owens before them, Carlos and Smith used sports as a conduit for addressing broader issues of discrimination based on identity. In so doing, they set the context for modern athletes to shape debates over group identity and injustice.

Shut Up and Dribble

NBA standout Lebron James has emerged as an activist on a range of causes related to racial justice and education equity. In spite of his fame and tremendous wealth, James has still been targeted by those who see his racial identity as problematic. In 2018, conservative talk-show host Laura Ingraham advised James and other athletes to "keep the political comments to yourselves. . . . Shut up and dribble" (Chavez 2018). A year earlier, vandals tagged his home with graffiti and racial slurs. Understanding the politicized nature of group identity helps better understand the uproar following the decision in 2016 by former NFL player Colin Kaepernick to kneel during the National

Anthem. Kaepernick and other players who refused to stand were branded as unpatriotic and reprimanded by President Trump for being "SOB's" who didn't deserve to be on the field. The move inspired other professional and collegiate athletes, such as Megan Rapinoe of the US women's soccer team and members of the University of New Mexico football team, to kneel in protest.

In the years leading up to Kaepernick's decision, uprisings spread across college campuses, public squares, and neighborhood streets over deadly interactions between law enforcement and citizens of color. While many questioned why violence was part of these contemporary conflicts, the response of Dr Martin Luther King, Jr, to riots in places such as Watts and Newark in the 1960s provides useful instruction: "I think that we've got to see that a riot is the language of the unheard. And, what is it that America has failed to hear?"[2] The desire to amplify the voices of the unheard motivated patrons of the Stonewall Inn in New York to resist laws criminalizing their gender identity and forms of expression. It inspired Bree Newsome to scale a flagpole in South Carolina to protest a symbol that has divided the nation since it was first adopted. This desire to address the unheard sparked the launch of the Me Too movement against sexual assault and the Seneca Falls Convention for women's rights. And it motivated protesters at Standing Rock just as it had for members of the Indians of All Tribes at Alcatraz decades earlier. The linkages between past movements for freedom and contemporary demands for inclusion are an important part of the American political fabric.

Context and Controversy

When I first conceived the themes for this book, I couldn't have imagined that a fierce debate would erupt over the revelation that the governor and attorney general of Virginia were immortalized in their college yearbooks wearing blackface. Just as the debate over Confederate monuments prompted conversations over past context and contemporary social understanding, this latest challenge revealed the difficulty of navigating identity. I also couldn't have predicted the firestorm that accompanied a presidential decision to separate migrant children from their families. Although many people expressed shock over the conditions of the makeshift detention camps, they resembled the internment camps authorized by Franklin Roosevelt's Executive Order 9066 which targeted US citizens of Japanese, Italian, and German descent. To be sure, the people being held in World War II-era camps were American citizens whose Fourteenth Amendment rights were violated. However, deciding which groups pose a threat to "US interests" and which groups are included within those interests remains a time-tested challenge.

One of the greatest arenas for gauging perceptions of group threat and "Americanness" is in the realm of electoral politics. Historically, access to voting and office-holding was reserved for those thought independent enough to participate. For the vast majority of US history, that standard excluded groups such as women, young people, people of color, and poor people. This denial of one of the most fundamental rights of US citizenship fueled a persistent quest for full citizenship via the franchise. Through a series of political movements, legal challenges, and constitutional amendments, the diversity among voters has increased while that of legislators has been more constrained. The results of the 2018 midterm elections highlight the possibility that many voters are ready to change that.

The 116th Congress is the most diverse in the history of the people's branch. While it is true that the number of women, African Americans, Latinx, and LGBTQI members of the legislature has increased, we also witnessed greater diversity along the lines of gender identity, religion, and age. And yet, even as some celebrated these victories, longstanding institutional norms and structures continue to shape their ability to translate those demographic changes into a more substantive representation of group interests. For some elected officials, their very presence in a legislative body that once denied their citizenship is evidence of democracy's promise. The changing demographic landscape of the United States, coupled with our increasingly polarized political space, means that candidates from underrepresented groups now have the potential to challenge traditional conventions. For example, Georgia voters chose Lucy McBath (D-Georgia) to unseat a Republican incumbent in a district once represented by former Speaker of the House Newt Gingrich. In conservative Mississippi, former US Agriculture Secretary Mike Espy stunned observers by narrowly losing the Senate race to frontrunner Susan Hyde-Smith. And yet the persistence of voter suppression and disenfranchisement in places such as Georgia, Florida, Nevada, Ohio, and Pennsylvania reminds us that mobilization breeds countermobilization. Those institutional attacks coupled with candidates' use of racial dog whistles in 2018 suggest that maneuvering the politics of identity in the twenty-first century is often marred by early twentieth-century tactics.

Beyond the electoral arena, I couldn't have predicted that the release of blockbuster films *Crazy Rich Asians* and *Black Panther* would capture theater audiences in record numbers while stimulating broader conversations about authentic representations of ethnic identities in film and culture. Likewise, the heightened tensions between the United States and other countries such as North Korea elevated concerns about military threats while shaping renewed calls to define "America first." These dimensions of foreign policy and international standing help shape domestic debates over which groups are, and which are not, included within that collective national identity. And yet, even as voters sift through rapidly changing news cycles and the increasingly polarized attempts at discourse, we are reminded that the past is in fact a prologue in politics. The intense public debate surrounding these flashpoints reflects longstanding efforts to define the rights, privileges, and protections afforded to certain groups. That debate rests at the heart of American political development and centers the chapters contained in this book.

Chapter Summary

Throughout this book I have asserted the primacy of two key concepts for understanding identity politics in the United States: intersectionality and federalism. Federalism reflects the division of power across the federal government, states, and localities. For underrepresented groups, federalism helps determine whether the protections embedded in the Constitution are enforced to shape the quality of our everyday experiences. Indeed, it is federalism that defines whether the First Amendment's guarantee of religious freedom protects same-sex couples seeking a vendor to bake their wedding cake. Federalism struck down grandfather clauses that barred white ethnic immigrants from voting in the North and literacy tests that limited Black voters in the South. Historically, federalism has also posed a tremendous challenge for Indian tribes who battle against state-level infringements on their sovereignty rights. This conflict highlights the subjective nature of freedom and democracy for many groups.

Similarly, intersectionality structures the importance of and opportunities for political presence within an increasingly competitive political space. Intersectionality is more than recognizing that we are all members of multiple groups at once. Rather, it cautions us to address how certain group identities are constructed based on prevailing norms, values, and understandings. Just as the composition of groups may change across time and context, so too does their meaning. How we see ourselves as individuals is important. Yet, in the context of politics, how others see us and those like us vis-à-vis group affiliation often becomes more predictive.

Chapter 1 took up this claim by introducing the concept of authentic power – the extent to which a group harmed by a policy can get policy-makers and other government officials to acknowledge the harm and, ultimately, change the policy to the group's benefit. The quest for authentic power shapes political efforts by underrepresented groups as well as those who already have significant power. In turn, efforts to mobilize in pursuit of authentic power trigger countermobilization efforts to stave off challenges to the existing political order. Notions of power are reflected in the names and labels we choose to define groups because they connote a sense of agency. Likewise, it reflects our understanding that power and identity are dynamic and constantly being negotiated and renegotiated as new interests emerge and old challenges remain.

Sidney Verba (2003) challenges the commonly held assumption that American political development is characterized by a persistent commitment to and fight for equality. Rather, it reflects a negotiation of competing interests and anticipated outcomes framed in the context of group identities. This negotiation helps explain shifting public support for immigration based on country of origin, as well as shifting views on assimilation and interracial marriage.

Chapter 2 explored how social constructions of identity help define how we see ourselves and others. Group identity can serve as a coping mechanism for those who feel underrepresented while stimulating the consciousness needed to transform this marginalized status. At times the biases we hold, whether implicit or explicit, can create conditions that enhance opportunities for group conflict. Group conflict can be violent, such as the attacks on a Sikh temple in Wisconsin or the draft riots in New York. The political importance of group identity is determined by various institutions and actors based on proximity to power.

Chapter 3 traced the disconnect between the three formal conceptions of US citizenship and the various groups for whom the pursuit of belonging has been elusive. Throughout history, military service has been a key means used by many groups to prove their loyalty to the United States. This embrace of American patriotism over ties to the home country helped Irish and Italian immigrants transcend their ethnic identity and acquire US citizenship. For other groups, however, their acceptance as American citizens entitled to the full benefits of inclusion was conditioned by the circumstances of their birth. Whether it was American Indians such as John Elk or African Americans such as Dred Scott, the Constitution has been interpreted as rendering certain groups permanently beyond the scope of citizenship. And yet, even as formal institutional barriers are relaxed, some groups find that their standing in the polity remains fractured. Citizenship in the United States continues to be hierarchical, relational, and contextual.

Chapter 4 extended this view of fractured citizenship by examining the peculiar nature of racial identity in the US. Debates over Confederate flags, monuments, and markers highlight the seemingly immutable nature of racial division. For some, these symbols convey reverence for history and heritage. Supporters defend their right to use them as a form of expression protected by the First Amendment. Yet, as we also know, the framers believed that no right was absolute. While race is indeed a constructed identity with no inherent biological meaning, its socio-political meaning continues to define access to and battles for power. This quest inspires political movements to dismantle institutional barriers as well as encouraging new actors to institutionalize political power by seeking elected office. The increasing levels of diversity within racial groups promote new policy priorities and shift opportunities for coalition-building.

Challenging ignorance has been a major focus throughout this book. After Hurricane Maria ravaged the Caribbean, residents of the island of Puerto Rico began moving to the mainland while demanding that the US government commit resources to helping the island rebuild. As I noted in *Chapter 5*, 52 percent of participants in a survey about hurricane relief didn't know that Puerto Ricans are US citizens. This ignorance has political consequences. Those who see Puerto Ricans as citizens are significantly more likely to support recovery aid for the island than those who understand them as non-citizens (see table 5.1, p. 96). It also challenges us to consider the diasporic nature of ethnoracial identity in the US.

The twin patterns of migration and immigration help shape the political meaning of ethnic identity. There were initially very few conditions for determining whether groups were eligible to be present and included as US citizens. Growing economic challenges and perceived threats to power helped fuel fears that certain groups had to be limited. In adopting the Chinese Exclusion Act in 1882, the United States simultaneously stigmatized group identity based on country of origin and ordered how other countries perceived each other. This stigma helped shape the path to whiteness and, in turn, Americanness for various groups while affirming the existence of fractured citizenship. As the demographic makeup of the United States continues to diversify, so too will political battles based on ethnic identity and fear.

The elevated political status of men was enshrined in the very formation of this nation when Thomas Jefferson wrote: "We hold these truths to be self-evident, that all men are created equal, that they are endowed by their Creator with certain unalienable Rights, that among these are Life, Liberty and the pursuit of Happiness." At the same time, the phrase "all men" was never intended to mean that all men should be included in the polity. Exclusions based on wealth, tribal affiliation, race, and ancestry defined who was and who was not embraced. Over time, efforts to move toward inclusion (e.g. Fifteenth Amendment) reified existing boundaries while erecting new barriers. These efforts to address discrimination inspired grassroots attempts to denounce policies and practices that defined certain groups as inferior and thus more vulnerable based on gender and sexual identity.

Chapter 6 affirmed the need to reject monolithic views of groups and examined the tremendous diversity that exists *within* groups based on self-definition and social categorization. Just as rights evolve, so too does our understanding of the complex and fluid nature of gender and sexual identity that shapes policy preferences and opportunities for representation. In January 2019, Pete Buttigieg announced he was running for the presidency. Most people had never heard of the small-town mayor and wondered why he would enter such a high-stakes election. As the first openly gay presidential candidate in US history, as one of the youngest, and as an Afghan War veteran, his bid challenges longstanding debates about identity, military service, and suitability for public office.

Chapter 7 addressed the popular myth that the United States was founded as a place of religious freedom. The reality is that freedom was extended to certain traditions while denied to others. Clashes between colonies and the subsequent battle for recognition within states made it clear that the barriers faced in England were replicated here. Over time, the fear that these unfamiliar religious traditions violated the norms of assimilation outlined in chapter 2 sparked formal and informal efforts to police the impact of religious identity. The Establishment and Free Exercise Clauses created a constitutional distinction between an unfettered freedom to believe or not believe and deliberate restrictions on the freedom to practice those beliefs. This distinction helped guide negotiations over immigration policies, candidates for elected office, and even the texts used in public schools. Religious identity in the United States is inherently intersectional because it captures the confluence of political power based on race, ethnicity, region, and country of origin.

Finally, *chapter 8* explored how various groups challenge their exclusion via political movements. Movement-building is necessarily messy, intersectional, and difficult. Even when groups share a common policy concern, it is challenging to overcome both institutional and individual constraints on collective action. Groups must carefully negotiate their agenda, leadership, and strategy while balancing threats of co-optation and dilution. For some groups, political movements have been an effective tool for demanding rights such as access to education and safe working conditions. For other groups, they focus on acquiring the resources necessary to pursue their interests on their own terms. Movements learn from each other. They observe successes and failures and attempt to overcome traditional collective action problems in pursuit of policy goals and heightened public awareness. Although movements vary in size, scope, and duration, they remain an important vehicle for channeling discontent and pain into substantive change. These lessons are captured in the burgeoning Never Again movement, which draws on the belief that those closest to the problem are best suited to change it.

Group Identity and the Never-Ending Pursuit of Freedom

In 1944, Fred Korematsu sued for his freedom. As John Elk had sixty years earlier, and like Dred Scott thirty years before him, Korematsu challenged whether the promises embedded in the US Constitution had been violated by those responsible for enforcing them.[3] Korematsu was a native-born US citizen whose parents had emigrated from Japan. In the wake of World War II and persistent questions about domestic security, President Franklin D. Roosevelt signed Executive Order 9066 – a sweeping Act that created military zones and

Karen Korematsu speaks following oral arguments on a proposed travel ban targeting Muslims. Her father, Fred T. Korematsu, sued the federal government in 1944, arguing that the forced internment of Japanese citizens violated his civil rights.

granted military commanders broad discretion to determine who could be forcibly removed and ordered into internment camps. The language of the order was purposely vague. It allowed military officers to "determine, from which any or all persons may be excluded,"[4] while also deciding the duration of exclusion for individual cases. Though Roosevelt's edict made no mention of particular countries or groups, its enforcement exclusively targeted people of Japanese, German, and Italian descent.

Korematsu was arrested for refusing to comply with an order to abandon his home and report to camp. He resisted on the grounds that Roosevelt's order violated his Fifth Amendment rights as a US citizen by targeting groups based on their shared racial identity and perceived threat to US interests. The Court rejected Korematsu's claim in a stunning 6–3 decision. However, Justice Frank Murphy's dissent directly addressed the role of discrimination in shaping the introduction and implementation of the order. He countered his colleagues by writing:

> I dissent, therefore, from this legalization of racism. Racial discrimina-
> tion in any form and in any degree has no justifiable part whatever in our
> democratic way of life. It is unattractive in any setting, but it is utterly
> revolting among a free people who have embraced the principles set
> forth in the Constitution of the United States. All residents of this nation
> are kin in some way by blood or culture to a foreign land. Yet they are

primarily and necessarily a part of the new and distinct civilization of the United States. They must, accordingly, be treated at all times as the heirs of the American experiment, and as entitled to all the rights and freedoms guaranteed by the Constitution.[5]

Nowhere in the Constitution is discrimination banned as the practice of treating groups differently. Rather, it provides the parameters by which we decide who can and cannot be excluded from public life. In the decades following Korematsu's conviction, advocacy organizations praised his commitment to protecting the civil liberties of all people regardless of race, ethnicity, or citizenship. Ironically, Korematsu was vindicated seventy years later in a Supreme Court case that questioned whether a travel ban imposed by the Trump administration violated the Constitution's Establishment Clause. The original focus on seven Muslim majority countries drew an international backlash and allegations that it discriminated on the basis of racial identity.[6] By its third and last iteration the ban remained at seven but included two non-Muslim countries (Venezuela and North Korea) to quell allegations of ethnoreligious profiling.

In delivering the majority opinion in *Trump v. Hawaii*, Chief Justice John Roberts criticized his predecessors for "getting it wrong" in 1944: "Korematsu . . . has been convicted of an act not commonly thought a crime . . . It consists merely of being present in the state whereof he is a citizen, near the place where he was born, and where all his life he has lived" (585 US 542). To some, Roberts's opinion of Korematsu was viewed as a sign of progress because it affirmed the protections of US citizenship regardless of ethnic heritage. However, the ruling in *Trump v. Hawaii* replaced one stigmatized identity (e.g. Japanese descent) with another (e.g. Muslim adherent). It also raised long-standing questions over the trade-off between protecting civil liberties and protecting public safety.

Justice Sonia Sotomayor wrote in her scathing dissent that:

> The United States of America is a Nation built upon the promise of religious liberty. Our Founders honored that core promise by embedding the principle of religious neutrality in the First Amendment. The Court's decision today fails to safeguard that fundamental principle. It leaves undisturbed a policy first advertised openly and unequivocally as a "total and complete shutdown of Muslims entering the United States" because the policy now masquerades behind a façade of national-security concerns.

The court codified fears of Islam at the same time that leaders from the Religious Right were demanding a repeal of the Johnson Amendment which has for decades protected the separation of church and state. This retreat, coupled with persistent clashes over the most basic tenets of democracy, highlights the inextricable link between group identity and freedom in the United States.

The next five years will prove critical for addressing how US democracy revolves around how we see ourselves and how we see others. The country will undertake a new census in 2020 alongside a presidential election season that promises to be one of the most expensive – and contentious – in history. Persistent debates over border security, religious freedom, voting rights, and federalism heighten the relationship between identity and political polarization. Though the individual actors may change, the quest to cultivate authentic power will remain.

Glossary

Glossary words in the text are emboldened upon first usage. Terms are italicized when they are introduced in the text as a term.

African American: References people of African descent now living in the United States.

Alien enemies: Classification imposed by the US government to categorize citizens, residents, and descendants of countries with which the United States is engaged in conflict. It was particularly influential during World War II, when President Roosevelt used this status to limit the movement of people from Japan, Germany, and Italy.

Alt-right: The term *alt-right* or *alternative right* refers to a collection of groups, individuals, and organizations which support a far-right, extremist view of conservatism. Adherents are loosely bound together by the belief that white identity is under attack and that racial and ethnic groups seek to erase American history. The term was popularized by self-identified Alt-Right movement leader Richard Spencer. The movement gained national notoriety following a gathering it held in Washington, DC, to celebrate the election in 2016 of Donald Trump.

American exceptionalism: The notion that the United States is unique in its professed commitment to the values of liberty and democracy because its citizens possess strong ties to the nation.

American Indian movement: A coalition of various tribes who protested the US government's seizure of Indian land and the failure to abide by treaties affirming sovereignty.

Assimilation: The process of giving up ties to the home country or culture of origin to fully adopt and adapt to traditions of the host country or culture. This can include changes in language, dress, religious practice, food, and holiday observances.

Authentic power: The extent to which a group harmed by a policy can get policy-makers and other government officials to acknowledge this harm and, ultimately, to change the policy to the group's benefit.

Birther movement: A movement initiated based on the belief that Barack Obama was born in Kenya and thus ineligible to serve as President of the United States.

Black: References people of African descent now living in the United States.

Black Church: The seven major Black Protestant denominations that developed in response to the legal, social, economic, and political exclusion of Blacks in American life.

Black liberation theology: A deliberate effort to empower Blacks to love themselves in the face of a complex history of racial segregation, state-sanctioned violence, and denials of citizenship.

Black Lives Matter: A movement that combined grassroots demonstrations and direct action to address the disproportionate number of African Americans killed by law enforcement and others with impunity.

Citizens United* v. *Federal Election Commission (2010): US Supreme Court case which ruled that communications expenditures for non-profits, labor unions, and other associations cannot be restricted due to the First Amendment protection of speech.

Civil disobedience: The practice of intentionally breaking the law in a non-violent manner to address a political issue, challenge, or controversy. It was popularized during the Civil Rights movement.

Civil Rights Act of 1964: Legislation that bans discrimination based on race, color, religion, sex, and national origin in public places, public facilities, and employment. The Act also boosted the integration of public schools.

Cognitive liberation: The sense of awareness shared by members of aggrieved groups that they can collectively act to challenge their standing.

Collective action: Group behavior that challenges or cements the political status quo. It often requires that people forego individual resources (e.g. power, time, money) in pursuit of broader group advancement.

Collective dilemma: A situation that creates a disconnect or dilemma between self-interests and group interests.

Combahee River Collective: An organization of Black queer women, active from 1974 to 1980, who worked to advance the standing of marginalized women across a range of identities.

Concentrated punishment: References communities with excessive rates of surveillance, incarceration, and disenfranchisement.

Cooper v. *Aaron* (1958): Supreme Court ruling that no legislator, executive, or judicial official could undermine his or her obligation to uphold the doctrines of the Constitution.

Dark money: Money donated to non-profit organizations that use the funds to influence elections. There are no limits on the amount of money these organizations can collect, and they are not required to disclose their donors.

De facto **discrimination:** Discrimination created and/or enforced by practice rather than law.

De jure **discrimination:** Discrimination created and/or enforced by law.

Defense of Marriage Act of 1996: Federal legislation that defined marriage as between one man and one woman and which allowed states to refuse to recognize same-sex marriages and deny partner benefits.

Descriptive representation: The extent to which members of legislative bodies mirror various demographic features of their constituents.

Discrimination: The practice of treating certain groups differently based on an assigned set of beliefs, values, perceptions, and practices.

Don't Ask, Don't Tell (DADT): Policy that allowed lesbian, gay, and bisexual military members to serve as long as they did not disclose their sexual identity.

Dred Scott v. *Sandford* (1857): US Supreme Court case that challenged the citizenship status of a formerly enslaved man named Dred Scott. The Court ruled that African descendants were never intended to become citizens and thus could lay no legal claim to freedom.

Enrollment Act of 1863: Civil War-era draft that required enrollment of every male citizen and every male immigrant who applied for citizenship. Men who were drafted could avoid service by finding a replacement or paying $300 to opt out. The Act heightened tensions between Irish immigrants and Black residents.

Environmental racism: The disproportionate exposure of underrepresented groups to pollution via water, air, and soil. Often this exposure results from patterns or residential segregation and economic displacement that relegates communities of color to land and neighborhoods that are either contaminated or compromised.

Establishment Clause: Enshrined in the First Amendment to the Constitution, the Establishment Clause prohibits Congress from establishing an official religion or privileging one religious tradition over another.

Ethnicity: Distinctions based on culture, language, or common descent that shape political standing.

Ethno-nationalism: Membership in ethnic and national communities.

Executive Order 9066: Presidential action that authorized the forced removal of thousands of people of Japanese descent. The order made no distinction between citizens and "resident aliens."

Federalism: The division of power between a central authority and various subordinates.

Fractured citizenship: The view that citizenship in the United States is a dynamic construct contingent on a collection of political decisions, strategies, and beliefs.

Free Exercise Clause: Provision of the First Amendment that allows citizens to practice their religious beliefs as long as they don't trigger a compelling government interest.

Free rider problem: The challenge of convincing people to participate in movements even when they can derive the same material benefits without contributing to collective action.

Gender gap: The persistent differences between men and women in reference to voting behavior, partisanship, policy preferences, political opportunities, and political ambitions.

Gender identity: Gender identity captures the myriad ways in which individuals are socialized to associate certain behaviors, characteristics, and traits as masculine or feminine and what it means to embrace those qualities in a consistent way. It is distinct from sex and the categories we are assigned at birth.

Griswold v. Connecticut (1965): US Supreme Court case that struck down state-level restrictions on married couples' rights to discuss, purchase, possess, and use contraception. It helped establish the implied right to privacy embedded in the US Constitution.

Group consciousness: A more politicized view of membership that focuses on using political action to improve the group's position in society.

Gurdwara: A place of worship for Sikhs.

Hart–Celler Immigration Act of 1965: Immigration reform which eliminated national origin quotas that privileged immigrants from Northern Europe and raised the ceiling on immigration from the rest of the world. By easing national origin quotas, the Hart–Celler Act dramatically transformed America's racial and ethnic makeup: more than 20 million immigrants have arrived from countries in Latin America, Asia, and the Caribbean since 1965.

Identity: The attachments we hold to the groups to which we belong or want to belong.

Identity politics: A set of beliefs, values, perceptions, laws, public policies, and practices that shape how groups experience politics.

Immigration Reform and Control Act of 1986 (IRCA): The first major attempt to regulate unauthorized immigration to the United States. It punished employers who knowingly hired undocumented immigrants while also creating a path toward legalization for unauthorized residents who met certain requirements.

Implicit bias: The thoughts about people you didn't know you had that result from the messages, experiences, and stereotypes encountered.

Insurgency: Acts of resistance, protest, and rebellion that challenge the political status quo. Insurgency is often used by underrepresented groups to pressure a response and cultivate authentic power.

Internment: The forced removal, detention, or incarceration of groups based on a prescribed set of criteria.

Johnson Amendment: The Johnson Amendment provides tax-exempt status to religious organizations that refrain from engaging in partisan activities such as collecting donations.

Johnson–Reed Act of 1924: Legislation that imposed limits on the number of immigrants from particular countries based on their current share of the US population. It was significant for changing the demographic composition of immigrants limiting white ethnic immigration.

Jones–Shafroth Act of 1917: Legislation signed by President Woodrow Wilson that recognized Puerto Rico as a US territory and granted American citizenship to residents of the island. However, the Act does not provide full voting rights to Puerto Ricans, nor does it provide them with voting representation in the US Congress.

Jordan Commission: Committee authorized by Congress (1990–97) to evaluate and make recommendations for comprehensive immigration reform. The commission was named after the late Barbara Jordan, who was the first African American woman to represent the state of Texas in Congress.

Judiciary Act of 1789: Signed into law by President George Washington, the Judiciary Act established the federal judicial system.

Jus sanguinis: The principle that citizenship is derived from having one or both parents who are US citizens.

Jus soli: The principle that citizenship is automatically conferred upon those born on US soil. It is commonly referred to as "birthright citizenship."

Know Nothing Party: Formed in 1850 as a nativist, anti-Catholic organization guided by the mantra that "Americans Must Rule America." The party successfully elected its supporters to local, state, and national office to solidify its influence over every aspect of public life.

Korematsu* v. *United States (1944): US Supreme Court case that challenged a presidential order forcing people of Japanese descent into internment camps during World War II. Korematsu was a native-born US citizen who refused to comply with the order. The Court ruled against him on the basis that public safety was more important than individual rights.

Lemon test: Establishes the guidelines by which government can assist religion without infringing upon the First Amendment's freedom of and freedom from religion. Government may only assist if the primary purpose of the assistance is secular, the assistance must neither promote nor inhibit religion, and there is no excessive entanglement between church and state.

LGBT: References those who identify as lesbian, gay, bisexual, or transgender.

LGBTQI: References those who identify as lesbian, gay, bisexual, transgender, queer, or intersexed.

Liberalism: Value associated with American citizenship that promotes personal liberty.

Majority-minority districts: Legislative districts where a single ethnoracial group or set of groups comprises the majority. Such districts are created to enhance the chances of electing a candidate of color but have also been used by some legislators to isolate minority influence.

McCarran–Walter Act of 1952: Revision to the 1924 Johnson Act that maintained national origin quotas but created preferences based on immigrant skills and family reunification. It lifted the ban on immigration from Asian countries and reflected broader concerns over communism and national security.

Media framing: The process of focusing on certain events or issues and then placing them in a broader field of meaning.

Mobilization of bias: Derived from the work of E. E. Schattschneider, it reflects the view that some interests or issues are organized into politics while others are organized out.

Moral Majority movement: Led by Reverend Jerry Falwell, the Moral Majority Movement was a hybrid blend of patriotism and evangelical tenets that condemned emerging political movements (e.g. Gay Rights movement, Women's movement, etc.) as threats to Christian principles.

Morrill Anti-Bigamy Act of 1862: A federal provision initiated to directly address the marriage practices of the Mormon faith.

National American Woman Suffrage Association: Led by Carrie Chapman Catt, the organization resulted from the merger of two competing suffrage groups who cultivated both state and federal pressure to help women gain the ability to vote.

National Farm Workers' movement: The organization of farm workers and their allies to demand better pay and safer work conditions.

Nation of Islam: Religious tradition created in 1931 by W. D. Fard Muhammad that combines elements of Islam and Black Nationalism. It was popularized by members such as Muhammad Ali, Malcolm X, and Elijah Muhammad.

Nativism: The commitment to favoring native-born citizens over immigrants coupled with concerns over immigrants' growing influence.

Naturalization: The formal process by which people born elsewhere pursue US citizenship.

Naturalization Act of 1790: The first formal statement outlining requirements for U.S. citizenship including a two-year period of residence in the country, one year of residence in the current state, and proof of good character. The Act also restricted citizenship to those classified as "white."

Nineteenth Amendment: Constitutional amendment that prohibits discrimination in voting on the basis of sex.

Obergefell v. Hodges (2015): Supreme Court Case that struck down state-level bans on same-sex marriage.

Plessy v. Ferguson (1896): US Supreme Court case which created the "separate but equal doctrine" that said racially separate public accommodations were legal as long as they were of equal quality.

Pluralism: The belief that the right to participate in elections is the ultimate guarantee of democracy by insuring that everyone has the opportunity to participate in the political process.

Plyer v. Doe (1982): Supreme Court ruling that undocumented children cannot be barred from attending public elementary and secondary schools because education is a public good.

Political movement: The harnessing of organized, purposive, collective strategies designed to bring about or resist political change.

Preclearance: A provision in the Voting Rights Act of 1965 that requires certain jurisdictions to submit to the US Department of Justice any proposed changes to their electoral qualifications before said policies can go into effect. Congress allocates the formula used to determine which jurisdictions qualify for preclearance.

Pregnancy Discrimination Act of 1978: Prohibited discrimination in employment and accommodation based on pregnancy, childbirth, or related medical conditions.

Protestant: Covers a host of Christian denominations that emerged after the Reformation. Protestants view the Bible as the sole holy text and build their houses of worship, religious practices, and beliefs upon a broad set of tenets.

Public goods: Products or services that are collectively created and available to all.

Race: Categories of difference based on social definitions rather than biological, anthropological, or genetic differences.

Racial categorization: The product of intense battles over which racial groups we belong to, the meaning of those assignments, and changing contexts for altering outcomes.

Racialization: The process of ascribing ethnic or racial identities to a relationship, social practice, or group that does not identify itself as such.

Reconstruction Act of 1867: A collection of policies that required states of the former Confederacy to adopt new state constitutions and provisions to uphold the mandates of the national Constitution before they could be admitted to the Union. For example, it required states to ratify the Fourteenth Amendment and adopt universal male suffrage regardless of race.

Refugees: Defined by the Refugee Resettlement Act of 1980 as a person with a well-founded fear of persecution.

Refugee Resettlement Act of 1980: Formalized efforts to assist people fleeing political turmoil in their home country by instituting strict requirements to minimize threats to domestic security. It granted the president statutory authority to accept refugees while requiring annual consultation with Congress.

Religiosity: An individual's relationship to formal religious institutions, frequency of attendance, and the overall importance of religion in daily life.

Religious Freedom Act of 1993: An Act designed to ensure religious freedom by preventing government from burdening the free exercise of religion without a compelling interest. Its provisions apply only to the actions of the federal government.

Religious identity: The socially constructed norms, conditions, expectations, and boundaries of how we practice our beliefs and respond to the practices of others.

Religious Right: A broad coalition of religious conservatives composed primarily of white Evangelicals who have deepened their political involvement and power via the creation of think tanks, advocacy organizations, and candidate training programs.

Republicanism: Value associated with American citizenship where the people hold popular sovereignty.

Roe v. Wade (1973): Landmark Supreme Court case that upheld a woman's right to choose whether to bear or beget a child. The case was also pivotal for setting the boundaries of individual rights and government's authority to define the universe of choices available to citizens.

Sanctuary city: Designation given to cities and municipalities who prefer to cooperate with the federal government to enforce federal immigration policy only when there is a clear concern for public safety and when it does not create economic hardship for the city.

Self-identity: The extent to which an individual feels they are part of a group.

Seneca Falls Convention: Gathering in New York in 1848 that was organized by women for women. The call for a convention resulted from the refusal to allow women to participate fully in the World Anti-Slavery Convention and a desire to draw attention to the invisibility of women within political movements.

Sexual identity: Captures how one thinks of oneself based on to whom one is sexually or romantically attracted.

Slaughterhouse Cases (1873): Set of Supreme Court cases which held that the Fourteenth Amendment to the Constitution protected citizenship of the United States rather than the individual states. They were pivotal in shaping subsequent appeals for federal intervention in state-level civil rights violations.

Social capital: The connections among individuals and the norms of reciprocity and trustworthiness that arise from them.

Social categorization: The extent to which society views individuals as belonging to a particular group.

Social distancing: The calculated assessment of the relative costs and benefits of affiliating with a particular group.

Stand Your Ground laws: State-level laws that determine when a person can use lethal force to defend herself or others against threats or perceived threats.

Stonewall Riots: Violent clashes in 1969 between activists from New York City's LGBTQI community and members of the New York Police Department who routinely raided gay establishments. It sparked the modern Gay Rights movement by denouncing legally sanctioned discrimination based on gendered and sexual identity.

Substantive representation: Addresses the question of whether the composition of voters and elected officials shapes the resulting votes and policy preferences of those in power.

Suffragists: Those who advocated for the full extension and protection of voting rights for women.

Symbolic racism: The blend of negative stereotypes of Blacks and the perception that Blacks violate cherished American values such as individualism, the Protestant work ethic, meritocracy, self-reliance, freedom, discipline, and impulse control.

Syncretic religion: The blending of two or more faith traditions to uniquely honor cultural and spiritual distinctions.

Tenth Amendment: Provides states with the authority to make laws regarding the health, safety, and wellbeing of its residents.

Transgender: Individuals whose gender identity, expression, and behavior do not fit with the sex they were assigned at birth.

Tribal sovereignty: The rights of over 560 federally recognized tribal nations to self-governance and control in various areas of decision-making.

United States v. Cruikshank (1876): US Supreme Court case that upheld the boundaries of federalism by not applying the Bill of Rights to the states.

United States* v. *Reese (1876): The first test of the provisions of the Fifteenth Amendment regarding voting rights. The Court held that the amendment did not confer an affirmative right to vote but did specify the conditions under which ballot access could not be denied.

USA PATRIOT Act: Comprehensive legislation passed by Congress in 2001 in direct response to the September 11th terror attacks. The Act significantly expanded government authority in the areas of intelligence, communications, and law enforcement to combat domestic terrorism. The Act was amended in 2011 to address civil rights and civil liberties concerns.

Voting Rights Act of 1965: Signed into law by President Lyndon B. Johnson, the Voting Rights Act of 1965 struck down decades of tactics used to restrict black access to voting and representation by removing grandfather clauses, white-only Primaries and poll taxes. Subsequent extensions of the Act helped extend protections for language-minorities such as American Indians, Asian Americans, and Latinos. The Voting Rights Act of 1965 ushered in more people of color as voters, candidates, and legislators.

Womanism: References the meaning of feminism and freedom for women of color who exist in spaces marked by multiple interlocking forms of oppression.

Notes

CHAPTER 1 THE PERSONAL IS POLITICAL

1 For more on the complicated history of addiction and public policy, see Hart (2013).
2 See Fact Sheets on Women of Color in Office from the Center for American Women and Politics, www.cawp.rutgers.edu/fact-sheets-women-color.
3 Tiger Woods, quoted in Carter (2013).
4 The term *intersexed* refers to individuals born with sexual anatomy that doesn't fit traditional definitions of male and female.
5 See Raquel Richard, "Why We Say Latinx: Trans & Gender Non-Conforming People Explain," www.latina.com/lifestyle/our-issues/why-we-say-latinx-trans-gender-non-conforming-people-explain.

CHAPTER 2 IDENTITY POLITICS AND THE BOUNDARIES OF BELONGING

1 The terms *trans* and *transgender* reference individuals whose sense of identity (gender identity) does not match the sex they were assigned at birth.
2 Jenée Desmond-Harris, "Rachel Dolezal: 'Well, I Definitely am Not White'," *Vox*, June 16, 2015.
3 Janet Mock, "Revealing Caitlyn Jenner: My Thoughts on Media, Privilege, Healthcare Access & Glamour," June 3, 2015, https://janetmock.com/2015/06/03/caitlyn-jenner-vanity-fair-transgender/.
4 *Transitioning/transitioned* is the process of undertaking a range of medical, legal, and personal measures to align gender identity with physical and emotional standing. For more information on related terminology, see the Gay and Lesbian Alliance against Defamation (GLAAD) Media Reference Guide, www.glaad.org/reference/covering-trans-community.
5 The term *colored* was used to refer to people of African descent. Over time the appellation has evolved from Negro to colored to Black to Afro American and now to African American.
6 The "One Drop Rule" declared that anyone with at least one drop of black blood should be properly identified as "Black." This form of *hypodescent* sets one's identity at birth and cannot be changed. Racial classifications vary across cultural contexts but are very rigid in the United States.

251

7 I use *Native American* here rather than American Indian because it is the term explicitly used by the organization.

8 Park's prolific work on ethnic assimilation defines social distance as an "attitude or human feeling rather than a spatial concept" (1924: 3). He believed that such attitudes derive from broader social and political processes that make distancing and distinctiveness necessary for a group's assimilation, acculturation, and acceptance into the dominant society.

9 As we will see in later chapters, these stereotypes can serve as useful heuristics for helping citizens make sense of the political world.

10 For a detailed description of the various benefit programs, eligibility criteria, and group coverage, visit the US Department of Health and Human Services, www.hhs.gov.

CHAPTER 3 THE SUBSTANCE OF US CITIZENSHIP

1 In 2017, President Donald J. Trump invited Indian code talkers to the White House for a special ceremony commemorating their military service. He drew criticism for referring to Massachusetts Senator Elizabeth Warren as "Pocahontas" while also suggesting tribal land could be a rich source of economic development.

2 The term *sanctuary city* has become highly controversial, with critics arguing that such cities undermine public safety by not prosecuting people who commit crimes. Advocates argue that a more appropriate term would be *safe city*, because it recognizes that cities do pursue violent and high-risk criminals while deferring action to the federal government for low-threat immigrants. According to Blanco (2017), each deportation costs taxpayers an average of $10,854.

3 Certain treaty stipulations relating to the Chinese, May 6, 1882; Enrolled Acts and Resolutions of Congress, 1789–1996; General Records of the United States Government; Record Group 11; National Archives.

4 Subsequent cases, such as *Ozawa v. United States* (1922) and *United States v. Bhagat Singh* (1923), tested whether groups from other countries (here Japan and India) could meet the qualifications for attaining US citizenship. In Singh's case his application to become a naturalized citizen was rejected because the law didn't allow him to meet the requirement of being a "free white person" even though he self-identified as a white "high caste Aryan."

5 David Wilkins (2002) highlights the inherent tensions of defining American Indian citizenship by citing the views of Chief Irving Powless, Jr, of the Onondaga Nation: "You have passed a law that says we are U.S. citizens . . . we did not agree to be citizens and we did not agree that your government could have jurisdiction over us. We do not accept these laws. We are not citizens of the U.S."

6 See Article II, Section 1, Clause 5 of the US Constitution.

7 The concept of *jus sanguinis* applied only to children born to married parents. Efforts to deny citizenship to children born illegitimately were shaped by broader notions of race (see the previous reference to Sally Hemings and Thomas Jefferson) and anti-miscegenation laws that prohibited mixed-race couples from officially marrying. For a detailed discussion, see Collins (2014).

8 See the work of Andrea Campbell (2003) for more on how public policies can activate interests and, in turn, bring more Americans into the decision-making process.

9 The VRA was originally intended to erase state-level restrictions on Black citizenship. Over time, several extensions of the Act also attacked the barriers faced by language minorities. See Jones-Correa (2005).

CHAPTER 4 RACIAL IDENTITY, CITIZENSHIP, AND VOTING

1 In 2017, the US Supreme Court declined to hear a case brought by a Mississippi resident who claimed the state's decision to include a portion of the Confederate flag in its state flag was an "official endorsement of white supremacy." The plaintiff, attorney Carlos Reeves, referenced research by Professor B. D'Andra Orey of Jackson State University that investigates physiological responses to seeing the Confederate flag. For more, see D'Andra Orey (2004).

2 Several photos released after the massacre in Charleston showed the shooter, Dylan Roof, proudly displaying the Confederate flag while spitting on the American flag and also visiting various Confederate history sites. A manifesto he published states: "I have no choice. I am not in the position to, alone, go into the ghetto and fight. I chose Charleston because it is the most historic city in my state, and at one time had the highest ratio of Blacks to Whites in the country. We have no skinheads, no real KKK, no one doing anything but talking on the internet. Well someone has to have the bravery to take it to the real world, and I guess that has to be me."

3 For the full transcript of President Barack H. Obama's eulogy delivered for Reverend Clementa Pinckney, see the *Washington Post*, June 26, 2015, www.washingtonpost.com/news/post-nation/wp/2015/06/26/transcript-obama-delivers-eulogy-for-charleston-pastor-the-rev-clementa-pinckney/?utm_term=.5dfe99aa1218.

4 Bree Newsome, June 27, 2015: video at https://bit.ly/2LLAjka.

5 Walter Scott was an unarmed Black motorist who was stopped by Officer Michael Slager in Charleston in April 2015 for a broken tail light. Slager fired eight shots into Mr Scott's back as he fled. He was convicted of violating Scott's civil rights and sentenced to twenty years in prison. Bree Newsome's use of the phrase "Whom shall I fear?" references a Bible verse popular within many African American religious traditions. Psalm 27

states: "The Lord is my light and my salvation; whom shall I fear? The Lord is the strength of my life; of whom shall I be afraid?" For a detailed discussion of the relationship between race, faith, and political activism, see Lewis (2012).

6 The United Daughters of the Confederacy (UDC) is the nation's oldest heritage organization in existence. Membership is restricted to women who can directly and proudly tie their ancestry to Confederate soldiers who fought during the Civil War. In response to the unrest in the United States in 2017 over Confederate symbols and monuments, the UDC reaffirmed its commitment to honoring its forefathers in spite of their contentious past:

> We are the descendants of Confederate soldiers, sailors, and patriots. Our members are the ones who have spent 123 years honoring their memory by various activities in the fields of education, history, and charity, promoting patriotism and good citizenship. Our members are the ones who, like our statues, have stayed quietly in the background, never engaging in public controversy . . . We are saddened that some people find anything connected with the Confederacy to be offensive. Our Confederate ancestors were and are Americans. We as an organization do not sit in judgement of them nor do we impose the standards of the 21st century on these Americans of the 19th century. (www.hqudc.org/)

7 For the full transcript of Mitch Landrieu's speech on May 23, 2017, see www.nytimes.com/2017/05/23/opinion/mitch-landrieus-speech-transcript.html?_r=0.

8 See Joe Heim, "A Sharp Contrast Inside and Outside a Charlottesville Church during the Torch March," *Washington Post*, August 19, 2017; www.washingtonpost.com/local/a-stark-contrast-inside-and-outside-a-charlottesville-church-during-the-torch-march/2017/08/19/a2311a7a-847a-11e7-902a-2a9f2d808496_story.html?utm_term=.f01b45cd0091.

9 Thomas Jefferson, *Notes on the State of Virginia*, Thomas Jefferson Foundation, www.monticello.org/site/research-and-collections/notes-state-virginia.

10 The term *alt-right* or *alternative right* refers to a collection of groups, individuals, and organizations which support a far-right, extremist view of conservatism. Adherents are loosely bound together by the belief that white identity is under attack and that racial and ethnic groups seek to erase American history. The term was popularized by self-identified alt-right movement leader Richard Spencer. The movement gained national notoriety following a gathering it held in Washington, DC, to celebrate the election of Donald Trump. Former White House strategist Steve Bannon declared that the media platform he chaired, Breitbart News, served as the media hub for the alt-right. For a detailed overview of the alt-right and

its role in contemporary US politics, see Taylor Hosking, "The Rise of the Alt-Right," *The Atlantic*, December 28, 2017.

11 The counterprotesters represented very diverse groups and interests. Some were from groups promoting nonviolence as an appropriate response to white supremacy. Others believed acts of violence should be met with reciprocal violence. President Trump also admonished members of the "Antifa" for committing acts of violence and harm during the rally and protests. Antifa (short for anti-fascist) refers to a collection of left-leaning groups who oppose neo-Nazi activity.

12 In "Remarks by President Donald J. Trump on Infrastructure," August 15, 2017, www.whitehouse.gov/briefings-statements/remarks-president-trump-infrastructure/.

13 *Brown* v. *Board* (1954) struck down the separate but equal doctrine on the grounds that state laws that established separate education facilities for Black and white children violated the Fourteenth Amendment's Equal Protection Clause.

14 W. E. B. DuBois (1906) "Address to the Country," second conference of the Niagara movement, Harper's Ferry, West Virginia, www.elegantbrain.com/academic/department/AandL/AAS/ANNOUNCE/niagaramovement/harpers/harperspeech.html.

15 It is common in political parlance to use the phrase "right to vote." However, it's important to note that the US Constitution does not contain an affirmative right to vote. This loophole allows states to set the conditions by which access to voting can be denied and/or restricted. For a detailed history, see Keyssar (2009).

16 The Supreme Court ruled in *Elk* v. *Wilkins* (1884) that the Fourteenth Amendment did not apply to Native Americans, and therefore Native Americans could not be considered citizens. It was not until the Indian Naturalization Act of 1890 that tribal members could begin *applying* for citizenship status.

17 See Arrington and Taylor (1993) for a detailed discussion of the contentious path to ratifying these amendments.

18 Shaffer (1998) argues that this process essentially represented a power contest between the Republican Congress and the Democrat President Andrew Johnson.

19 According to Foner (1988), the Klan was the creation of a group of ex-Confederate veterans in Pulaski, Tennessee. Reflecting the "invisible empire of the South," the Klan would grow to become one of the largest groups that opposed the Reconstruction government's attempts to extend rights to Blacks.

20 Lynching was not restricted to Black victims.

21 *United States* v. *Cruikshank* (1876) (92 US 542). The case challenged the 1870 Enforcement Act, initially designed to disrupt Klan activity, which

prohibited two or more people from conspiring to deprive people of their civil rights. The Court held that it violated First Amendment freedoms of speech and assembly.

22 James and Lawson (1999) define the *Gilded Age* as a "period of rampant political corruption that flowed from both partisan and private business sources" (p. 116).

23 The Slaughterhouse Cases combined *The Butchers' Benevolent Association of New Orleans* v. *The Crescent City Live-Stock Landing and Slaughter-House Company* and *Esteban et al.* v. *State of Louisiana*.

24 The Civil Rights Act of 1957 established the Civil Rights division of the US Department of Justice and allowed federal oversight of state or local efforts to abridge access to voting.

25 In issuing its decision on May 18, 1896, the Supreme Court asserted: "[we] cannot say that a law that authorizes or even requires the separation of the two races in public conveyances is unreasonable." Although this particular case involved the physical separation of the races (e.g. separate dining and travel facilities for Blacks and whites), the decision was later interpreted to apply to political and economic separation as well.

26 Mr McLaurin of Sharkey County, quoted in *Clarion Ledger* (Jacksonville), September 25, 1890, p. 3.

27 C. Vann Woodard (1981) documents an 1892 Alabama editorial suggesting that the state "would do well to imitate the wise politicians of Mississippi" in shaping the priorities of its constitutional convention.

28 For detailed time series data of wages based on state, occupation, and year, see the annual *Statistical Abstract of the United States* published by the US Bureau of Statistics.

29 As of 2018, the Twenty-Fourth Amendment had not been ratified by Arkansas, Arizona, Georgia, Louisiana, Oklahoma, South Carolina, and Wyoming. Mississippi rejected the proposed amendment when it was first introduced.

30 Matthews and Prothro (1966) suggest that there has been a great deal of scholarly debate regarding the actual impact of these constitutional changes on immediate participation rates. Key (1949), for example, uses Texas election data to suggest that these changes simply legalized the Black disenfranchisement that had already been achieved via violence. However, Lewinson (1959) uses voter registration data from Louisiana to argue that these changes were responsible for the dramatic decline in Black voting.

31 Benjamin Rattner, "Kentucky's Disturbing Disenfranchisement Numbers," Brennan Center for Justice, March 12, 2010, www.brennancenter.org/blog/archives/kentuckys_disturbing_disenfranchisement_numbers/.

32 Section 2 is a permanent provision of the Voting Rights Act of 1965 that prohibits discrimination on the basis of race, creed, color, or membership

in one of the federally identified language groups. It is designed to ensure that minority voters have equal access to the political process. In 1982 the provision was amended to address electoral rules that have a discriminatory *impact* even when intent cannot be proven.

33 *Hunter* v. *Underwood* (1985) struck down an Alabama clause that disenfranchised people convicted of the vaguely defined "crimes of moral turpitude."

34 "Census Treatment of Incarcerated Felons Unfairly Dilutes Voting Strength of Non-Prison Communities," June 22, 2005, www.prisonpolicy.org/news/pr06222005.html.

35 Virginia and Texas are two of the most popular states for receiving out-of-state inmates. A report issued by the Connecticut Department of Corrections estimated that the state spent approximately $40,000 per inmate housed in another state; it terminated its inmate transfer program in order to be more cost-efficient.

CHAPTER 5 ETHNIC IDENTITY: DEMOGRAPHY AND DESTINY

1 The New Haven Public Schools District, like many other districts across the country, does not collect comparable accurate data on enrollment patterns for American Indian and Pacific Islander students. A number of advocacy organizations have filed suit, given the presence of multiple tribes within the state and the need to fully assess the challenges facing students across a range of identity markers. In a 1996 case (*Sheff* v. *O'Neill*), the Connecticut Supreme Court ruled that local schools were heavily segregated by race and class. The ruling ordered state officials to take immediate steps to remedy this segregation. At the time of this writing, however, a number of school districts were embroiled in legal battles over the continued hypersegregation of public schools based on race, class, and geography.

2 Krogstad, Starr, and Sandstrom (2017) found that, between 2005 and 2015, Puerto Rico suffered a net loss of 446,000 people. Florida was the most popular destination for those leaving the island: the number of people of Puerto Rican descent living in the state numbers around 1 million.

3 The Merchant Marine Act of 1920 (also called the Jones Act) requires that all goods shipped between US ports are transported by vessels that were built in the United States and operated primarily by Americans. Though this Act has often been used to address foreign shipping, it holds special significance for the island of Puerto Rico as a US port. In the aftermath of Hurricane Maria, advocates requested that President Donald Trump relax the Act's restrictions to help expedite the delivery of valuable goods to aid the island's recovery efforts.

4 Although many people use the terms *race* and *ethnicity* interchangeably and refer to Latinos as a racial group, the term *Hispanic* refers to ethnicity and, often, country of origin. The most commonly reported race for Hispanics

was white alone (48 percent). Beginning with the 2000 census, respondents of all races were asked if they were Spanish, Hispanic, or Latino and were given the opportunity to differentiate between: (1) Mexican, Mexican American, Chicano; (2) Puerto Rican; (3) Cuban; and (4) other Spanish/Hispanic/Latino. The Department of Commerce has considered proposals to allow people to identify just as Latino/Hispanic rather than having to choose an additional category.

5 The concerns raised about single men emigrating to the United States weren't restricted to those coming from Asian countries. A number of legislators opposed Italian immigrants, who were most often single men, who intended to temporarily move to the US to earn money and return home. Referred to as "Birds of Passage," the flock of men who saw working in America as a temporary means of improving conditions in the home country intensified anti-immigrant sentiment.

6 The eugenics movement was based on the belief that improving the human race required selective breeding that avoided "less desirable" groups (based on race, country of origin, etc.) while preserving the purity of highly desirable groups. The movement and its supporters heightened ethnoracial and religious tensions by endorsing policies and practices that often mistreated members of less desirable groups.

7 Speech by Ellison DuRant Smith, April 9, 1924, *Congressional Record*, 68th Congress, 1st Session, vol. 65: 5961.

8 In a Supreme Court case evaluating the constitutionality of a presidential effort to restrict travel from certain countries, Chief Justice John Roberts argued that the Court had incorrectly ruled against Korematsu. Although the opinion did not overturn Korematsu's conviction, it highlighted the significance of the case for restricting citizenship rights based on ethnicity and country of origin. See *Trump* v. *Hawaii* (2018).

9 Section 212(a) of the Act deemed certain people inadmissible for entry, including those "who write or publish . . . or who knowingly circulate, distribute, print, or display, any written or printed matter, advocating or teaching opposition to all organized government, or advocating or teaching . . . the economic, international, and governmental doctrines of world communism."

10 Scholars such as Greer (2013), Smith (2014), and Carter and Perez (2016) examine the rise of "black ethnics" who represent a distinct political class from native-born African Americans, and whose experiences based on country of origin, generational status, and cultural beliefs shape their political presence and attachments in the United States.

11 See Department of Homeland Security, *2012 Yearbook of Immigration Statistics*, Table 2, pp. 8–12 (author's calculations). Across the United States, more than 37.6 million people speak Spanish and 70 percent of Asian Americans speak a language other than English at home. Camille Ryan, *Language Use*

in the United States: 2011 (US Census Bureau), Table 1, p. 3; Asian American Center for Advancing Justice, *A Community of Contrasts: Asian Americans in the United States, 2011*, p. 24. Some 25 million Americans are classified as possessing limited English proficiency. Monica Whatley and Jeanne Batalova, *Limited English Proficient Population of the United States*, Migration Policy Institute, 2013.

12 Despite these dramatic demographic changes, few studies have statistically examined the impact of the Voting Rights Act on groups other than African Americans. The most notable exception is Jones-Correa's study of the 2000 presidential election. He finds that 67 percent of Blacks registered, and 57 percent actually voted. In comparison, 52 percent of Asian Americans and 57 percent of Latinos registered; 43 percent of Asian Americans and 45 percent of Latinos actually cast a ballot.

13 An additional four states were added to the list of covered jurisdictions and three new Asian groups were added to the list of covered groups based on the results of the 2010 census.

14 See Hajnal (2010), who finds that, in cities where Latinos represent 5 percent or more of the population, their representation on city councils averages 13 points below parity; for Asian Americans, the figure is 9 points below; and, for African Americans, it is 8 points below. See also Richard Fausset, "Mostly Black Cities, Mostly White City Halls," *New York Times*, September 28, 2014, which cites analysis provided by the International City/County Management Association and Professor Jessica Trounstine and observes that, "among 340 American cities where more than 20 percent of the population is Black, two had councils on which Blacks were overrepresented compared with their population; 209 were within one seat of their population, and 129 underrepresented Blacks by more than one seat.

15 See the national website for the National Caucus of Native American State Legislators, www.ncsl.org/research/state-tribal-institute/national-caucus-native-american-state-legislators.aspx.

16 The United States may extend refugee status to those who fear imminent persecution based on their race, religion, nationality, political opinion, or membership in a particular group. It does not protect those who have called for or committed acts of violence against others based on the aforementioned factors.

17 US Commission on Immigration Reform, www.fairus.org/issue/legal-immigration/us-commission-immigration-reform.

18 The Uniting and Strengthening America by Providing Appropriate Tools Required to Intercept and Obstruct Terrorism Act of 2001 (USA PATRIOT Act) authorized the indefinite detention of those suspected of terrorism, stripped the citizenship of Americans suspected of terroristic involvement, and significantly expanded surveillance powers of the federal government.

19 For a detailed overview of the public opinion data on public support for civil liberties restrictions in the wake of the attacks of 9/11, see Jeffrey M. Jones, "The Impact of the Attacks on America," September 25, 2001, https:// news.gallup.com/poll/4894/impact-attacks-america.aspx.

20 *Shelby* v. *Holder*, 133 S.Ct. 2612 (2013).

21 The following fourteen states adopted new voter restrictions in advance of the 2016 presidential election: Alabama, Arizona, Indiana, Kansas, Mississippi, Nebraska, New Hampshire, Ohio, Rhode Island, South Carolina, Tennessee, Texas, Virginia, and Wisconsin.

22 Comprehensive data on American Indian voter registration and turnout are elusive. Scholars such as Laughlin McDonald of the ACLU's Voting Rights Project have documented the paucity of data, which is often complicated by issues of access and protection. Further, his research shows that, within the scope of voting rights cases, the US Department of Justice has been least likely to enforce the protections of the Voting Rights Act in cases involving American Indian plaintiffs. He attributes this hesitance to a range of factors, including economic depression, limited organizational pressure, and a general oversight of American Indian voting on reservations.

23 See https://standwithstandingrock.net/.

24 Traditionally, American Indian legislators at the national level have run as Republicans. Given the long history of federal government intrusion on tribal sovereignty, Indian legislators tend to prefer limited government. Across all ethnoracial groups we see that American Indian voters are more willing to support third-party candidates than other groups. In 1996 and 2000, Green Party candidate Ralph Nader ran for president with Winona LaDuke as his running mate. LaDuke is a member of the Ojiwe tribe and has been a prominent activist in the environmental justice movement. In 2000, the Green Party's platform emphasized support for treaty rights, tribal sovereignty, and sustainable energy. In 2018, a record number of American Indian women ran for state and national office on a platform of increased public support for education, health, economic development, and public safety.

CHAPTER 6 GENDER, SEXUAL IDENTITY, AND THE CHALLENGE OF INCLUSION

1 In 2018, New York City health officials began allowing parents to use the non-gender binary designation of "X" rather than male or female on their children's birth certificates.

2 See Allen J. Beck and Marcus Berzofsky, *Sexual Victimization in Prisons and Jails Reported by Inmates, 2011–12* (Washington, DC: Bureau of Justice Statistics, 2013).

3 Elizabeth Cady Stanton, *Eighty Years and More: Reminiscences 1815–1897* (New York: T. Fisher Unwin, 1898).

4 Report of the Woman's Rights Convention, Seneca Falls, New York, July 19–20, 1848.

5 Corrine McConnaughey, quoted in Linton Weeks, "American Women Who Were Anti-Suffragettes," *NPR News*, October 22, 2015.

6 For a detailed discussion of the gender gap, see Inglehart and Norris (2000).

7 Report of the Governmental Affairs Division, Committee on General Welfare, Intro. no. 24, to amend the administrative code of the city of New York in relation to gender-based discrimination. Accessible via http://legistar.council.nyc.gov/Legislation.aspx.

8 The policy never directly addressed the question of transgender recruits.

9 The Charter and Bylaws of the Democratic National Committee, amended August 2015.

10 See amicus brief filed by the US Justice Department in *Zarda* v. *Altitude Express* (July 26, 2017).

11 For a detailed discussion of the relationship between trans identity and political incorporation, see Murib (2015).

12 https://now.org/about/history/statement-of-purpose/.

13 www.ncai.org/resources/resolutions/creation-of-two-spirit-task-force.

CHAPTER 7 RELIGIOUS IDENTITY AND POLITICAL PRESENCE

1 A small but growing number of Sikhs have been elected to office across the United States. In 2009 Kashmir Gill was elected the first Sikh mayor, and in 2018 Gurbir Grewal became the first Sikh to be appointed attorney general, for the state of New Jersey. Later that year the sheriff of New Jersey's largest county was forced to resign after audio recordings surfaced of him using derogatory racial slurs toward Mr Grewal and African American residents. In his official response to the controversy, Grewal wrote: "The fact that a top official could make racist comments about the African-American community – and that no one in the room would challenge or correct him – raises serious concerns" (Grewal 2018).

2 See Shawn D. Lewis, "Post-9/11 Discrimination Plagues Detroit Area Sikhs," *Detroit News*, September 11, 2009.

3 In their *New York Times* op-ed "How Hate Gets Counted," Singh and Singh (2012) argue that the FBI needs to officially track bias crimes targeting Sikhs rather than classifying them as cases of mistaken Muslim identity.

4 Mark 16:18 (King James Bible).

5 John Burnett, "Snake-Handling Preachers Open up about 'Takin' up Serpents'," *NPR News*, October 4, 2013, www.npr.org/2013/10/04/226838383/snake-handling-preachers-open-up-about-takin-up-serpents.

6 Historians have sharply debated Lopez's role in the slave trade in the West Indies. Some argue that he amassed his wealth trading enslaved Africans, while others suggest human trafficking was a small part of his overall shipping business.

7 See Zola and Dollinger (2014).

8 George Washington, "Letter to Moses Seixas," August 17, 1790, www.loc. gov/item/today-in-history/august-17/.

9 See *Employment Division* v. *Smith* (1990).

10 A test of New Mexico's RFRA determined that the policy protected private business owners only from government action rather than private lawsuits. At issue was a photography company which refused to photograph a same-sex commitment ceremony. The New Mexico Human Rights Commission ordered the photographer to pay the couple's legal fees and damages. The Supreme Court refused to hear an appeal in that case. In 2018, however, the Court ruled that the Colorado Human Rights Commission's sanction of a baker who refused to make a cake for a same-sex wedding violated his religious freedom. See *Master Piece Cake Shop* v. *Colorado Human Rights Commission*.

11 Official statement from Kim Davis via legal counsel: www.lc.org/protect ing-marriage-and-family.

12 *Lemon* v. *Kurtzman*, 403 US 602 (1971).

13 Though some hailed the decision as a victory, groups such as the Anti-Defamation League cautioned that classifying Jews as a racial group harkened back to Nazi claims that Jews were an inferior racial class. This social classification was used to justify decades of violence and harm meant to extinguish an entire racial group and preserve the purity of the so-called Aryan race.

14 See Council on American-Islamic Relations, www.cair.com/candidates_ and_constituents_american_muslim_election_victories_and_voter_attitudes_ survey.

CHAPTER 8 IDENTITY AND POLITICAL MOVEMENTS

1 "Malloy, Foley Neck and Neck in Connecticut Gov Race," Quinnipiac University poll, October 22, 2014, https://poll.qu.edu/connecticut/release-detail?ReleaseID=2097.

2 The value of social media platforms for connecting protesters and stigmatized groups was best exemplified via the "Arab Spring" that spread across a number of Middle Eastern countries in 2011. Those who feared government repression and retaliation used technology to communicate their discontent, build support, and share information.

3 Orval Eugene Faubus Papers, Special Collections, University of Arkansas.

4 While Eisenhower's efforts were certainly beneficial, perhaps his greatest contribution to the civil rights movement was his nomination of Earl Warren as chief justice of the Supreme Court.

5 Scholars refer to this as *respectability politics*. Respectability politics occurs when members of underrepresented groups attempt to police members of their own group to show that their values and norms are compatible

with those of the mainstream. In her book *The Boundaries of Blackness* (1999), Cathy Cohen identifies this phenomenon as *secondary marginalization* and advances that it undermines group efforts to pursue full political incorporation.

6 The Big Six civil rights leaders were John Lewis of the Student Nonviolent Coordinating Committee; labor organizer A. Philip Randolph; Whitney Young, Jr, of the National Urban League; James Farmer, Jr, of the Congress of Racial Equality; Roy Wilkins of the National Association for the Advancement of Colored People; and Reverend Dr Martin Luther King, Jr, of the Southern Christian Leadership Conference.

7 Lyndon B. Johnson. "Speech before Congress on Voting Rights," March 15, 1965, http://movies2.nytimes.com/books/98/04/12/specials/johnson-rig htsadd.html.

8 The eleven states of the Confederacy in order of secession from the Union are South Carolina, Mississippi, Florida, Alabama, Georgia, Louisiana, Texas, Virginia, Arkansas, North Carolina, and Tennessee.

9 FL Stat. 776.032. Twenty-six states currently have similar laws on their books.

10 I use the phrase "Native Lives Matter" because it is used by groups such as the Red Nation who advocate for "addressing the invisibility of Native struggles within mainstream social justice organizing."

11 "Fatal Injury Reports, National, Regional and State, 1981–2017," https://webappa.cdc.gov/sasweb/ncipc/mortrate.html.

12 "Guiding Vision and Definition of Principles," https://march.womensmar ch.com/mission-and-principles.

13 Connecticut Students for a Dream, www.ct4adream.org/our-story.

14 Connecticut passed legislation in 2018 that provides in-state tuition rates for certain undocumented students attending public colleges and universities. Eligible students must have attended a high school in the state for at least two years and to have been a resident before they were seventeen and younger than thirty-six by June 15, 2018. Those qualifications are relaxed for undocumented veterans who were honorably discharged. Students convicted of a felony are not eligible for tuition equity. For more information, see Sullivan (2018).

15 United We Dream: https://unitedwedream.org/about/.

16 Tweets from Emma González (@Emma4Change), March 4, 2018.

CHAPTER 9 THE INESCAPABILITY OF IDENTITY POLITICS

1 In 1971, the Supreme Court overturned Muhammad Ali's conviction for violating the rules of the US Selective Service draft requirement. The ruling, *Clay* v. *United States*, supported Ali's claim that his Muslim faith prevented him from fighting and that he should thus be protected as a conscientious objector.

2 Interview with CBS News, September 27, 1966.
3 Legal scholars refer to a handful of cases as comprising the "anti-canon" of jurisprudence. These are cases whose decisions have not stood the test of time because their foundational arguments are inconsistent with contemporary understanding.
4 Executive Order Authorizing the Secretary of War to Prescribe Military Areas, https://catalog.archives.gov/id/5730250.
5 *Korematsu* v. *United States*, 323 US 214.
6 The original travel ban targeted people coming from seven Muslim-majority countries: Iraq, Iran, Libya, Somalia, Sudan, Syria, and Yemen. The final iteration of the ban covered Iran, Libya, North Korea, Somalia, Syria, Venezuela, and Yemen.

References

Abraham, Mark, and Mary Buchanan (2016) *Greater New Haven Community Index: Understanding Well-Being, Economic Opportunity, and Change in Greater New Haven Neighborhoods*. New Haven, CT: DataHaven.

Abrajano, Marisa (2010) "Are Blacks and Latinos Responsible for the Passage of Proposition 8? Analyzing Voter Attitudes on California's Proposal to Ban Same-Sex Marriage in 2008," *Political Research Quarterly*, 63/4: 922–32.

Ajzen, Icek, and Martin Fishbein (1980) *Understanding Attitudes and Predicting Social Behavior*. Englewood Cliffs, NJ: Prentice-Hall.

Alcoff, Linda Martin (2005) *Visible Identities: Race, Gender, and the Self*. New York: Oxford University Press.

Alexander, Michelle (2010) *The New Jim Crow: Mass Incarceration in the Age of Colorblindness*. New York: New Press.

Alexander-Floyd, Nikol G. (2012) "Disappearing Acts: Reclaiming Intersectionality in the Social Sciences in a Post-Black Feminist Era," *Feminist Formations*, 24/1: 1–25.

American Medical Association (2018) "AMA Adopts New Policies at 2018 Interim Meeting," press release, November 13.

Anderson, Carol (2017) *White Rage: The Unspoken Truth of Our Racial Divide*. London: Bloomsbury Press.

Anderson, Mary R. (2010) "Community Psychology, Political Efficacy, and Trust," *Political Psychology*, 31/1: 59–84.

Ansolabehere, Stephen, and Eitan Hersh (2013) "Gender, Race, Age and Voting: A Research Note," *Politics and Governance*, 1/2: 132–7.

Appiah, Kwame Anthony (2018) "Should I Go to a Gender Reveal Party?" *New York Times Magazine*, September 25.

Arrington, Karen McGill, and William L. Taylor (1993) *Voting Rights in America: Continuing the Quest for Full Participation*. Lanham, MD: University Press of America.

Arthur, Rob, and Allison McCann (2018) "How the Gutting of the Voting Rights Act Led to Hundreds of Closed Polls," *Vice News*, October 16, https://news.vice.com/en_us/article/kz58qx/how-the-gutting-of-the-voting-rights-act-led-to-closed-polls.

Asiatic Exclusion League (1908) *Proceedings of the Asiatic Exclusion League*, http://moses.law.umn.edu/darrow/documents/Dec%2008%20Asiatic.pdf, p. 15.

Associated Press (2008) "McCain Counters Obama 'Arab' Question," www. youtube.com/watch?v=jrnRU3ocIH4&feature=youtu.be.

—— (2014) "Connecticut is Increasing Minimum Wage to $10.10 an Hour," *New York Times*, March 26.

Audette, Andre P. (2016) *The Political Mobilization of Latino/a Religious Beliefs*, paper presented at the Western Political Science Association Annual Meeting, San Diego, March 25.

Bachrach, Peter, and Morton S. Baratz (1973) "Two Faces of Power," in William E. Conley (ed.), *The Bias of Pluralism*. New York: Atherton Press.

Bailey, Michael A., and Forrest Maltzman (2011) *The Constrained Court: Law, Politics, and the Decisions Justices Make*. Princeton, NJ: Princeton University Press.

Bailey, Sarah Pulliam (2015) "Jerry Falwell, Jr: If More Good People Had Concealed-Carry Permits, Then We Could End Those Islamist Terrorists," *Washington Post*, December 5.

Baldwin, James (1955) *Notes of a Native Son*. Boston: Beacon Press.

Banaji, Mahzarin, and Anthony Greenwald (2013) *Blindspot: Hidden Biases of Good People*. New York: Delacorte Press.

Banaszak, Lee Ann (1996) *Why Movements Succeed or Fail: Opportunity, Culture, and the Struggle for Woman Suffrage*. Princeton, NJ: Princeton University Press.

Barker, Lucius J., Mack H. Jones, and Katherine Tate (1999) *African Americans and the American Political System*. 4th edn, Upper Saddle River, NJ: Prentice Hall.

Barreto, Matt A. (2007) "¡Sí Se Puede! Latino Candidates and the Mobilization of Latino Voters," *American Political Science* Review, 101/3: 425–41.

Barreto, Matt A., and Dino N. Bozonelos (2009) "Democrat, Republican, or None of the Above? The Role of Religiosity in Muslim American Party Identification," *Politics and Religion*, 2/2: 200–29.

Bass, Paul (2014) "DREAMer Takes Michelle Obama Off-Script," *New Haven Independent*, October 30, www.newhavenindependent.org/index.php/archives/entry/dreamer_takes_michelle_obama_off-script/.

Baumgartner, Frank R., and Bryan D. Jones (2009) *Agendas and Instability in American Politics*. Chicago: University of Chicago Press.

Baxter Corporation (2017) "A Global Response to Hurricane Maria," www.baxter.com/perspectives/community-engagement/global-response-hurricane-maria.

Belcher, Cornell (2016) *A Black Man in the White House: Barack Obama and the Triggering of America's Racial-Aversion Crisis*. Healdsburg, CA: Water Street Press.

Bell, Derrick A. (1973) *Race, Racism, and American Law*. Boston: Little, Brown.

—— (1989) *And We Are Not Saved: The Elusive Quest for Racial Justice*. New York: Basic Books.

Beltrán, Cristina (2010) *The Trouble with Unity: Latino Politics and the Creation of Identity*. Oxford: Oxford University Press.

Berman, Ari (2017) "Rigged: How Voter Suppression Threw Wisconsin to Trump, and Possibly Handed Him the Whole Election," *Mother Jones*, November/

December. www.motherjones.com/politics/2017/10/voter-suppression-wisco nsin-election-2016/.

Bhaba, Jacqueline (2011) *Children without a State: A Global Human Rights Challenge.* Cambridge, MA: MIT Press.

Blalock, Hubert (1967) *Toward a Theory of Minority-Group Relations.* New York: John Wiley.

Blanco, Octavio (2017) "How Much It Costs ICE to Deport an Undocumented Immigrant," CNN Business, April 13, https://money.cnn.com/2017/04/13/news/economy/deportation-costs-undocumented-immigrant/index.html.

Blee, Kathleen M. (1996) "Becoming a Racist: Women in Contemporary Ku Klux Klan and Neo-Nazi Groups," *Gender and Society*, 10/6: 680–702.

Blumer, Herbert (1958) "Race Prejudice as a Sense of Group Position," *Pacific Sociological Review*, 1/1: 3–7.

Bobo, Lawrence (1983) "Whites' Opposition to Busing: Symbolic Racism or Realistic Group Conflict?" *Journal of Personality and Social Psychology*, 45/6: 1196–210.

Bobo, Lawrence, and Franklin D. Gilliam (1990) "Race, Sociopolitical Participation, and Black Empowerment," *American Political Science Review*, 84/2: 377–93.

Bobo, Lawrence, and Vincent L. Hutchings (1996) "Perceptions of Racial Group Competition: Extending Blumer's Theory of Group Position to a Multiracial Social Context," *American Sociological Review*, 61: 951–72.

Boyle, Kaitlin M., and Chase B. Meyer (2018) "Who is Presidential? Women's Political Representation, Deflection, and the 2016 Election," *Socius*, January, https://doi.org/10.1177/2378023117737898.

Branum, Tara L. (2002) "President or King: The Use and Abuse of Executive Orders in Modern-Day America," *Journal of Legislation*, 2/1: 1–86.

Brennan Center for Justice (2006) *Citizens without Proof: A Survey of Americans' Possession of Documentary Proof of Citizenship and Photo Identification.* New York: Brennan Center for Justice, New York University School of Law.

Brockes, Emily (2018) "MeToo Founder Tarana Burke: 'You Have to Use Your Privilege to Serve Other People'," *The Guardian*, January 15.

Brown, Nadia (2014) *Sisters in the Statehouse: Black Women and Legislative Decision Making.* Oxford: Oxford University Press.

Brown-Dean, Khalilah L. (2003) "One Lens, Multiple Views: Felon Disenfranchisement Laws and American Political Inequality," PhD dissertation, Ohio State University.

—— (2016) "Counting Bodies and Ballots: Prison Gerrymandering and the Paradox of Urban Political Representation," in Amy Bridges and Michael Javen Fortner (eds), *Urban Citizenship and American Democracy: The Historical and Institutional Roots of Local Politics and Policy.* Albany: SUNY Press.

Brown-Dean, Khalilah, and Ben Jones (2017) "Building Authentic Power: A Study of the Campaign to Repeal Connecticut's Death Penalty," *Politics, Groups, and Identities,* 5/2: 321–42.

Brown-Dean, Khalilah, Zoltan Hajnal, Christina Rivers, and Ismail White (2015) *50 Years of the Voting Rights Act: The State of Race in Politics.* Washington, DC: Joint Center for Political and Economic Studies.

Bullock, Charles S. III, and Ronald Keith Gaddie (2009) *The Triumph of Voting Rights in the South.* Norman: University of Oklahoma Press.

Burch, Traci R. (2013) *Trading Democracy for Justice: Criminal Convictions and the Decline of Neighborhood Political Participation.* Chicago: University of Chicago Press.

Burrell, Barbara C. (1994) *A Woman's Place is in the House: Campaigning for Congress in the Feminist Era.* Ann Arbor: University of Michigan Press.

Butler, Daniel M., and David E. Broockman (2012) "Do Politicians Racially Discriminate against Constituents? A Field Experiment on State Legislators," *American Journal of Political Science,* 55/3: 463–77.

Cacciatore, Michael A., Sara K. Yeo, Dietram A. Scheufele, Michael A. Xenos, Doo Hun Choi, Dominique Brossard, Amy B. Becker, and Elizabeth Corley (2014) "Misperceptions in Polarized Politics: The Role of Knowledge, Religiosity, and Media," *PS: Political Science and Politics,* 47/3: 654–61.

Calahan, Margaret Werner, and Lee Anne Parsons (1986) *Historical Corrections Statistics in the United States, 1850–1984.* Rockville, MD: Westat.

Calhoun-Brown, Allison (1996) "African American Churches and Political Mobilization: The Psychological Impact of Organizational Resources," *Journal of Politics,* 58/4: 935–53.

Campbell, Andrea Louise (2003) *How Policies Make Citizens: Senior Political Activism and the American Welfare State.* Princeton, NJ: Princeton University Press.

Campbell, David E., and J. Quin Monson (2008) "The Religion Card: Gay Marriage and the 2004 Presidential Election," *Public Opinion Quarterly,* 72/3: 399–419.

Campbell, David E., John C. Green, and J. Quin Monson (2014) *Seeking the Promised Land: Mormons and American Politics.* Cambridge: Cambridge University Press.

Carnes, Nicholas, and John B. Holbein (2018) *Do Public Officials Exhibit Social Class Biases when They Handle Casework? Evidence from Multiple Correspondence Experiments,* Working Paper, Duke University.

Carpenter, Zoë, and Tracie Williams (2018) "Since Standing Rock, 56 Bills Have Been Introduced in 30 States to Restrict Protests," *The Nation,* February 16.

Carroll, Susan J., and Richard L. Fox (2018) *Gender and Elections: Shaping the Future of American Politics.* 4th edn, Cambridge: Cambridge University Press.

Carter, Greg (2013) *The United States of the United Races: A Utopian History of Racial Mixing.* New York: New York University Press.

Carter, Niambi, and Efren Perez (2016) "Race and Nation: How Racial Hierarchy Shapes National Attachments," *Political Psychology,* 37/4: 497–513.

CAWP (Center for American Women and Politics) (2017) "Gender Differences in Voter Turnout," www.cawp.rutgers.edu/sites/default/files/resources/gen derdiff.pdf.

Chavez, Chris (2018) "Fox News' Laura Ingraham: LeBron Should 'Shut Up and Dribble' after Criticism of President Trump," *Sports Illustrated*, February 16.

Chávez, Maria, Jessica L. Monforti, and Melissa R. Michelson (2014) *Living the Dream: New Immigration Policies and the Lives of Undocumented Latino Youth*. New York: Routledge.

Chisholm, Shirley (1970) *Unbought and Unbossed*. Boston: Houghton Mifflin.

Cillizza, Chris, and Sean Sullivan (2013) "How Proposition 8 Passed in California – and Why," *Washington Post*, March 26.

Clear, Tom (2012) "FBI Arrests Four East Haven Cops," *Connecticut Post*, January 25.

Clinton, Hillary (2016) Full Text of the 2016 Democratic National Convention Speech, www.politico.com/story/2016/07/full-text-hillary-clintons-dnc-speech-226410.

Coates, Ta-Nehesi (2015) "There Is No Post-Racial America," *The Atlantic*, July/August.

Cobb, William Jelani (2010) *The Substance of Hope*. New York: Walker.

Cohen, Cathy J. (1999) *The Boundaries of Blackness: AIDS and the Breakdown of Black Politics*. Chicago: University of Chicago Press.

Cohen, Elizabeth F. (2010) "Jus Soli, Jus Sanguinis and Jus Tempus," paper presented at the Western Political Science Association Annual Meeting, San Francisco; https://papers.ssrn.com/sol3/papers.cfm?abstract_id=1580633.

Cole, Justin (2008) "More Media Coverage of Rick Warren Inaugural Controversy," December 19, www.glaad.org/2008/12/19/more-media-coverage-of-rick-warren-inaugural-controversy.

Collier-Thomas, Bettye, and V. P. Franklin (2001) *Sisters in the Struggle: African American Women in the Civil Rights–Black Power Movement*. New York: New York University Press.

Collins, Kristin A. (2014) "Illegitimate Borders: *Jus Sanguinis* Citizenship and the Legal Construction of Family, Race, and Nation," *Yale Law Journal*, 123/7: 2134–235.

Collins, Patricia Hill (1998) "It's All in the Family: Intersections of Race, Gender, and Nation," *Hypatia*, 13/3: 62–82.

Cone, James H. (1970) *A Black Theology of Liberation*. New York: Orbis Books.

Connor, Walker (1993) *Ethnonationalism: The Quest for Understanding*. Princeton, NJ: Princeton University Press.

Cook, Philip J., and Kristin A. Goss (2014) *The Gun Debate: What Everyone Needs to Know*. Oxford: Oxford University Press.

Cose, Ellis (1995) *The Rage of a Privileged Class*. New York: HarperCollins.

Cox, Daniel, and Robert P. Jones (2017) "America's Changing Religious Identity," Public Religion Research Institute, September 6, www.prri.org/research/american-religious-landscape-christian-religiously-unaffiliated/.

Cox, Karen L. (2003) *Dixie's Daughters: The United Daughters of the Confederacy and the Preservation of Confederate Culture.* Gainesville: University of Florida Press.

Craven, Julia (2016) "Black Lives Matter Co-Founder Wants to Live in 'a World Where All Lives Matter'," *Huffington Post*, June 20.

Crenshaw, Kimberlé (1991) "Mapping the Margins: Intersectionality, Identity Politics, and Violence against Women of Color," *Stanford Law Review*, 43/6: 1241–99.

C-SPAN (2011) "2011 White House Correspondents' Dinner," April 30, www.c-span.org/video/?c4649273/obama-lion-king.

Dahl, Robert A. (1957) "The Concept of Power," *Behavioral Science*, 2/3: 201–15.

—— (1961) *Who Governs? Democracy and Power in an American City.* New Haven, CT: Yale University Press.

—— (1989) *Democracy and its Critics.* New Haven, CT: Yale University Press.

Dana, Karam, Bryan Wilcox-Archuleta, and Matt Barreto (2017) "The Political Incorporation of Muslims in the United States: The Mobilizing Role of Religiosity in Islam," *Journal of Race, Ethnicity, and Politics*, 2/2: 170–200.

Dawson, Michael C. (1993) *Behind the Mule: Race and Class in African-American Politics.* Princeton, NJ: Princeton University Press.

Dawson, Michael C., and Lawrence D. Bobo (2009) "One Year Later and the Myth of a Post-Racial Society," *DuBois Review: Social Science Research on Race*, 6/2: 247–9.

Day, John Kyle (2014) *The Southern Manifesto: Massive Resistance and the Fight to Preserve Segregation.* Jackson: University of Mississippi Press.

Demaret, Kent (1982) "Raised White, a Louisiana Belle Challenges Race Records That Call Her 'Colored'," *People Magazine*, December 6.

D'Emilio, John (2003) *Lost Prophet: The Life and Times of Bayard Rustin.* Chicago: University of Chicago Press.

Devos, Thierry, and Mazarin R. Banaji (2005) "American = White?" *Journal of Personality and Social Psychology*, 88/3: 447–66.

Dias, Elizabeth (2016) "How Evangelicals Helped Donald Trump Win," *Time Magazine*, November 9.

Dittmar, Kelly, Kira Sanbonmatsu, and Susan J. Carroll (2018) *A Seat at the Table: Congresswomen's Perspectives on Why Their Presence Matters.* Oxford: Oxford University Press.

Dodge, Mrs Arthur M. (1915) "Mrs. Arthur M. Dodge Declares Suffrage Unnecessary," *Columbia Daily Spectator*, LIX/28, October 29.

Dolan, Julie, Melissa M. Deckman, and Michele L. Swers (2016) *Women and Politics: Paths to Power and Political Influence.* 3rd edn, Lanham, MD: Rowman & Littlefield.

Domke, David, and Kevin Coe (2008) *The God Strategy: How Religion Became a Political Weapon in America.* New York: Oxford University Press.

Eagle, Adam Fortunate (1992) *Alcatraz! Alcatraz!* Berkeley, CA: Heyday Books.

Eagly, Alice H., and Shelly Chaiken (1993) *The Psychology of Attitudes.* Fort Worth, TX: Harcourt, Brace, Jovanovich.

Ebenstein, Julie A. (2018) "The Geography of Mass Incarceration: Prison Gerrymandering and the Dilution of Prisoners' Political Representation," *Fordham Urban Law Journal*, 45/2: 322–72.

Engel, Stephen M. (2015) "Developmental Perspectives on Lesbian and Gay Politics: Fragmented Citizenship in a Fragmented State," *Perspectives on Politics*, 13/2: 287–311.

Erie, Steven P. (1988) *Rainbow's End: Irish-Americans and the Dilemmas of Urban Machine Politics, 1840–1985.* Berkeley: University of California Press.

Espiritu, Yen Le (1992) *Asian American Panethnicity: Bridging Institutions and Identities.* Philadelphia: Temple University Press.

Esses, Victoria M., Geoffrey Haddock, and Mark P. Zanna (1993) "Values, Stereotypes, and Emotions as Determinants of Intergroup Attitudes," in Diane M. Mackie and David L. Hamilton (eds), *Affect, Cognition, and Stereotyping: Interactive Processes in Group Perception.* San Diego: Academic Press, pp. 137–66.

Feimster, Crystal N. (2009) *Southern Horrors: Women and the Politics of Rape and Lynching.* Cambridge, MA: Harvard University Press.

Fenno, Richard F. (1978) *Home Style: House Members in Their Districts.* Boston: Little, Brown.

Flores, Juan, and George Yudice (1990) "Living Borders/Buscondo America: Languages of Latino Self-Formation," *Social Text*, no. 24: 57–84.

Foley, Elise (2017) "Dreamer Lorella Praeli to be a Leader of Trump Resistance on Immigration," *Huffington Post*, April 28.

Foner, Eric (1988) *Reconstruction: America's Unfinished Revolution, 1863–1877.* New York: Harper & Row.

Ford, Richard Thompson (2008) *The Race Card: How Bluffing about Bias Makes Race Relations Worse.* New York: Farrar, Strauss, & Giroux.

Forman, James (2018) *Locking Up Our Own: Crime and Punishment in Black America.* New York: Farrar, Strauss, & Giroux.

Fortner, Michael Javen (2015) *Black Silent Majority: The Rockefeller Drug Laws and the Politics of Punishment.* Cambridge, MA: Harvard University Press.

Fox, Richard L. (2011) "Studying Gender in US Politics: Where Do We Go From Here?" *Politics and Gender*, 7/1: 94–9.

Frankovic, Kathy (2017) "Trump's Domestic Crisis: Charlottesville and White Nationalists," *YouGov Politics and Current Affairs*, August 16, https://today.you gov.com/topics/politics/articles-reports/2017/08/16/trumps-domestic-crisis-charlottesville-and-white-n.

Frazier, Edward Franklin (1963) *The Negro Church in America.* New York: Shocken Books.

Freeman, Jo, and Victoria Johnson (1999) *Waves of Protest: Social Movements since the Sixties*. Lanham, MD: Rowman & Littlefield.

Freund, Ernst (1904) *Police Power: Public Policy and Constitutional Rights*. Chicago: University of Chicago Press.

Fujino, Diane C. (2012) *Samurai among Panthers: Richard Aoki on Race, Resistance, and a Paradoxical Life*. Minneapolis: University of Minnesota Press.

Gaither, Gerald H. (2005) *Blacks and the Populist Movement: Ballots and Bigotry in the New South*. Tuscaloosa: University of Alabama Press.

Gamson, William A. (1975) *The Strategy of Social Protest*. Homewood, IL: Dorsey Press.

Gans, Ray (2016) *The Influence of Religion on United States Supreme Court Decision Making*, undergraduate research thesis, Ohio State University.

Garcia, Matt (2014) *From the Jaws of Victory: The Triumph and Tragedy of Cesar Chavez and the Farm Worker Movement*. Berkeley: University of California Press.

Garcia Bedolla, Lisa (2003) "The Identity Paradox: Latino Language, Politics and Selection Dissociation," *Latino Studies*, 1/2: 264–83.

Gates, Henry Louis, Jr, and Cornel West (2000) *The African-American Century: How Black Americans Have Shaped our Country*. New York: Free Press.

Gay, Claudine (2002) "Spirals of Trust? The Effect of Descriptive Representation on the Relationship between Citizens and Their Government," *American Journal of Political Science*, 46/4: 717–32.

Gerteis, Joseph (2007) *Class and the Color Line: Interracial Class Coalition in the Knights of Labor and the Populist Movement*. Durham, NC: Duke University Press.

Gilens, Martin (1996) "'Race Coding' and White Opposition to Welfare," *American Political Science Review*, 90/3: 593–604.

Gillespie, Andra (2009) *Whose Black Politics? Cases in Post-Racial Black Leadership*. New York: Routledge.

Githens, Marianne, and Jewel Limar Prestage (1977) *A Portrait of Marginality: The Political Behavior of the American Woman*. New York: Longman.

Gonzalez, David (1992) "What's the Problem with 'Hispanic'? Just Ask a 'Latino'," *New York Times*, November 15.

Gonzales-Day, Ken (2006) *Lynching in the West, 1850–1935*. Durham, NC: Duke University Press.

Gordon, Milton M. (1964) *Assimilation in American Life*. New York: Oxford University Press.

Gordon-Reed, Annette (1998) *Thomas Jefferson and Sally Hemings: An American Controversy*. Charlottesville: University Press of Virginia.

——(2018) "America's Original Sin: Slavery and the Legacy of White Supremacy," *Foreign Affairs*, 97/1: 2–7.

Graham, David A. (2018) "From 'I Alone Can Fix It', to 'Change the Laws!'" *The Atlantic*, June 19.

Grant, Jacquelyn (1989) *White Women's Christ and Black Women's Jesus*. Atlanta: Scholars Press.

Green, John C., and James L. Guth (1988) "The Christian Right in the Republican Party: The Case of Pat Robertson's Supporters," *Journal of Politics*, 50/1: 150–65.

Green, John C., Lyman A. Kellstedt, Corwin E. Smidt, and James L. Guth (2013) "The Soul of the South: Religion and Southern Politics in the New Millennium," in Charles S. Bullock III and Mark J. Rozell (eds), *The New Politics of the Old South: An Introduction to Southern Politics*. Lanham, MD: Rowman & Littlefield, pp. 291–312.

Greenfeld, Liah (1993) *Nationalism: Five Roads to Modernity*. Cambridge, MA: Harvard University Press.

Greer, Christina M. (2013) *Black Ethnics: Race, Immigration, and the Pursuit of the American Dream*. Oxford: Oxford University Press.

Grewal, Gurbir S. (2018) "Statement of Attorney General Gurbir S. Grewal regarding Bergen County Sheriff Saudino's Resignation," September 21, https://nj.gov/oag/newsreleases18/pr20180921b.html.

Griffin, Jonathan (2017) "2017 Religious Freedom Restoration Act Legislation," National Conference of State Legislators, www.ncsl.org/research/civil-and-criminal-justice/2017-religious-freedom-restoration-act-legislation.aspx.

Grzymala-Busse, Anna (2012) "Why Comparative Politics Should Take Religion (More) Seriously," *Annual Review of Political Science*, 15: 421–42.

Gurin, Patricia, Arthur H. Miller, and Gerald Gurin (1980) "Stratum Identification and Consciousness," *Social Psychology Quarterly*, 43/1: 30–47.

Hajnal, Zoltan (2010) *America's Uneven Democracy: Race, Turnout, and Representation in City Politics*. Cambridge: Cambridge University Press.

Hajnal, Zoltan, and Taeku Lee (2011) *Why Americans Don't Join the Party: Race, Immigration and the Failure (of Political Parties) to Engage the Electorate*. Princeton, NJ: Princeton University Press.

Hajnal, Zoltan, Nazita Lajevardi, and Lindsay Nielson (2017) "Voter Identification Laws and the Suppression of Minority Votes," *Journal of Politics*, 79/2: 363–79.

Hamilton, Charles V. (1986) "Social Policy and the Welfare of Black Americans: From Rights to Resources," *Political Science Quarterly*, 101/2: 239–55.

Hannah-Jones, Nikole (2016) "The End of the Postracial Myth," *New York Times Magazine*, November 15.

Hanson, Gordon (2016) "Executive Power Can Still Affect Immigration Enforcement," *New York Times*, September 12.

Harding, Vincent (1981) *There is a River: The Black Struggle for Freedom in America*. Cambridge, MA: Harvard University Press.

Hardy-Fanta, Carol, Pei-te Lien, Dianne Pinderhughes, and Christine Marie Sierra (2016) *Contested Transformation: Race, Gender, and Political Leadership in 21st Century America*. Cambridge: Cambridge University Press.

Harris, Frederick C. (2001) *Something Within: Religion in African-American Political Activism*. Oxford: Oxford University Press.

—— (2012) *The Price of the Ticket: Barack Obama and the Rise and Decline of Black Politics*. Oxford: Oxford University Press.

Harris-Lacewell, Melissa Victoria (2004) *Bibles, Barbershops, and BET: Everyday Talk and Black Political Thought*. Princeton, NJ: Princeton University Press.

Hart, Carl (2013) *High Price: A Neuroscientist's Journey of Self-Discovery that Challenges Everything You Know about Drugs and Society*. New York: HarperCollins.

Hartz, Louis (1955) *The Liberal Tradition in America*. New York: Harcourt, Brace.

Harvard Law Review Editors (2017) "The Harvard Plan that Failed Asian Americans," *Harvard Law Review*, 131: 604–25.

Hasen, Richard L. (2012) *The Voting Wars: From Florida 2000 to the Next Election Meltdown*. New Haven, CT: Yale University Press.

Hawkesworth, Mary (2003) "Congressional Enactments of Race-Gender: Toward a Theory of Raced-Gendered Institutions," *American Political Science Review*, 97/4: 529–50.

Hayward, Clarissa R. (2000) *De-Facing Power*. Cambridge: Cambridge University Press.

Healy, Kieran (2015) "America is a Violent Country," https://kieranhealy.org/blog/archives/2012/07/20/america-is-a-violent-country/.

Heaney, Michael T. (2018) "The New Wave of the Women's Movement in the United States," *Mobilizing Ideas*, January 22, https://mobilizingideas.word press.com/2018/01/22/the-new-wave-of-the-womens-movement-in-the-uni ted-states/.

Heaney, Michael T., and Fabio Rojas (2015) *Party in the Street: The Antiwar Movement and the Democratic Party after 9/11*. Cambridge: Cambridge University Press.

Hedgeman, Anna Arnold (1964) *The Trumpet Sounds: A Memoir of Negro Leadership*. New York: Holt, Rinehart, & Winston.

Hero, Rodney (1992) *Latinos and the U.S. Political System: Two-Tiered Pluralism*. Philadelphia: Temple University Press.

—— (1998) *Faces of Inequality: Social Diversity in American Politics*. New York: Oxford University Press.

Hicks, William D., Seth C. McKee, Mitchell D. Sellers, and Daniel A. Smith (2014) "A Principle or a Strategy? Voter Identification Laws and Partisan Competition in the American States," *Political Research Quarterly*, 68/1: 18–33.

Higgins, Nicholas (2014) "Religious Influences on Latino Ideology and Vote Choice: Are Evangelical Catholics Different?" *Politics, Groups, and Identities*, 2/3: 402–21.

Hinton, Elizabeth (2016) *From the War on Poverty to the War on Crime: The Making of Mass Incarceration in America*. Cambridge, MA: Harvard University Press.

Hippler, Mike (1989) *Matlovich: The Good Soldier*. New York: Alyson Books.

Hochschild, Jennifer L. (1984) *The New American Dilemma: Liberal Democracy and School Desegregation*. New Haven, CT: Yale University Press.

hooks, bell (1981) *Ain't I a Woman: Black Women and Feminism*. New York: Routledge.

Huckfeldt, Robert, and Carol Weitzel Kohfeld (1989) *Race and the Decline of Class in American Politics*. Urbana: University of Illinois Press.

Hume, David (1875) "That Politics May Be Reduced to a Science," in *The Philosophical Works*, ed. T. H. Green and T. H. Grose. London: Longmans, Green.

Husain, Atiya (2018) "Are Jews White?" *Slate*, August 14.

Ichioka, Yuji (2006) *Before Internment: Essays in Prewar Japanese American History*, ed. Gordon H. Chang and Eiichiro Azuma. Stanford, CA: Stanford University Press.

Inglehart, Ronald, and Pippa Norris (2000) "The Developmental Theory of the Gender Gap: Women's and Men's Voting Behavior in Global Perspective," *International Political Science Review*, 21/4: 441–63.

Ingram, Helen M., and Anne L. Schneider (2005) "Introduction: Public Policy and the Social Construction of Deservedness," in Anne L. Schneider and Helen M. Ingram (eds), *Deserving and Entitled: Social Constructions and Public Policy*. Albany: State University of New York Press, pp. 1–34.

Ishizuka, Karen L. (2016) *Serve the People: Making Asian America in the Long Sixties*. New York: Verso Books.

Jackson, David (2019) "President Trump Says He Rejected Plan to Reopen the Government to Negotiate Border Wall," *USA Today*, January 14.

James, Scott C., and Brian L. Lawson (1999) "The Political Economy of Voting Rights Enforcement in America's Gilded Age: Electoral College Competition, Partisan Commitment, and the Federal Election Law," *American Political Science Review*, 93/1: 115–31.

Jenkins, J. Craig, and Charles Perrow (1977) "Insurgency of the Powerless: Farm Worker Movements (1946–1972)," *American Sociological Review*, 42/2: 249–68.

Jennings, James (1992) *The Politics of Black Empowerment: The Transformation of Black Activism in Urban America*. Detroit: Wayne State University Press.

Jones-Correa, Michael (2005) "Language Provisions under the Voting Rights Act: How Effective Are They?" *Social Science Quarterly*, 86/3: 549–64.

Jones-Correa, Michael, and David L. Leal (2001) "Political Participation: Does Religion Matter," *Political Research Quarterly*, 54/4: 751–70.

Kahangi, Linda (2018) "We Believe Women Should Make Their Own Choices," media press release, Alpha Phi International Fraternity, https://d28htnjz2 elwuj.cloudfront.net/wp-content/uploads/2017/12/14115317/Harvard-Recrui tment-121217.pdf.

Kaleka, Amardeep, and Pardeep Kaleka (2013) "The American Dream," www. youtube.com/watch?v=AlHYYQNVyYA&feature=youtu.be.

Kelly, Jason P. (2012) "The Strategic Use of Prisons in Partisan Gerrymandering," *Legislative Studies Quarterly*, 37/1: 117–34.

Key, V. O. (1949) *Southern Politics in State and Nation*. New York: Knopf.

Keyes, Elizabeth (2013) *Defining American: The DREAM Act, Immigration Reform and Citizenship*. Baltimore School of Law Legal Studies Research Paper no. 2013-15.

Keyssar, Alexander (2009) *The Right to Vote: The Contested History of Democracy in the United States*. New York: Basic Books.

Khan-Cullors, Patrisse (2018) *When They Call You a Terrorist: A Black Lives Matter Memoir*. New York: St Martin's Press.

Kim, Claire Jean (2000) *Bitter Fruit: The Politics of Black–Korean Conflict in New York City*. New Haven, CT: Yale University Press.

Kinder, Donald R., and David O. Sears (1981) "Prejudice and Politics: Symbolic Racism versus Racial Threats to the Good Life," *Journal of Personality and Social Psychology*, 40/3: 414–31.

King, Coretta Scott (1993) *My Life with Martin Luther King, Jr.* New York: Holt, Rinehart, & Winston.

Klingenfuss, Melody (2017) "Please Raise Your Voice to Keep Our Dreams Alive," *Long Beach Press Telegram*, March 15.

Klinkner, Philip A., and Rogers M. Smith (1999) *The Unsteady March: The Rise and Decline of Racial Equality in America*. Chicago: University of Chicago Press.

Kluger, Richard (1979) *Simple Justice*. New York: Random House.

Kousser, J. Morgan (1974) *The Shaping of Southern Politics: Suffrage Restriction and the Establishment of the One-Party South, 1880–1910*. New Haven, CT: Yale University Press.

—— (1999) *Colorblind Injustice: Minority Voting Rights and the Undoing of the Second Reconstruction*. Chapel Hill: University of North Carolina Press.

Krauss, Robert M., and Susan R. Fussell (1996) "Social Psychological Models of Interpersonal Communication," in Edward T. Higgins and Arie W. Kruglanski (eds), *Social Psychology: Handbook of Basic Principles*. New York: Guilford Press, pp. 655–701.

Krogstad, Jens Manuel, Kelsey Jo Starr, and Aleksandra Sandstrom (2017) "Key Findings About Puerto Rico," Pew Research Center, March 29.

Krogstad, Jens Manuel, Antonio Flores, and Mark Hugo Lopez (2018) "Key Takeaways about Latino Voters in the 2018 Midterm Elections," Pew Research Center, November 9.

Ladson-Billings, Gloria (2006) "From the Achievement Gap to the Education Debt: Understanding Achievement in U.S. Schools," *Educational Researcher*, 35/7: 3–12.

Landrieu, Mitch (2018) *In the Shadow of Statues: A White Southerner Confronts History*. New York: Viking Press.

Lau, Richard R., and David P. Redlawsk (2001) "Advantages and Disadvantages of Cognitive Heuristics in Political Decision Making," *American Journal of Political Science*, 45/4: 951–71.

Laughland, Oliver (2018) "Federal Judge Rules against Trump's Crackdown on 'Sanctuary Cities'," *The Guardian*, November 30, www.theguardian.com/us-news/2018/nov/30/federal-judge-rules-against-trumps-crackdown-on-sanctuary-cities.

Lawless, Jennifer L., and Richard L. Fox (2010) *It Takes a Candidate: Why Women Don't Run for Office*. Cambridge: Cambridge University Press.

Lawson, Steven F. (ed.) (2003) *To Secure These Rights: The Report of President Harry S. Truman's Committee on Civil Rights*. New York: Bedford/St Martin's Press.

Layman, Geoffrey (2001) *The Great Divide: Religious and Cultural Conflict in American Party Politics*. New York: Columbia University Press.

Leal, David L., Jerod Patterson, and Joe R. Tafoya (2016) "Religion and the Political Engagement of Latino Immigrants: Bridging Capital or Segmented Religious Assimilation?," *RSF: The Russell Sage Foundation Journal of the Social Sciences*, 2/3: 125–46.

Lebron, Christopher J. (2017) *The Making of Black Lives Matter: A Brief History of an Idea*. Oxford: Oxford University Press.

Lee, Gordon (2003) "The Forgotten Revolution," *Hyphen: Asian America Unabridged*, June 1, https://hyphenmagazine.com/magazine/issue-1-premiere-summer-2003/forgotten-revolution.

Lee, Taeku, S. Karthick Ramakrishnan, and Ricardo Ramírez (2007) *Transforming Politics, Transforming America: The Political and Civic Incorporation of Immigrants in the United States*. Charlottesville: University of Virginia Press.

Leonard, David J. (2017) *Playing While White: Privilege and Power On and Off the Field*. Seattle: University of Washington Press.

Levine, Robert A., and Donald T. Campbell (1972) *Ethnocentrism: Theories of Conflict, Ethnic Attitudes, and Group Behavior*. New York: John Wiley.

Lewinson, Paul (1959) *Race, Class, & Party: A History of Negro Suffrage and White Politics in the South*. New York: Oxford University Press.

Lewis, Donna (2018) "Trump–Cohen Tape Mentioned 'Use' of President's Black Surrogates, But Why?" NBC News, July 26, www.nbcnews.com/news/nbcblk/trump-cohen-tape-mentioned-use-president-s-black-surrogates-why-n894586.

Lewis, John (2012) *Across That Bridge: A Vision for Change and the Future of America*. New York: Hachette.

Lien, Pei-te, M. Margaret Conway, and Janelle Wong (2004) *The Politics of Asian Americans: Diversity and Community*. New York: Routledge.

Lincoln, C. Eric, and Lawrence H. Mamiya (1990) *The Black Church in the African American Experience*. Durham, NC: Duke University Press.

Lipka, Michael (2014) "Americans are Somewhat More Open to the Idea of an Atheist President," Pew Research Center, May 29.

Locke, John (1689) *Second Treatise on Government*. London: Awnsham Churchill.

Lockhart, P. R. (2018) "Why Women's March Leaders are Being Accused of Anti-Semitism," *Vox*, March 8.

Long, Michael G. (ed.) (2012) *I Must Resist: Bayard Rustin's Life in Letters*. San Francisco: City Lights.

Lopez, German (2018) "Voter Suppression Really May Have Made the Difference for Republicans in Georgia," *Vox*, November 7.

Lowndes, Joseph, and Dorian Warren (2011) "Occupy Wall Street: A Twenty-First Century Political Movement?" *Dissent*, October 21, www.dissentmag azine.org/online_articles/occupy-wall-street-a-twenty-first-century-populist-movement.

Luders, Joseph E. (2010) *The Civil Rights Movement and the Logic of Social Change*. Cambridge: Cambridge University Press.

Lugo, Luis (2013) *A Portrait of Jewish Americans*, Pew Research Center, http://assets. pewresearch.org/wp-content/uploads/sites/11/2013/10/jewish-american-full-report-for-web.pdf.

Madej, Patricia (2018) "Men Arrested at Philadelphia Starbucks: 'It's Not Just a Black People Thing it's a People Thing'," *Chicago Tribune*, April 19.

Manley, John F. (1983) "Neo-Pluralism: A Class Analysis of Pluralism I and Pluralism II," *American Political Science Review*, 77/2: 368–83.

Margolis, Michele F. (2018) "How Politics Affects Religion: Partisanship, Socialization, and Religiosity in America," *Journal of Politics*, 80/1: 30–43.

Marschall, Melissa J., and Amanda Rutherford (2016) "Voting Rights for Whom? Examining the Effects of the Voting Rights Act on Latino Political Incorporation," *American Journal of Political Science*, 60/3: 590–606.

Maslow, Abraham H. (1954) *Motivation and Personality*. New York: Harper & Row.

Matthews, Donald R., and James W. Prothro (1966) *Negroes and the New Southern Politics*. New York: Harcourt, Brace.

Mauer, Marc, and Ryan S. King (2007) *A 25-Year Quagmire: The War on Drugs and its Impact on American Society*. Washington, DC: The Sentencing Project.

Maynard, Douglas H. (1960) "The World's Anti-Slavery Convention of 1840," *Journal of American History*, 47/3: 452–71.

Mazzola, Jessica, and Karen Yi (2017) "Sanctuary City? Welcoming Town? 5 Questions Break Down Divisive Issue," October 31, www.nj.com/essex/index.ssf/2017/10/what_are_sanctuary_cities_and_what_do_they_mean_fo.html.

McAdam, Doug (1982) *Political Process and the Development of Black Insurgency, 1930–1970*. 2nd edn, Chicago: University of Chicago Press.

McCarthy, John D., and Mayer N. Zald (1973) *The Trend of Social Movements in America: Professionalization and Resource Mobilization*. Morristown, NJ: General Learning Press.

McClain, Paula D. (1993) "The Changing Dynamics of Urban Politics," *Journal of Politics*, 55/2: 399–414.

McClerking, Harwood K., and Tasha S. Philpot (2008) "Struggling to be Noticed: The Civil Rights Movement as an Academic Agenda Setter," *PS: Political Science and Politics*, 41/4: 813–17.

McCloud, Aminah Beverly (1995) *African American Islam*. New York: Routledge.

McConnaughy, Corrine (2013) *The Woman Suffrage Movement in America: A Reassessment*. Cambridge: Cambridge University Press.

McCool, Daniel, Susan M. Olson, and Jennifer L. Robinson (2007) *Native Vote: American Indians, the Voting Rights Act, and the Right to Vote*. Cambridge: Cambridge University Press.

McCormick, Joseph II, and Charles E. Jones (1993) "The Conceptualization of Deracialization," in *Dilemmas of Black Politics*, ed. Georgia A. Persons. New York: HarperCollins, pp. 66–84.

McDaniel, Eric L. (2008) *Politics in the Pews: The Political Mobilization of Black Churches*. Ann Arbor: University of Michigan Press.

McDaniel, Eric L., and Christopher G. Ellison (2008) "God's Party? Race, Religion, and Partisanship over Time," *Political Research Quarterly*, 61/2: 180–91.

McKenzie, Brian D. (2011) "Barack Obama, Jeremiah Wright, and Public Opinion in the 2008 Presidential Primaries," *Political Psychology*, 32/6: 943–61.

McWhorter, John (2008) "Racism in America is Over," *Forbes*, December 30.

Mettler, Suzanne B. (1998) *Dividing Citizens: Gender and Federalism in New Deal Public Policy*. Ithaca, NY: Cornell University Press.

Meyer, Robinson (2017) "What's Happening with the Relief Effort in Puerto Rico?" *The Atlantic*, October 4.

Michaelis, Arno, and Pardeep Singh Kaleka (2018) *The Gift of Our Wounds: A Sikh and a Former White Supremacist Find Forgiveness after Hate*. New York: St Martin's Press.

Morris, Aldon D. (1984) *The Origins of the Civil Rights Movement: Black Communities Organizing for Change*. New York: Free Press.

Moses, Paul (2017) "White Catholics & Nativism: The Church's Future under Trump," *Commonweal*, September 1.

Muhammad, Khalil G. (2011) *The Condemnation of Blackness: Race, Crime, and the Making of Modern Urban America*. Cambridge, MA: Harvard University Press.

Muñoz, Carlos, Jr (2007) *Youth, Identity, Power: The Chicano Movement*. New York: Verso.

Murib, Zein (2015) "Transgender: Examining an Emerging Political Identity Using Three Political Processes," *Politics, Groups, and Identities*, 3/3: 381–97.

— (2018) "Trumpism, Citizenship, and the Future of the LGBTQ Movement," *Politics and Gender*, 14/4: 649–72.

Myrdal, Gunnar (1944) *An American Dilemma*, Vol. 1: *The Negro Problem and Modern Democracy*. New York: Harper & Row.

Needleman, Rafe (2009) "Starbucks: Stay as Long as You Want," *Cnet*, August 15.

Nelson, Louis (2017) "From 'Locker Room Talk' on, Trump Fends off Misconduct Claims," *Politico*, December 12, www.politico.com/story/2017/12/12/trump-timeline-sexual-misconduct-allegations-defense-292146.

Neuhaus, Richard John (1984) *The Naked Public Square: Religion and Democracy in America*. 2nd edn, Grand Rapids, MI: William B. Eerdmans.

Neuman, Scott (2015) "Indiana's 'Religious Freedom' Bill Sparks Firestorm of Controversy," *National Public Radio*, March 28.

Nunnally, Shayla C. (2012) *Trust in Black America: Race, Discrimination, and Politics*. New York: New York University Press.

Obama, Barack H. (2014) "Remarks by the President in Address to the Nation on Immigration," November 20, https://obamawhitehouse.archives.gov/the-press-office/2014/11/20/remarks-president-address-nation-immigration.

—— (2015) "Remarks by the President at Nationalization Ceremony," December 15, https://obamawhitehouse.archives.gov/the-press-office/2015/12/15/remarks-president-naturalization-ceremony.

O'Connor, Clare (2012) "Donald Trump Tells Forbes Why He's Offering $5 Million for Obama's Records," *Forbes*, October 24, www.forbes.com/sites/clareoconnor/2012/10/24/trump-tells-forbes-why-hes-offered-5-million-for-obamas-records/#2586a86b3e9a.

Ogbar, Jeffrey O. G. (2001) "Yellow Power: The Formation of Asian-American Nationalism in the Age of Black Power, 1966–1975," *Souls*, 3/3: 29–38.

O'Leary, Mary (2013) "Connecticut Gun Laws: Breakdown of When New Laws Go into Effect," *New Haven Register*, April 6.

Olson, Mancur (1971) *The Logic of Collective Action: Public Goods and the Theory of Groups*. Cambridge, MA: Harvard University Press.

Omelicheva, Mariya Y., and Ranya Ahmed (2017) "Religion and Politics: Examining the Impact of Faith on Political Participation," *Religion, State and Society*, 46/1: 4–25.

Omi, Michael, and Howard Winant (1986) *Racial Formation in the United States*. New York: Routledge & Kegan Paul.

Orey, Byron D'Andra (2004) "White Racial Attitudes and Support for the Mississippi State Flag," *American Politics Research*, 32/1: 102–16.

Orfield, Gary, and Chungmei Lee (2007) "Historic Reversals, Accelerating Resegregation, and the Need for New Integration Strategies," UCLA Civil Rights Project, August 29.

Orrenius, Pia M., and Madeline Zavodny (2003) "Do Amnesty Programs Reduce Undocumented Immigration? Evidence from IRCA," *Demography*, 40/3: 437–50.

Orum, Anthony M. (1974) "On Participation in Political Protest Movements," *Journal of Applied Behavioral Science*, 10/2: 181–207.

Owens, Michael Leo (2007) *God and Government in the Ghetto: The Politics of Church–State Collaboration in Black America*. Chicago: University of Chicago Press.

Packard, Jerrold M. (2002) *American Nightmare: The History of Jim Crow*. New York: St Martin's Griffin.

Pager, Devah (2007) *Marked: Race, Crime, and Finding Work in an Era of Mass Incarceration*. Chicago: University of Chicago Press.

Parenti, Michael (1983) *Democracy for the Few*. 4th edn, New York: St Martin's Press.

Park, Bernadette, Carey S. Ryan, and Charles M. Judd (1992) "Role of Meaningful Subgroups in Explaining Differences in Perceived Variability for In-Groups and Out-Groups," *Journal of Personality and Social Psychology*, 63/4: 553–67.

Park, Robert E. (1924) "The Concept of Social Distance as Applied to the Study of Racial Attitudes and Racial Relations," *Journal of Applied Sociology*, 8: 339–44.

Parker, Christopher S. (2009) *Fighting for Democracy: Black Veterans and the Struggle against White Supremacy in the Postwar South*. Princeton, NJ: Princeton University Press.

Parker, Christopher S., and Matt A. Barreto (2013) *Change They Can't Believe in: The Tea Party and Reactionary Politics in America*. Princeton, NJ: Princeton University Press.

Parvini, Sarah (2017) "Being Sikh in Trump's America," *Los Angeles Times*, June 11.

Paulson, Michael (2009) "Obama Nomination Would Boost Ranks of Catholics on Court," *Boston Globe*, May 30.

Peak, Christopher (2018) "Blumenthal, Murphy Fight for Puerto Rico," *New Haven Independent*, January 7.

Peterson, Brandie (2015) "Election 2016: Why Ted Cruz Picked Liberty University," *CNN Politics*, March 23.

Pettigrew, Thomas (1982) *Prejudice*. Cambridge, MA: Harvard University Press.

Pevar, Stephen L. (2012) *The Rights of Indians and Tribes*. 4th edn, Oxford: Oxford University Press.

Pew Research Center (2010) "Most Continue to Favor Gays Serving Openly in Military," November 29, www.people-press.org/2010/11/29/most-continue-to-favor-gays-serving-openly-in-military/.

—— (2013) "Big Racial Divide over Zimmerman Verdict: Whites Say Too Much Focus on Race, Blacks Disagree," July 22, www.people-press.org/2013/07/22/big-racial-divide-over-zimmerman-verdict/.

—— (2015) "America's Changing Racial Landscape," May 12, www.pewforum.org/2015/05/12/americas-changing-religious-landscape/.

—— (2016) "Faith and the 2016 Campaign," January 27, www.pewforum.org/2016/01/27/faith-and-the-2016-campaign/.

Pitkin, Hanna Fenichel (1972) *The Concept of Representation*. Berkeley: University of California Press.

Piven, Frances Fox, and Richard A. Cloward (1979) *Poor People's Movements: Why They Succeed, How They Fail*. New York: Vintage Books.

Pratt, Dorothy Overstreet (2017) *Sowing the Wind: The Mississippi Constitutional Convention of 1890*. Jackson: University Press of Mississippi.

Price, Melanye T. (2016) *The Race Whisperer: Barack Obama and the Political Uses of Race*. New York: New York University Press.

Prucha, Francis Paul (ed.) (1973) *Americanizing the American Indians: Writings by the "Friends of the Indian," 1880–1900*. Cambridge, MA: Harvard University Press.

Pulido, Laura (2006) *Black, Brown, Yellow, and Left: Radical Activism in Los Angeles.* Berkeley: University of California Press.

Purdie-Vaughns, Valerie, and Richard P. Eibach (2008) "Intersectional Invisibility: The Distinctive Advantages and Disadvantages of Multiple Subordinate-Group Identities," *Sex Roles*, 59/5–6: 377–91.

Quarantotto, Marcelo A. (2010) "Students Address City Council on Polling Place," *Liberty News*, February 24.

Rasor, Paul, and Richard E. Bond (2011) *From Jamestown to Jefferson: The Evolution of Religious Freedom in Virginia.* Charlottesville: University of Virginia Press.

Rawls, John (1971) *A Theory of Justice.* Cambridge, MA: Harvard University Press.

Robinson, Shirleene (2017) "Witch-Hunts and Surveillance: The Hidden Lives of Queer People in the Military," *The Conversation*, April 24.

Rodrik, Dani (2016) "What's the Biggest Fear of a Trump Presidency?" *New York Times*, November 9.

Rosenberg, Morton (2008) *Presidential Claims of Executive Privilege: History, Law, Practice and Recent Developments.* Washington, DC: Congressional Research Service.

Rosentiel, Tom (2012) "How Many US Sikhs?" August 6, www.pewresearch. org/2012/08/06/ask-the-expert-how-many-us-sikhs/.

Ross, Gyasi (2012) "Yes, the Death of Trayvon Martin is about You," *Huffington Post*, March 27.

Ross, Lawrence C. (2001) *The Divine Nine: The History of African American Fraternities and Sororities.* New York: Kensington Press.

Roth, Michael S. (2014) "Campus Conversations on Fraternities," *Roth on Wesleyan*, April 30, http://roth.blogs.wesleyan.edu/2014/04/30/campus-conver sations-on-fraternities/.

Rule, James, and Charles Tilly (1975) "Political Process in Revolutionary France: 1830–1832," in John M. Merriman (ed.), *1830 in France.* New York: New Viewpoints.

Rustin, Bayard (1965) "From Protest to Politics: The Future of the Civil Rights Movement," *Commentary Magazine*, www.commentarymagazine.com/articles/ from-protest-to-politics-the-future-of-the-civil-rights-movement/.

Rutenberg, Jim (2008) "The Man behind the Whispers about Obama," *New York Times*, October 12, www.nytimes.com/2008/10/13/us/politics/13martin. html.

Sanchez, Gabriel R., and Edward D. Vargas (2016) "Taking a Closer Look at Group Identity: The Link between Theory and Measurement of Group Consciousness and Linked Fate," *Political Research Quarterly*, 69/1: 160–74.

Schattschneider, E. E. (1960) *The Semisovereign People: A Realist's View of Democracy in America.* Hinsdale, IL: Dryden Press.

Schermerhorn, R. A. (1970) *Comparative Ethnic Relations: A Framework for Theory and Research.* New York: Random House.

Schmidt, Ronald Sr, Yvette M. Alex-Assensoh, Andrew L. Aoki, and Rodney E. Hero (2009) *Newcomers, Outsiders, and Insiders: Immigrants and American Racial Politics in the Early Twenty-First Century*. Ann Arbor: University of Michigan Press.

Schneider, Anne, and Helen Ingram (1993) "Social Construction of Target Populations: Implications for Politics and Policy," *American Political Science Review*, 87/2: 334–47.

Schram, Sanford F., Joe Soss, and Richard C. Fording (eds) (2003) *Race and the Politics of Welfare Reform*. Ann Arbor: University of Michigan Press.

Schroedel, Jean Reith, and Roger J. Chin (2017) "Whose Lives Matter: The Media's Failure to Cover Police Use of Lethal Force against Native Americans," *Race and Justice*, https://doi.org/10.1177/2153368717734614.

Schuit, Sophie, and Jon C. Rogowski (2017) "Race, Representation, and the Voting Rights Act," *American Journal of Political Science*, 61/3: 513–26.

Sears, David O., and Funk, Carolyn L. (1991) "The Role of Self-Interest in Social and Political Attitudes," *Advances in Experimental Social Psychology*, 24: 1–91.

Sears, David O., and Kinder, Donald R. (1971) *Racial Tension and Voting in Los Angeles*. Los Angeles: University of California, Institute of Government and Public Affairs.

Shaffer, Donald R. (1998) "Why Clinton Will Survive," *ORIGINS: Current Events in Historical Perspective*, November 5, http://origins.osu.edu/history-news/why-clinton-will-survive.

Shaw, Anna Howard (1915) *The Story of a Pioneer*. New York: Harper.

Shaw, Todd, Louis DeSipio, Dianne Pinderhughes, and Toni-Michelle C. Travis (2015) *Uneven Roads: An Introduction to U.S. Racial and Ethnic Politics*. Los Angeles: CQ Press.

Shear, Michael D. (2015) "A 'Dreamer' Activist Becomes a Citizen, but Her Fight is Not Over," *New York Times*, December 15, www.nytimes.com/2015/12/16/us/lorella-praeli-dreamer-us-citizen-obama.html.

Sherrill, Kenneth (1993) "On Gay People as a Politically Powerless Group," in *Gays and the Military: Joseph Steffan versus the United States*, ed. Marc Wolinsky and Kenneth Sherrill. Princeton, NJ: Princeton University Press, pp. 84–120.

Sherrill, Kenneth, and Alan Yang (2000) "From Outlaws to In-Laws: Anti-Gay Attitudes Thaw," *Public Perspective*, 11/1: 20–3.

Shklar, Judith N. (1991) *American Citizenship: The Quest for Inclusion*. Cambridge, MA: Harvard University Press.

Sides, John, Michael Tesler, and Lynn Vavreck (2018) *Identity Crisis: The 2016 Presidential Campaign and the Battle for the Meaning of America*. Princeton, NJ: Princeton University Press.

Silbey, Joel H., Allan G. Bogue, and William H. Flanigan (1978) *The History of American Electoral Behavior*. Princeton, NJ: Princeton University Press.

Simien, Evelyn M. (2007) "Doing Intersectionality Research: From Conceptual Issues to Practical Examples," *Politics and Gender*, 3/2: 264–71.

Simpson, John A. (1975) "The Cult of the 'Lost Cause'," *Tennessee Historical Quarterly*, 34/4: 350–61.

Singh, Simran Jeet, and Prabhjot Singh (2012) "How Hate Gets Counted," *New York Times*, August 24, www.nytimes.com/2012/08/24/opinion/do-american-sikhs-count.html.

Smith, Candis Watts (2014) *Black Mosaic: The Politics of Black Pan-Ethnic Diversity*. New York: New York University Press.

Smith, Gregory, and Jessica Martínez (2016) "How the Faithful Voted: A Preliminary Analysis," November 9, www.pewresearch.org/fact-tank/2016/11/09/how-the-faithful-voted-a-preliminary-2016-analysis/.

Smith, Robert C. (1996) *We Have No Leaders: African Americans in the Post-Civil Rights Era*. Albany: State University of New York Press.

Smith, Rogers M. (1985) "The Meaning of American Citizenship," www.academia.edu/2806585/The_Meaning_of_American_Citizenship.

—— (1993) "Beyond Tocqueville, Myrdal, and Hartz: The Multiple Traditions in America," *American Political Science Review*, 87/3: 549–66.

—— (1999) *Civic Ideals: Conflicting Visions of Citizenship in U.S. History*. New Haven, CT: Yale University Press.

Smooth, Wendy (2006) "Intersectionality in Electoral Politics: A Mess Worth Making," *Politics and Gender*, 2/3: 400–14.

—— (2011) "Standing for Women? Which Women? The Substantive Representation of Women's Interests and the Research Imperative of Intersectionality," *Politics and Gender*, 7/3: 436–41.

Southern Poverty Law Center (2018) *Whose Heritage: Public Symbols of the Confederacy*. Montgomery, AL: Southern Poverty Law Center.

Sowell, Thomas (1984) *Civil Rights: Rhetoric or Reality?* New York: Morrow.

Stanley, Harold W. (1987) *Voter Mobilization and the Politics of Race: The South and Universal Suffrage, 1952–1984*. New York: Praeger.

Steele, Shelby (1990) *The Content of Our Character: A New Vision of Race in America*. New York: St Martin's Press.

Stein, Marc (2012) *Rethinking the Gay and Lesbian Movement*. New York: Routledge.

Stokes-Brown, Atiya Kai (2012) "America's Shifting Color line? Reexamining Determinants of Latino Racial Self-Identification," *Social Science Quarterly*, 93/2: 309–32.

Strolovitch, Dara Z. (2008) *Affirmative Advocacy: Race, Class, and Gender in Interest Group Politics*. Chicago: University of Chicago Press.

Strother, Logan Ray (2017) *Impact: The Supreme Court in American Politics*, doctoral dissertation, Syracuse University, https://surface.syr.edu/cgi/viewcontent.cgi?article=1741&context=etd.

Sullivan, Marybeth (2018) *Institutional Aid for Undocumented Students*. Hartford: Connecticut Office of Legislative Research.

Swain, Carol M. (1993) *Black Faces, Black Interests: The Representation of African American Interests in Congress*. Cambridge, MA: Harvard University Press.

Swavola, Elizabeth, Kristine Riley, and Ram Subramanian (2016) *Overlooked: Women and Jails in an Era of Reform*. New York: Vera Institute of Justice.

Tajfel, Henri (1979) "Individuals and Groups in Social Psychology," *British Journal of Social and Clinical Psychology*, 18/2: 183–90.

Tajfel, Henri, and John Turner (1979) "An Integrative Theory of Intergroup Conflict," in William G. Austin and Stephen Worchel (eds), *The Social Psychology of Intergroup Relations*. Monterey, CA: Brooks-Cole.

Tarrow, Sidney (1994) *Power in Movement: Social Movements and Contentious Politics*. Cambridge: Cambridge University Press.

Tate, Katherine (1994) *From Protest to Politics: The New Black Voters in American Elections*. Cambridge, MA: Harvard University Press.

Taylor, Keeanga-Yamahtta (2016) *From #BlackLivesMatter to Black Liberation*. Chicago: Haymarket Books.

Tesler, Michael (2016) *Post-Racial or Most-Racial? Race and Politics in the Obama Era*. Chicago: University of Chicago Press.

Thrush, Glenn, and Jeremy W. Peters (2018) "Charges of Vote Stealing in Florida Portend More Distrust in System for 2020," *New York Times*, November 18, www.nytimes.com/2018/11/18/us/politics/florida-recount-voter-fraud.html.

Thurston, Chloe N. (2018) "Black Lives Matter, American Political Development, and the Politics of Visibility," *Politics, Groups, and Identities*, 6/1: 162–70.

Tilly, Charles, and Sidney Tarrow (2006) *Contentious Politics*. London: Paradigm.

Tilly, Charles, Louise Tilly, and Richard Tilly (1975) *The Rebellious Century, 1830–1930*. Cambridge, MA: Harvard University Press.

Tocqueville, Alexis de (1835) *Democracy in America*, trans. Henry Reeve. New York: G. Dearborn.

Traister, Rebecca (2017) "The Complicated, Controversial, Historic, Inspiring Women's March," *The Cut*, January 20.

Tumulty, Karen (2008) "Will Obama's Anti-Rumor Plan Work?" *Time Magazine*, June 12, http://content.time.com/time/subscriber/article/0,33009,1813978,00.html.

Tyson, Vanessa C. (2017) *Twists of Fate: Multiracial Coalitions and Minority Representation in the US House of Representatives*. Oxford: Oxford University Press.

Umhoefer, Dave, and Gina Barton (2012) "What Brought Wade Michael Page to Milwaukee?" *Milwaukee-Wisconsin Journal Sentinel*, August 7.

US Citizenship and Immigration Services (2018) "Approximate Active DACA Recipients: Country of Birth," www.uscis.gov/sites/default/files/USCIS/Resources/Reports%20and%20Studies/Immigration%20Forms%20Data/All%20Form%20Types/DACA/DACA_Population_Data_August_31_2018.pdf.

US Commission on Immigration Reform (1990), www.fairus.org/issue/legal-immigration/us-commission-immigration-reform.

US Department of Justice (2017) "Attorney General Sessions Announces Immigration Compliance Requirements for Edward Byrne Memorial Justice

Assistance Grant Programs," July 25, www.justice.gov/opa/pr/attorney-general-sessions-announces-immigration-compliance-requirements-edward-byrne-memorial.

Valelly, Richard M. (2004) *The Two Reconstructions: The Struggle for Black Enfranchisement*. Chicago: University of Chicago Press.

Vasilogambros, Matt (2018) "Hundreds of New State Gun Laws: Most Expand Access," *Pew Stateline*, March 2.

Verba, Sidney (2003) "Would the Dream of Political Inequality Turn out to be a Nightmare?" *Perspectives on Politics*, 1/4: 663–79.

Verba, Sidney, Kay Lehman Schlozman, and Henry E. Brady (1995) *Voice and Equality: Civic Voluntarism in American Politics*. Cambridge, MA: Harvard University Press.

Volpp, Leti (2016) "Immigrants Outside the Law: President Obama, Discretionary Executive Power, and Regime Change," *Critical Analysis of Law*, 3/2: 385–404.

Wadsworth, Nancy D. (2011) "Intersectionality in California's Same-Sex Marriage Battles: A Complex Proposition," *Political Research Quarterly*, 64/1: 200–16.

Wald, Kenneth D., and Allison Calhoun-Brown (2018) *Religion and Politics in the United States*. 8th edn, Lanham, MD: Rowman & Littlefield.

Walker, Clarence E., and Gregory D. Smithers (2012) *The Preacher and the Politician: Jeremiah Wright, Barack Obama, and Race in America*. Charlottesville: University of Virginia Press.

Walters, Ronald W. (2005) *Freedom is Not Enough: Black Voters, Black Candidates, and American Presidential Politics*. Lanham, MD: Rowman & Littlefield.

Walton, Hanes (1985) *Invisible Politics: Black Political Behavior*. Albany: State University of New York Press.

Walton, Hanes, and Robert C. Smith (2000) *American Politics and the African American Quest for Universal Freedom*. New York: Longman.

Warren, Dorian T. (2010) "The American Labor Movement in the Age of Obama: The Challenges and Opportunities of a Racialized Political Economy," *Perspectives on Politics*, 8/3: 847–60.

Wei, William (2016) *Asians in Colorado: A History of Persecution and Perseverance in the Centennial State*. Seattle: University of Washington Press.

Wells-Barnett, Ida B. (1895) *A Red Record: Tabulated Statistics and Alleged Causes of Lynchings in the United States: 1892, 1893, and 1894, Respectfully Submitted to the Nineteenth Century Civilization in "the Land of the Free and the Home of the Brave"*. Chicago: Donohue & Henneberry.

Wides-Muñoz, Laura (2018) *The Making of a Dream: How a Group of Young Undocumented Immigrants Helped Change What it Means to be American*. New York: HarperCollins.

Wilcox, Clyde (1989) "The Fundamentalist Voter: Politicized Religious Identity and Political Attitudes and Behavior," *Review of Religious Research*, 31/1: 54–67.

Wilkins, David E. (2002) *American Indian Politics and the American Political System.* Lanham, MD: Rowman & Littlefield.

Wilkins, David E., and Heidi Kiiwetinepinesiik Stark (2011) *American Indian Politics and the American Political System.* 3rd edn, Lanham, MD: Rowman & Littlefield.

Williamson, Vanessa, Theda Skocpol, and John Coggin (2011) "The Tea Party and the Remaking of Republican Conservatism," *Perspectives on Politics*, 9/1: 25–43.

Wilson, David C., and Matthew O. Hunt (2013) "The First Black President? Cross-Racial Perceptions of Barack Obama's Race," in Amilcar Antonio Barreto and Richard L. O'Bryan (eds), *American Identity in the Age of Obama.* New York: Routledge, pp. 222–44.

Wilson, David C., Michael Leo Owens, and Darren W. Davis (2015) "How Racial Attitudes and Ideology Affect Political Rights for Felons," *Du Bois Review: Social Science Research on Race*, 12/1: 73–93.

Woodard, Stephanie (2016) "The Police Killings No One is Talking About," *In These Times*, October 17, http://inthesetimes.com/features/native_american_police_killings_native_lives_matter.html.

Woodward, C. Vann (1981) *Origins of the New South, 1877–1913: A History of the South.* Rev. edn, Baton Rouge: Louisiana State University Press.

Zelinsky, Wilbur (2001) *The Enigma of Ethnicity: Another American Dilemma.* Iowa City: University of Iowa Press.

Zepeda-Millán, Chris, and Sophia J. Wallace (2013) "Racialization in Times of Contention: How Social Movements Influence Latino Racial Identity," *Politics, Groups, and Identities*, 1/4: 510–27.

Zirin, Dave (2005) *What's My Name, Fool? Sports and Resistance in the United States.* Chicago: Haymarket Books.

Zola, Gary Phillip, and Marc Dollinger (2014) *American Jewish History: A Primary Source Reader.* Waltham, MA: Brandeis University Press.

Index

Bold page numbers indicate tables
Italicized page numbers indicate figures